the
complete illustrated
TOOL BOOK

Edited by
Stephen Clark and Daniel Lyman

GALAHAD BOOKS · NEW YORK CITY

Library of Congress Catalog Card Number: 74-16563
ISBN 0-88365-262-5

Published by arrangement with Pathfinder Publications, Inc.
Formerly published as The Incredible Illustrated Tool Book
Manufactured in the United States of America

Contents

Introduction

With construction costs climbing daily, and with a rejuvenated interest in handicrafts, more and more people are discovering the advantages of making home repairs and improvements. Others have *always* enjoyed working with tools and know the relaxation and satisfaction of building and repairing their own furniture or of tinkering with automobiles. Still others earn their livings using their hands. All of these people need to be aware of the most efficient methods of utilizing tools and of the procedures necessary for their proper maintenance.

The Complete Illustrated Tool Book is a remarkably complete guide to the names, uses, and maintenance requirements of virtually every tool commonly employed today. It is fully supplemented with over three hundred illustrations, which serve to enhance the meticulous explanations of each tool's uses and capabilities. The book is designed to be a reference work for the experienced professional as well as a primer for the beginning do-it-yourselfer. It is so complete that it might as easily be found in a construction worker's tool box as in a home library.

The book is divided into seven chapters, each of which is a detailed and systematic review of one of the major groups. Chapter 1 describes impact tools, twisting and turning tools, wood-cutting tools, metal-cutting tools, miscellaneous tools, safety equipment, and safety rules. Chapter 2 describes pneumatic and electrically-powered tools such as drills, grinders, sanders, and scalers.

Certain tools are especially useful for measuring purposes. Rules, tapes, calipers, micrometers, and squares, together with techniques for using them, are detailed in Chapter 3. Fasteners, not properly classified as tools, are nevertheless used extensively in wood and metalworking projects; Chapter 4 therefore outlines the uses of bolts, cotter pins, nails, nuts, rivets, and screws.

Chapter 5 discusses abrasive wheels and methods for grinding and sharpening chisels, drills, punches, and snips. Metal-cutting operations using the chisel, drill, reamer, and several types of thread cutters are described in Chapter 6. The final chapter describes miscellaneous problems the reader may encounter, such as bending and flaring tubing, removing broken bolts, studs, and taps, stripping insulated wire, and several soldering techniques and lubrication procedures.

Upon completion of this handbook, the reader should be able to identify tools and fastening devices by their correct names, understand the specific uses of each tool, and be able to keep them in perfect working order. The book not only explains in detail tools and their uses, but also helps the reader overcome especially difficult problems by acquainting him with tools he may not have known existed. The novice will find that some of the tools he encounters in the book will seem highly sophisticated and will therefore be of no use to him. His budget, too, may prevent him from purchasing such tools. As his proficiency increases, however, he will be able to turn to this handbook for solutions to very specific problems, while monetary obstacles may be overcome by making use of a tool rental store.

The editors of this book believe that The Complete Illustrated Tool Book is a thorough, up-to-date reference book and guide which will prove invaluable to anyone who works with tools. With the help of this book, and a little ingenuity, the reader should be able to tackle practically any home repair, hobby, or construction project he may encounter.

CHAPTER 1
COMMON HANDTOOLS

Tools are designed to make a job easier and enable you to work more efficiently. Tools are a craftsman's best friend. If the tools are not used properly or cared for, their advantages will be lost. Without them a craftsman is as helpless as he would be without his eyes. In fact, he would be more helpless, for a blind mechanic or craftsman skilled in the use of good tools and having them available, can do more than the most expert mechanic without tools.

Regardless of the type of work to be done, a craftsman must have, choose, and use the correct tools in order to do his work quickly, accurately, and safely. Without the proper tools and the knowledge of how to use them, he wastes time, reduces his efficiency, and may even injure himself. This chapter explains the specific purposes, correct use, and proper care of the more common tools you may encounter.

THE MOST VALUABLE TOOLS IN THE WORLD

What would you pay for THE MOST VALUABLE TOOLS IN THE WORLD? These tools can help you grip, grasp, push, twist and help you operate equipment. Furthermore, these remarkable tools can distinguish temperature variations and are sensitive to touch. It is impossible to purchase such tools . . . they are your HANDS.

1

These fabulous tools are subject to injury by being caught in machines, crushed by objects, or cut by a variety of sharp edged tools such as chisels, knives, or saws. Additionally, your hands can be damaged by being burnt, fractured or sprained unless you are always alert.

Why? Because they cannot THINK for themselves. PROTECT THEM. They are invaluable. KEEP ALERT while you work. THINK as you work. THINK before you make adjustments to machinery. Has the electric power been turned off? Are the required guards on the machinery? Is the object on which you are going to work properly secured and clamped?

Protect your hands from injury as directed by the applicable safety instructions whenever you use tools. You will be working under severe handicaps without the full use of both hands. Make it a habit to FOLLOW ALL SAFETY RULES.

TOOL HABITS

"A place for everything and everything in its place" is just common sense. You can't do an efficient, fast repair job if you have to stop and look around for each tool you need. The following rules, if followed, will make your job easier for you.

KEEP EACH TOOL IN ITS PROPER STOWAGE PLACE.—A tool is useless if you cannot find it. If you return each tool to its proper place, you'll know where it is the next time you need it.

KEEP YOUR TOOLS IN GOOD CONDITION.—Protect them from rust, nicks, burrs, and breakage.

USE EACH TOOL ONLY ON THE JOB FOR WHICH IT WAS DESIGNED.—If you use the wrong tool to make an adjustment, the results will probably be unsatisfactory. For example, if you use a socket wrench that's a trifle too big, you'll round off the corners of the wrench or nut.

KEEP YOUR TOOLS WITHIN EASY REACH AND WHERE THEY CANNOT FALL ON THE FLOOR OR MACHINERY.—Avoid placing tools anywhere above machinery or electrical apparatus. Serious damage will result if the tool falls into the machinery after the equipment is energized.

NEVER USE DAMAGED TOOLS.—A battered screwdriver may slip and spoil the screw slot, damage other parts, or cause painful injury. A gage strained out of shape will result in inaccurate measurements.

Remember, the efficiency of a craftsman and the tools he uses are determined to a great extent by the way he keeps his tools. Likewise, he is frequently judged by the manner in which he handles and cares for them. Anyone watching a skilled craftsman at his work notices the care and precision with which he uses the tools of his trade.

The care of hand tools should follow the same pattern as for personal articles; that is, always keep hand tools clean and free from dirt, grease, and foreign matter. After use, return tools promptly to their proper place in the toolbox. Improve your own efficiency by organizing your tools so that those used most frequently can be reached easily without digging through the entire contents of the box. Avoid accumulating unnecessary junk.

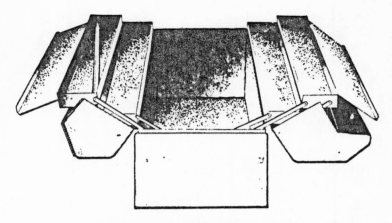

Figure 1-1.—Standard toolbox

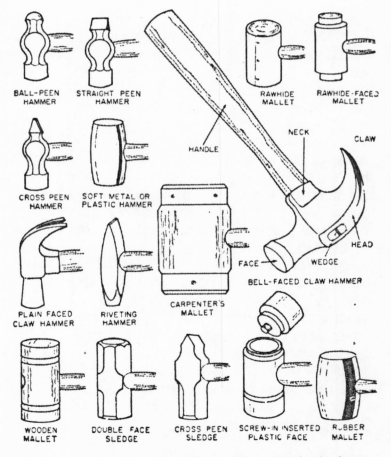

BALL-PEEN HAMMER   STRAIGHT PEEN HAMMER   RAWHIDE MALLET   RAWHIDE-FACED MALLET

HANDLE   NECK   CLAW

CROSS PEEN HAMMER   SOFT METAL OR PLASTIC HAMMER

PLAIN FACED CLAW HAMMER   RIVETING HAMMER   CARPENTER'S MALLET   FACE   WEDGE   HEAD

BELL-FACED CLAW HAMMER

WOODEN MALLET   DOUBLE FACE SLEDGE   CROSS PEEN SLEDGE   SCREW-IN INSERTED PLASTIC FACE   RUBBER MALLET

Figure 1-2.—Hammers, mallets and sledges.

4

STRIKING TOOLS

Hammers, mallets, and sledges are used to apply a striking force. The tool you select (fig. 1-2) will depend upon the intended application.

HAMMERS

Carpenter's Hammer

The primary use of the carpenter's hammer is to drive or draw (pull) nails. Note the names of the various parts of the hammer shown in figure 1-2. The carpenter's hammer has either a curved or straight claw. The face may be either bell-faced or plain-faced, and the handle may be made of wood or steel.

Machinist's Hammer

Machinist's hammers are mostly used by people who work with metal or around machinery. These hammers are distinguished from carpenter hammers by a variable-shaped peen, rather than a claw, at the opposite end of the face (fig. 1-2). The ball-peen hammer is probably most familiar to you.

The ball-peen hammer, as its name implies, has a ball which is smaller in diameter than the face. It is therefore useful for striking areas that are too small for the face to enter.

Ball-peen hammers are made in different weights, usually 4, 6, 8, and 12 ounces and 1, 1 1/2, and 2 pounds. For most work a 1 1/2-pound and a 12-ounce hammer will suffice. However, a 4- or 6-ounce hammer will often be used for light work such as tapping a punch to cut gaskets out of sheet gasket material.

Machinist's hammers may be further divided into hard-face and soft-face classifications. The hard-faced hammer is made of forged tool steel while the soft-faced hammers have a head made from brass, lead, or a tightly rolled strip of rawhide. Plastic-tipped hammers, or solid plastic with a lead core for added weight, are becoming increasingly popular.

Soft-faced hammers, (fig. 1-2) should be used when there is danger of damaging the surface of the work, as when pounding on a machined surface. Most soft-faced hammers have heads that can be replaced as the need arises. Lead-faced hammers, for instance, quickly become battered and must be replaced, but have the advantage of striking a solid, heavy nonrebounding blow that is useful for such jobs as driving shafts into or out of tight holes. If a soft-faced hammer is not available, the surface to be hammered may be protected by covering it with a piece of soft brass, copper, or hard wood.

Using Hammers

Simple as the hammer is, there is a right and wrong way of using it. (See fig. 1-3.) The most common fault is holding the handle too close to the head. This is known as choking the

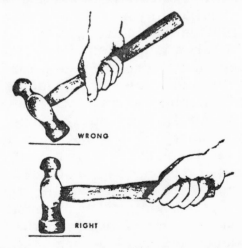

Figure 1-3.—Right and wrong way to use a ball-peen hammer.

hammer, and reduces the force of the blow. It also makes it harder to hold the head in an upright position. Except for light blows, hold the handle close to the end to increase the lever arm and produce a more effective blow. Hold the handle with the fingers underneath and the thumb along side or on top of the handle. The thumb should rest on the handle and never overlap the fingers. Try to hit the object with the full force of the hammer. Hold the hammer at such an angle that the face of the hammer and the surface of the object being hit will be parallel. This distributes the force of the blow over the full face and prevents damage to both the surface being struck and the face of the hammer.

MALLETS AND SLEDGES

The mallet is a short-handled tool used to drive wooden-handled chisels, gouges, wooden pins, or form or shape sheet metal where hard-faced hammers would mar or injure the finished work. Mallet heads are made from a soft material, usually wood, rawhide, or rubber. For example, a rubber-faced mallet is used for knocking out dents in an automobile. It is cylindrically shaped with two flat driving faces that are reinforced with iron bands. (See fig. 1-2.) Never use a mallet to drive nails, screws, or any object that may cause damage to the face.

The sledge is a steel headed, heavy duty driving tool that can be used for a number of purposes. Short-handled sledges are used to drive bolts, driftpins, and large nails, and to strike cold chisels and small hand rock drills. Long-handled sledges are used to break rock and concrete, to drive spikes, bolts, or stakes, and to strike rock drills and chisels.

The head of a sledge is generally made of a high carbon steel and may weigh from 6 to 16 lb. The shape of the head will vary according to the job for which the sledge is designed.

MAINTENANCE OF STRIKING TOOLS

Hammers, sledges, or mallets should be cleaned and repaired if necessary before they are stored. Before using, ensure that the faces are free from oil or other material that would cause the tool to glance off nails, spikes, or stakes. The heads should be dressed to remove any battered edges.

Never leave a wooden or rawhide mallet in the sun, as it will dry out and may cause the head to crack. A light film of oil should be left on the mallet to maintain a little moisture in the head.

The hammer handle should always be tight in the head. If it is loose the head may fly off and cause an injury. The eye or hole in the hammer head is made with a slight taper in both directions from the center. After the handle, which is tapered to fit the eye, is inserted in the head, a steel or wooden wedge is driven into the end of the handle that is inserted into the head. This wedge expands the handle and causes it to fill the opposite taper in the eye. Thus the handle is wedged in both directions as shown in figure 1-4. If the wedge starts to come out, it should be driven in again to tighten the handle. If the wedge comes out, replace it before continuing to use the hammer. If you cannot get another wedge right away, you may file one out of a piece of flat steel.

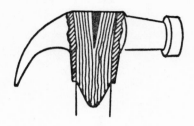

Figure 1-4.—Handle expanded
in hammer head by wedges.

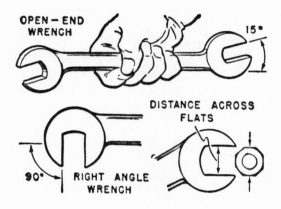

Figure 1-5.—Open-end wrenches

SAFETY PRECAUTIONS

Some important things to remember when using a hammer or mallet follow:

● Do not use a hammer handle for bumping parts in assembly, and never use it as a pry bar. Such abuses will cause the handle to split, and a split handle can produce bad cuts or pinches. When a handle splits or cracks, do not try to repair it by binding with string or wire. REPLACE IT.

9

● Make sure the handle fits tightly on the head.

● Do not strike a hardened steel surface with a steel hammer. Small pieces of steel may break off and injure someone in the eye or damage the work. However, it is permissible to strike a punch or chisel directly with the ball-peen hammer because the steel in the heads of punches and chisels is slightly softer than that of the hammerhead.

TURNING TOOLS (WRENCHES)

A wrench is a basic tool that is used to exert a twisting force on bolt heads, nuts, studs and pipes. The special wrenches designed to do certain jobs are, in most cases, variations of the basic wrenches that will be described in this section.

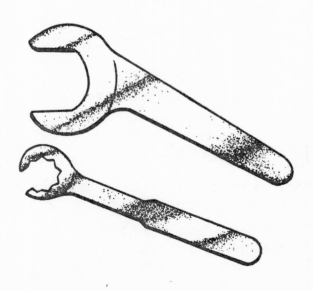

Figure 1-6.—Hydraulic wrenches.

The size of any wrench used on bolt-heads or nuts is determined by the size of the opening between the jaws of the wrench. The opening of a wrench is manufactured slightly larger than the bolt head or nut that it is designed to fit. Hex-nuts (six-sided) and other types of nut or bolt heads are measured across opposite flats (fig. 1-5). A wrench that is designed to fit a 3/8-inch nut or bolt usually has a clearance of from 5 to 8 thousandths of an inch. This clearance allows the wrench to slide on and off the nut or bolt with a minimum of "play." If the wrench is too large, the points of the nut or bolt head will be rounded and destroyed.

There are many types of wrenches. Each type is designed for a specific use.

OPEN-END WRENCHES

Solid, nonadjustable wrenches with openings in one or both ends are called open-end wrenches. (See fig. 1-5.) Usually they come in sets of from 6 to 10 wrenches with sizes ranging from 5/16 to 1 inch. Wrenches with small openings are usually shorter than wrenches with large openings. This proportions the lever advantage of the wrench to the bolt or stud and helps prevent wrench breakage or damage to the bolt or stud. One exception exists.

Open-end wrenches may have their jaws parallel to the handle or at angles anywhere up to 90 degrees. The average angle is 15 degrees (fig. 1-5). This angular displacement variation permits selection of a wrench suited for places where there is room to make only a part of a complete turn of a nut or bolt. If the wrench is turned over after the first swing, it will fit on the same flats and turn the nut farther. After two swings on the wrench, the nut is turned far enough so that a new set of flats are

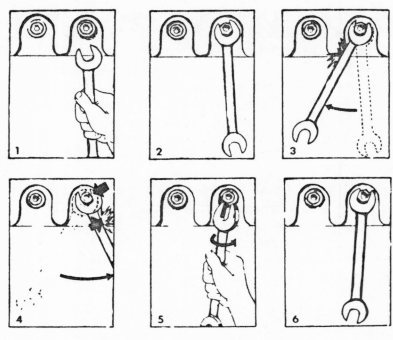

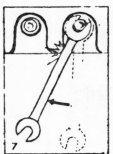

1. WRENCH, WITH OPENING SLOPING TO THE LEFT, ABOUT TO BE PLACED ON NUT

2. WRENCH POSITIONED AND READY TO TIGHTEN NUT. NOTE THAT SPACE FOR SWINGING THE WRENCH IS LIMITED.

3. WRENCH HAS BEEN MOVED CLOCKWISE TO TIGHTEN THE NUT AND NOW STRIKES THE CASTING WHICH PREVENTS FURTHER MOVEMENT

4. WRENCH IS REMOVED FROM NUT AND TURNED COUNTER CLOCKWISE TO BE PLACED ON THE NEXT SET OF FLATS ON NUT BUT CORNER OF CASTING PREVENTS WRENCH FROM FITTING ONTO THE NUT

5. WRENCH IS BEING FLOPPED OVER SO THAT WRENCH OPENING WILL SLOPE TO THE RIGHT

6. IN THIS FLOPPED POSITION, THE WRENCH WILL FIT THE NEXT TWO FLATS ON THE NUT

7. WRENCH NOW IS PULLED CLOCKWISE TO FURTHER TIGHTEN NUT UNTIL WRENCH AGAIN STRIKES CASTING BY REPEATING THE FLOPPING PROCEDURE, THE NUT CAN BE TURNED UNTIL IT IS TIGHT

Figure 1-7.—Use of open-end wrench.

in position for the wrench as shown in figure 1-7.

Handles are usually straight, but may be curved. Those with curved handles are called S-wrenches. Other open-end wrenches may have offset handles. This allows the head to reach nut or bolt heads that are sunk below the surface.

BOX WRENCHES

Box wrenches (fig. 1-8) are safer than open-end wrenches since there is less likelihood they will slip off the work. They completely surround or box a nut or bolt head.

The most frequently used box wrench has 12 points or notches arranged in a circle in the head and can be used with a minimum swing angle of 30 degrees. Six and eight point wrenches are used for heavy, 12 for medium, and 16 for light duty only.

Figure 1-8.—12-point box-end wrench.

One advantage of the 12 point construction is the thin wall. It is more suitable for turning nuts which are hard to get at with an open-end wrench. Another advantage is that the wrench will operate between obstructions where the space for handle swing is limited. A very short swing of the handle will turn the nut far enough to allow the wrench to be lifted and the next set of points fitted to the corners of the nut.

One disadvantage of the box-end wrench is the loss of time which occurs whenever a craftsman has to lift the wrench off and place it back on the nut in another position in case there is insufficient clearance to spin the wrench in a full circle.

COMBINATION WRENCH

After a tight nut is broken loose, it can be unscrewed much more quickly with an open-end wrench than with a box-wrench. This is where a combination box-open end wrench (fig. 1-9) comes in handy. You can use the box-end for breaking nuts loose or for snugging them down, and the open-end for faster turning.

The box-end portion of the wrench can be designed with an offset in the handle. Notice in figure 1-9, how the 15-degree offset allows clearance over nearby parts.

The correct use of open-end and box-end wrenches can be summed up in a few simple rules, most important of which is to be sure that the wrench properly fits the nut or bolt head.

When you have to pull hard on the wrench, as in loosening a tight nut, make sure the wrench is seated squarely on the flats of the nut.

PULL on the wrench—DO NOT PUSH. Pushing a wrench is a good way to skin your knuckles if the wrench slips or the nut breaks loose unexpectedly. If it is impossible to pull the wrench, and you must push, do it with the palm of your hand and hold your palm open.

Only actual practice will tell you if you are using the right amount of force on the wrench. The best way to tighten a nut is to turn it until the wrench has a firm, solid "feel." This will turn the nut to proper tightness without stripping the threads or twisting off the bolt.

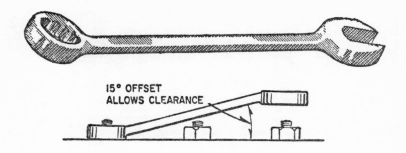

Figure 1-9.—Combination wrench.

SOCKET WRENCH

The socket wrench is one of the most versatile wrenches in the toolbox. Basically, it consists of a handle and a socket type wrench which can be attached to the handle.

The "Spintite" wrench shown in figure 1-10, is a special type of socket wrench. It has a hollow shaft to accommodate a bolt protruding through a nut, has a hexagonal head, and is used like a screwdriver. It is supplied in small sizes only and is useful for assembly and electrical work. When used for the latter purpose, it must have an insulated handle.

A complete socket wrench set consists of several types of handles along with bar extensions, adapters, and a variety of sockets (fig. 1-10).

Sockets

A socket (fig. 1-11) has a square opening cut in one end to fit a square drive lug on a detachable handle. In the other end of the socket is a 6-point or 12-point opening very much like the opening in the box end wrench. The 12-point socket needs to be swung only half as far as the 6-point socket before it has to be lifted and fitted on the nut for a new grip. It can therefore be used in closer quarters where there is less room to move the handle. A ratchet

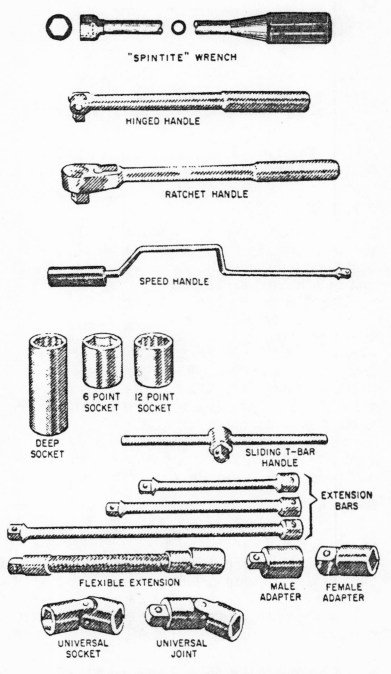

"SPINTITE" WRENCH

HINGED HANDLE

RATCHET HANDLE

SPEED HANDLE

6 POINT SOCKET

12 POINT SOCKET

DEEP SOCKET

SLIDING T-BAR HANDLE

EXTENSION BARS

FLEXIBLE EXTENSION

MALE ADAPTER

FEMALE ADAPTER

UNIVERSAL SOCKET

UNIVERSAL JOINT

Figure 1-10.—Socket set components.

handle eliminates the necessity of lifting the socket and refitting it on the nut again and again.

Sockets are classified for size according to two factors. One is the size of the square opening, which fits on the square drive lug of the handle. This size is known as the drive size. The other is the size of the opening in the opposite end, which fits the nut or bolt.

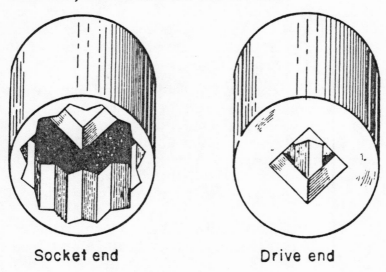

Socket end   Drive end

Figure 1-11.—12-point sockets.

Socket Handles

There are four types of handles used with these sockets. (See fig. 1-10.) Each type has special advantages, and the experienced worker chooses the one best suited for the job at hand. The square driving lug on the socket wrench handles has a spring-loaded ball that fits into a recess in the socket receptacle. This mated ball-recess feature keeps the socket engaged with the drive lug during normal usage. A slight pull on the socket, however, disassembles the connection.

17

RATCHET.—The ratchet handle has a reversing lever which operates a pawl (or dog) inside the head of the tool. Pulling the handle in one direction causes the pawl to engage in the ratchet teeth and turn the socket. Moving the handle in the opposite direction causes the pawl to slide over the teeth, permitting the handle to back up without moving the socket. This allows rapid turning of the nut or bolt after each partial turn of the handle. With the reversing lever in one position, the handle can be used for tightening. In the other position, it can be used for loosening.

HINGED HANDLE.—The hinged handle is also very convenient. To loosen tight nuts, swing the handle at right angles to the socket. This gives the greatest possible leverage. After loosening the nut to the point where it turns easily, move the handle into the vertical position and then turn the handle with the fingers.

SLIDING T-BAR HANDLE.—When using the sliding bar or T-handle, the head can be positioned anywhere along the sliding bar. Select the position which is needed for the job at hand.

SPEED HANDLE.—The speed handle is worked like the wood-worker's brace. After the nuts are first loosened with the sliding bar handle or the ratchet handle, the speed handle can be used to remove the nuts more quickly. In many instances the speed handle is not strong enough to be used for breaking loose or tightening the nut. The speed socket wrench should be used carefully to avoid damaging the nut threads.

Accessories

To complete the socket wrench set, there are several accessory items. Extension bars of different lengths are made to extend the distance from the socket to the handle. A universal joint allows the nut to be turned with the wrench handle at an angle. Universal sockets are also available. The use of universal joints, bar extensions, and universal sockets in combination with appropriate handles makes it possible to form a variety of tools that will reach otherwise inaccessible nuts and bolts.

Another accessory item is an adapter which allows you to use a handle having one size of drive and a socket having a different size drive. For example, a 3/8- by 1/4-inch adapter makes it possible to turn all 1/4-inch square drive sockets with any 3/8-inch-square drive handle.

TORQUE WRENCHES

There are times when, for engineering reasons, a definite force must be applied to a nut or bolt head. In such cases a torque wrench must be used. For example, equal force must be applied to all the head bolts of an engine. Otherwise, one bolt may bear the brunt of the force of internal combustion and ultimately cause engine failure.

The three most commonly used torque wrenches are the Deflecting Beam, Dial Indicating, and Micrometer Setting types (fig. 1-12). When using the Deflecting Beam and the Dial Indicating torque wrenches, the torque is read visually on a dial or scale mounted on the handle of the wrench.

To use the Micrometer Setting type, unlock the grip and adjust the handle to the desired setting on the micrometer type scale, then relock the grip. Install the required socket or adapter to the square drive of the handle. Place the wrench assembly on the nut or bolt and pull in a clockwise direction with a smooth, steady motion. (A fast or jerky motion will result in an improperly torqued unit.) When the torque

19

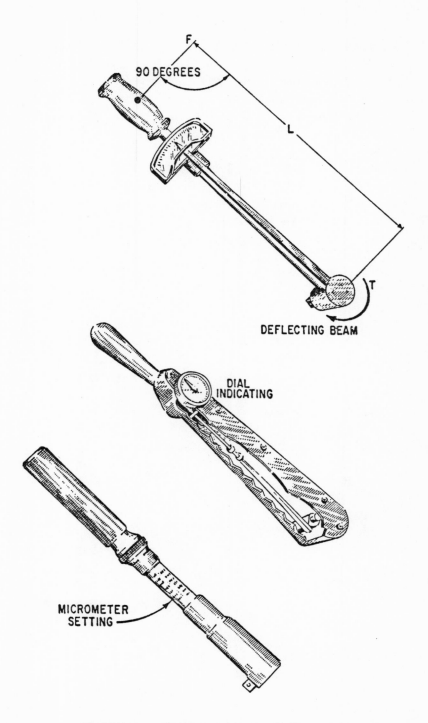

Figure 1-12.—Torque wrenches.

applied reaches the torque value, which is indicated on the handle setting, a signal mechanism will automatically issue an audible click, and the handle will release or "break," and move freely for a short distance. The release and free travel is easily felt, so there is no doubt about when the torquing process is complete.

Manufacturers' and technical manuals generally specify the amount of torque to be applied. To assure getting the correct amount of torque on the fasteners, it is important that the wrench be used properly in accordance with manufacturers' instructions.

Use that torque wrench which will read about mid-range for the amount of torque to be applied. BE SURE THAT THE TORQUE WRENCH HAS BEEN CALIBRATED BEFORE YOU USE IT. Remember, too, that the accuracy of torque-measuring depends a lot on how the threads are cut and the cleanliness of the threads. Make sure you inspect and clean the threads. If the manufacturer specifies a thread lubricant, it must be used to obtain the most accurate torque reading. When using the Deflecting Beam or Dial Indicating wrenches, hold the torque at the desired value until the reading is steady.

Torque wrenches are delicate and expensive tools. The following precautions should be observed when using them:

1. When using the Micrometer Setting type, do not move the setting handle below the lowest torque setting. However, it should be placed at its lowest setting prior to returning to storage.

2. Do not use the torque wrench to apply greater amounts of torque than its rated capacity.

3. Do not use the torque wrench to break loose bolts which have been previously tightened.

4. Do not drop the wrench. If dropped, the accuracy will be affected.

21

5. Do not apply a torque wrench to a nut that has been tightened. Back off the nut one turn with a non-torque wrench and retighten to the correct torque with the indicating torque wrench.

ADJUSTABLE WRENCHES

A handy all-round wrench that is generally included in every toolbox is the adjustable open-end wrench. This wrench is not intended to take the place of the regular solid open-end wrench. Additionally, it is not built for use on extremely hard-to-turn items. Its usefulness is achieved by being capable of fitting odd-sized nuts. This flexibility is achieved although one jaw of the adjustable open-end wrench is fixed because the other jaw is moved along a slide by a thumbscrew adjustment (fig. 1-13). By turning the thumbscrew, the jaw opening may be adjusted to fit various sizes of nuts.

Adjustable wrenches are available in varying sizes ranging from 4 to 24 inches in length. The size of the wrench selected for a particular job is dependent upon the size of nut or bolt head to which the wrench is to be applied. As the jaw opening increases the length of the wrench increases.

Adjustable wrenches are often called "knuckle busters," because mechanics frequently suffer these consequences as a result of improper usage of these tools. To avoid accidents, follow four simple steps. First, choose a wrench of the correct size; that is, do not pick

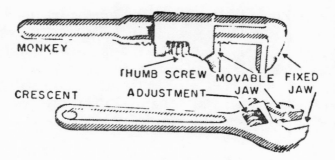

Figure 1-13.—Adjustable wrenches

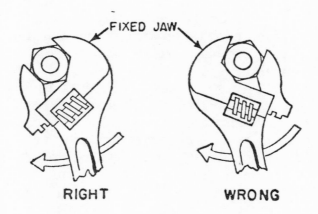

Figure 1-14.—Proper procedure for pulling adjustable wrenches.

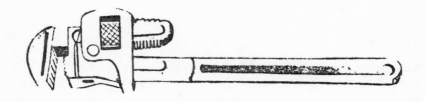

Figure 1-15.—Adjustable pipe wrench.

pivoted to permit a gripping action on the work. This tool must be used with discretion, as the jaws are serrated and always make marks on the work unless adequate precautions are observed. The jaws should be adjusted so the bite on the work will be taken at about the center of the jaws.

Chain Pipe Wrench

A different type pipe wrench, used mostly on large sizes of pipe, is the chain/pipe wrench (fig. 1-16). This tool works in one direction only, but can be backed partly around the work and a fresh hold taken without freeing the chain. To reverse the operation the grip is taken on the opposite side of the head. The head is a large 12-inch wrench and adjust the jaw for use on a 3/8-inch nut. This could result in a broken bolt and a bloody hand. Second, be sure the jaws of the correct size wrench are adjusted to fit snugly on the nut. Third, position the wrench around the nut until the nut is all the way into the throat of the jaws. If not used in this manner, the result is apt to be as bloody as before. Fourth, pull the handle toward the side having the adjustable jaw (fig. 1-14). This will prevent the adjustable jaw from springing open and slipping off the nut. If the location of the work will not allow for all four steps to be followed when using an adjustable wrench, then select another type of wrench for the job.

Pipe Wrench (Stillson)

When rotating or holding round work an adjustable pipe wrench (Stillson) may be used (fig. 1-15). The movable jaw on a pipe wrench is double ended and can be reversed when the teeth on one end are worn out.

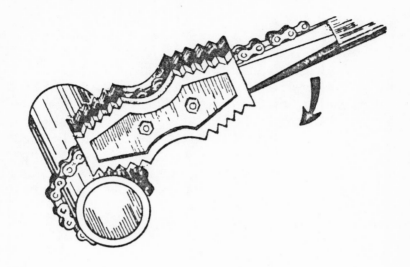

Figure 1-16.—Chain pipe wrench.

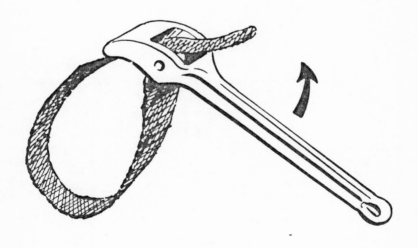

Figure 1-17.—Strap wrench.

Strap Wrench

The strap wrench (fig. 1-17) is similar to the chain pipe wrench but uses a heavy web strap in place of the chain. This wrench is used for turning pipe or cylinders where you do not want to mar the surface of the work. To use this wrench, the webbed strap is placed around the cylinder and passed through the slot in the metal body of the wrench. The strap is then pulled up tight and as the mechanic turns the wrench in the desired direction, the webbed strap tightens further around the cylinder. This gripping action causes the cylinder to turn.

SPANNER WRENCHES

Many special nuts are made with notches cut into their outer edge. For these nuts a hook spanner (fig. 1-18) is required. This wrench has a curved arm with a lug or hook on the end. This lug fits into one of the notches of the nut and the handle turned to loosen or tighten the nut. This spanner may be made for just one particular size of notched nut, or it may have a hinged arm to adjust it to a range of sizes.

Another type of spanner is the pin spanner. Pin spanners have a pin in place of a hook. This pin fits into a hole in the outer part of the nut.

Face pin spanners are designed so that the pins fit into holes in the face of the nut (fig. 1-18).

When you use a spanner wrench, you must ensure that the pins, lugs, or hooks make firm contact with the nut while the turning force is transferred from the wrench to the nut.

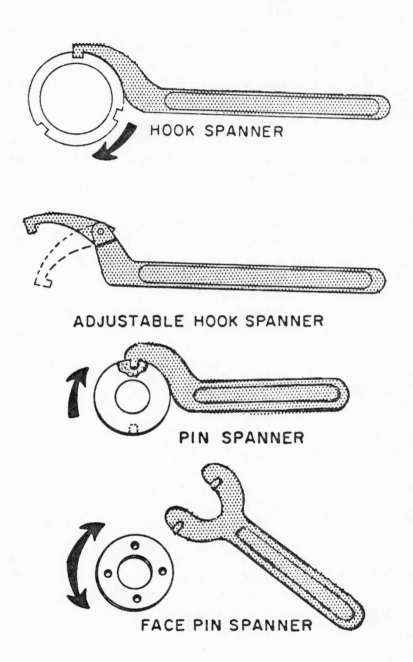

HOOK SPANNER

ADJUSTABLE HOOK SPANNER

PIN SPANNER

FACE PIN SPANNER

Figure 1-18.—General-purpose spanner wrenches.

27

SETSCREW WRENCHES
(ALLEN AND BRISTOL)

In some places it is desirable to use recessed heads on setscrews and capscrews. One type (Allen) screw is used extensively on office machines and in machine shops. The other type (Bristol) is used infrequently.

Recessed head screws usually have a hex-shaped (six-sided) recess. To remove or tighten this type screw requires a special wrench that will fit in the recess. This wrench is called an Allen-type wrench. Allen-type wrenches are made from hexagonal L-shaped bars of tool steel (fig. 1-19). They range in size up to 3/4 inch. When using the Allen-type wrench make sure you use the correct size to prevent rounding or spreading the head of the screw. A snug fit within the recessed head of the screw is an indication that you have the correct size.

The Bristol wrench is made from round stock. It is also L-shaped, but one end is fluted to fit the flutes or little splines in the Bristol setscrew (fig. 1-19).

NONSPARKING WRENCHES

Nonsparking wrenches are wrenches that will not cause sparks to be generated when working with steel nuts and bolts. They are generally made from a copper alloy (bronze). However, they may be made from other nonsparking materials.

Nonsparking wrenches must be used in areas where flammable materials are present. These tools are used extensively when working around gasoline-carrying vehicles.

SAFETY RULES FOR WRENCHES

There are a few basic rules that you should keep in mind when using wrenches. They are:

1. Always use a wrench that fits the nut properly.

2. Keep wrenches clean and free from oil. Otherwise they may slip, resulting in possible serious injury to you or damage to the work.

3. Do not increase the leverage of a wrench by placing a pipe over the handle. Increased leverage may damage the wrench or the work.

4. Provide some sort of kit or case for all wrenches. Return them to it at the completion of each job. This saves time and trouble and facilitates selection of tools for the next job.

5. Determine which way a nut should be turned before trying to loosen it. Most nuts are turned counterclockwise for removal. This may seem obvious, but even experienced men have been observed straining at the wrench in the tightening direction when they wanted to loosen it.

6. Learn to select your wrenches to fit the type of work you are doing.

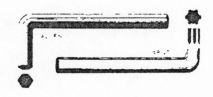

Figure 1-19.—Allen and Bristol type wrenches.

METAL CUTTING TOOLS

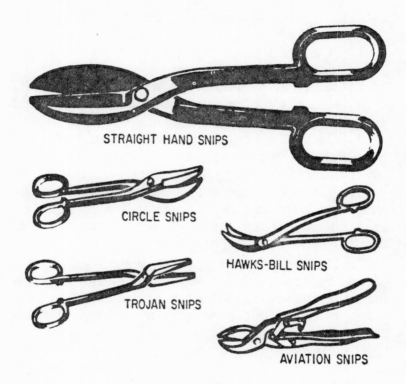

STRAIGHT HAND SNIPS

CIRCLE SNIPS

HAWKS-BILL SNIPS

TROJAN SNIPS

AVIATION SNIPS

Figure 1-20.—Snips.

SNIPS AND SHEARS

Snips and shears are used for cutting sheet metal and steel of various thicknesses and shapes. Normally, the heavier or thicker materials are cut by shears.

One of the handiest tools for cutting light (up to 1/16 inch thick) sheet metal is the hand snip (tip snips). The STRAIGHT HAND SNIPS shown in fig. 1-20 have blades that are straight and cutting edges that are sharpened to an 85-degree angle. Snips like this can be obtained in different sizes ranging from the small 6-inch to the large 14-inch snip. Tin snips will also work on slightly heavier gages of soft metals such as aluminum alloys.

Snips will not remove any metal when a cut is made. There is danger, though, of causing minute metal fractures along the edges of the metal during the shearing process. For this reason, it is better to cut just outside the layout line. This procedure will allow you to dress the cutting edge while keeping the material within required dimensions.

Cutting extremely heavy gage metal always presents the possibility of springing the blades. Once the blades are sprung, hand snips are useless. When cutting heavy material use the rear portion of the blades. This procedure not only avoids the possibility of springing the blades but also gives you greater cutting leverage.

Many snips have small serrations (notches) on the cutting edges of the blades. These serrations tend to prevent the snips from slipping backwards when a cut is being made. Although this feature does make the actual cutting easier, it mars the edges of the metal slightly. You can remove these small cutting marks if you allow proper clearance for dressing the metal to size. There are many other types of hand snips used for special jobs but the snips discussed here can be used for almost any common type of work.

Cutting Sheet Metal with Snips

It is hard to cut circles or small arcs with straight snips. There are snips especially designed for circular cutting. They are called CIRCLE SNIPS, HAWKS-BILL SNIPS, TROJAN SNIPS, and AVIATION SNIPS (fig. 1-20).

To cut large holes in the lighter gages of sheet metal, start the cut by punching or otherwise making a hole in the center of the area to be cut out. With an aviation snips, as shown in figure 1-21, or some other narrow-bladed snips, make a spiral cut from the starting hole out toward the scribed circle and continue cutting until the scrap falls away.

To cut a disk in the lighter gages of sheet metal, use a combination snips or a straight blade snips as shown in figure 1-22. First, cut away any surplus material outside of the scribed circle leaving only a narrow piece to be removed by the final cut. Make the final cut just outside of the layout line. This will permit you to see the scribed line while you are cutting and will cause the scrap to curl up below the blade of the snips where it will be out of the way while the complete cut is being made.

Figure 1-21.—Cutting an inside
hole with snips.

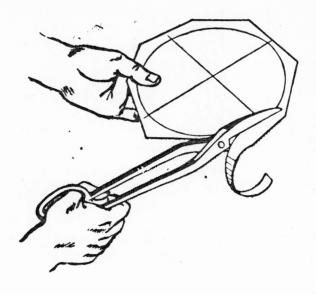

Figure 1-22.—Cutting a disk out of
sheet metal.

To make straight cuts, place the sheet metal
on a bench with the marked guideline over the
edge of the bench and hold the sheet down with
one hand. With the other hand hold the snips so
that the flat sides of the blades are at right
angles to the surface of the work. If the blades
are not at right angles to the surface of the
work, the edges of the cut will be slightly bent
and burred. The bench edge will also act as a
guide when cutting with the snips. The snips
will force the scrap metal down so that it does
not interfere with cutting. Any of the hand snips
may be used for straight cuts. When notches
are too narrow to be cut out with a pair of
snips, make the side cuts with the snips and cut
the base of the notch with a cold chisel.

Safety and Care

Learn to use snips properly. They should always be oiled and adjusted to permit ease of cutting and to produce a surface that is free from burrs. If the blades bind, or if they are too far 'apart, the snips should be adjusted.

Never use snips as screwdrivers, hammers, or pry bars. They break easily.

Do not attempt to cut heavier materials than the snips are designed for. Never use tin snips to cut hardened steel wire or other similar objects. Such use will dent or nick the cutting edges of the blades.

Never toss snips in a toolbox where the cutting edges can come into contact with other tools. This dulls the cutting edges and may even break the blades.

When snips are not in use, hang them on hooks or lay them on an uncrowded shelf or bench.

BOLT CUTTERS

Bolt cutters (fig. 1-23) are giant shears with very short blades and long handles. The handles are hinged at one end. The cutters are at the ends of extensions which are jointed in such a way that the inside joint is forced outwards when the handles are closed, thus forcing the cutting edges together with great force.

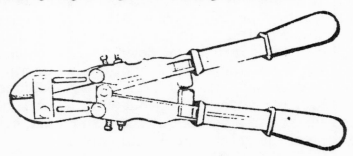

Figure 1-23.—Bolt cutters.

Bolt cutters are made in lengths of 18 to 36 inches. The larger ones will cut mild steel bolts and rods up to 1/2 inch. The material to be cut should be kept as far back in the jaws as possible. Never attempt to cut spring wire or other tempered metal with bolt cutters. This will cause the jaws to be sprung or nicked.

Adjusting screws near the middle hinges provide a means for ensuring that both jaws move the same amount when the handles are pressed together. Keep the adjusting screws just tight enough to ensure that the cutting edges meet along their entire length when the jaws are closed. The hinges should be kept well oiled at all times.

When using bolt cutters make sure your fingers are clear of the jaws and hinges. Take care that the bolt head or piece of rod cut off does not fly and injure you or someone else. If the cutters are brought together rapidly, sometimes a bolt-head or piece of rod being cut off will fly some distance.

Bolt cutters are fairly heavy, so make sure that they are stored in a safe place where they will not fall and injure someone.

HACKSAWS

Hacksaws are used to cut metal that is too heavy for snips or boltcutters. Thus, metal bar stock can be cut readily with hacksaws.

There are two parts to a hacksaw: the frame and the blade. Common hacksaws have either an adjustable or solid frame (fig. 1-24). Most hacksaws ordinarily in use are of the adjustable frame type. Adjustable frames can be made to hold blades from 8 to 16 inches long, while those with solid frames take only the length blade for which they are made. This length is the distance between the two pins that hold the blade in place.

Hacksaw blades are made of high-grade tool steel, hardened and tempered. There are two types: the all-hard and the flexible. All hard blades are hardened throughout, whereas only the teeth of the flexible blades are hardened. Hacksaw blades are about one-half inch wide, have from 14 to 32 teeth per inch, and are from 8 to 16 inches long. The blades have a hole at each end which hooks to a pin in the frame. All hacksaw frames which hold the blades either parallel or at right angles to the frame are provided with a wingnut or screw to permit tightening or removing the blade.

The SET in a saw refers to how much the teeth are pushed out in opposite directions from the sides of the blade. The four different kinds of set are ALTERNATE set, DOUBLE ALTER-NATE set, RAKER set, and WAVE set. Three of these are shown in figure 1-25.

The teeth in the alternate set are staggered, one to the left and one to the right throughout the length of the blade. On the double alternate set blade, two adjoining teeth are staggered to the right, two to the left, and so on. On the raker set blade, every third tooth remains straight and the other two are set alternately. On the wave (undulated) set blade, short sections of teeth are bent in opposite directions.

The hacksaw is often used improperly. Although it can be used with limited success by an inexperienced man, a little thought and study given to its proper use will result in faster and better work and less dulling and breaking of blades.

Good work with a hacksaw depends not only upon the proper use of the saw, but also upon the proper selection of the blades for the work to be done. Figure 1-26 will help you select the proper blade to use when sawing metal with a hacksaw. Coarse blades with fewer teeth per inch cut faster and are less liable to choke up with chips. However, finer blades with more teeth per inch are necessary when thin sections are being cut. The selection should be made so that, as each tooth starts its cut, the tooth ahead of it will still be cutting.

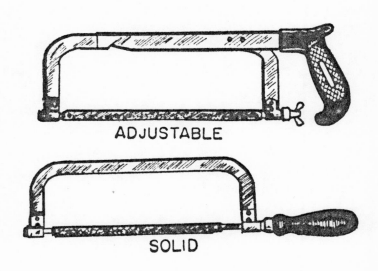

Figure 1-24.—Hacksaws.

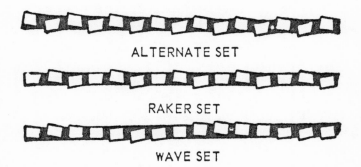

Figure 1-25.—"Set" of hacksaw
blade teeth.

14 TEETH PER INCH

FOR LARGE SECTIONS
OF MILD MATERIAL

18 TEETH PER INCH

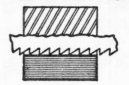

FOR LARGE SECTIONS
OF TOUGH STEEL

24 TEETH PER INCH

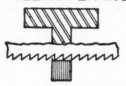

FOR ANGLE IRON, HEAVY
PIPE, BRASS, COPPER

32 TEETH PER INCH

FOR THIN TUBING

**KEEP AT LEAST TWO TEETH CUTTING
TO AVOID THIS**

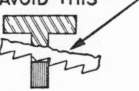

Figure 1-26.—Selecting the proper
hacksaw blade.

To make the cut, first install the blade in the
hacksaw frame (fig. 1-27) so that the teeth point
away from the handle of the hacksaw. (Hand
hacksaws cut on the push stroke.) Tighten the
wingnut so that the blade is definitely under
tension. This helps make straight cuts.

Place the material to be cut in a vise. A
minimum of overhang will reduce vibration,
give a better cut, and lengthen the life of the
blade. Have the layout line outside of the vise
jaw so that the line is visible while you work.

38

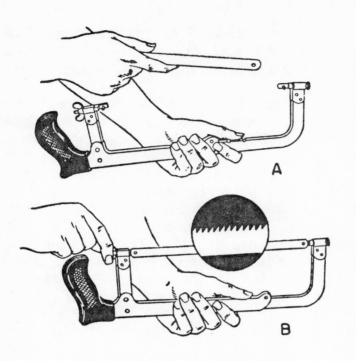

Figure 1-27.—Installing a
hacksaw blade.

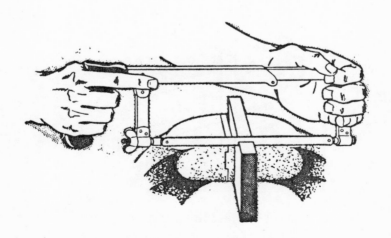

Figure 1-28.—Proper way to hold
a hacksaw.

The proper method of holding the hacksaw is depicted in figure 1-28. See how the index finger of the right hand, pointed forward, aids in guiding the frame.

When cutting, let your body sway ahead and back with each stroke. Apply pressure on the forward stroke, which is the cutting stroke, but not on the return stroke. From 40 to 50 strokes per minute is the usual speed. Long, slow, steady strokes are preferred.

For long cuts (fig. 1-29) rotate the blade in the frame so that the length of the cut is not limited by the depth of the frame. Hold the work with the layout line close to the vise jaws, raising the work in the vise as the sawing proceeds.

Saw thin metal as shown in figure 1-30. Notice the long angle at which the blade enters the saw groove (kerf). This permits several teeth to be cutting at the same time.

Metal which is too thin to be held, as shown in figure 1-30, can be placed between blocks of wood, as shown in figure 1-31. The wood provides support for several teeth as they are

Figure 1-29.—Making a long cut
near the edge of stock.

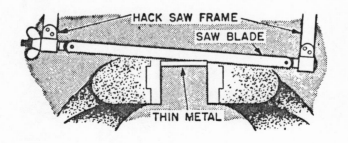

Figure 1-30.—Cutting thin metal
with a hacksaw.

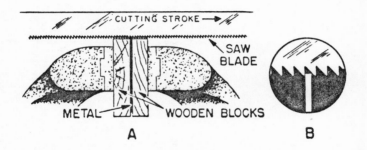

Figure 1-31.—Cutting thin metal
between two wooden blocks.

cutting. Without the wood, as shown at B in figure 1-31, teeth will be broken due to excessive
vibration of the stock and because individual
teeth have to absorb the full power of the stroke.

Cut thin metal with layout lines on the face
by using a piece of wood behind it (fig. 1-32).
Hold the wood and the metal in the jaws of the
vise, using a C-clamp when necessary. The
wood block helps support the blade and produces a smoother cut. Using the wood only in
back of the metal permits the layout lines to be
seen.

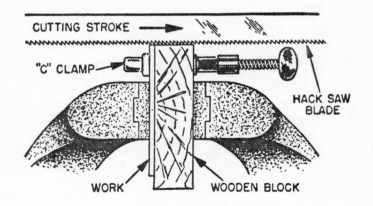

Figure 1-32.—Cutting thin metal using
wood block with layout lines.

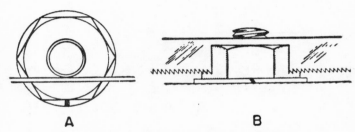

A   B

Figure 1-33.—Removing a frozen
nut with a hacksaw.

To remove a frozen nut with a hacksaw, saw
into the nut as shown in figure 1-33, starting
the blade close to the threads on the bolt or stud
and parallel to one face of the nut as shown in
figure 1-33A. Saw parallel to the bolt until the
teeth of the blade almost reach the lockwasher.
Lockwashers are hard and will ruin hacksaw
blades, so do not try to saw them. Figure 1-33B
shows when to stop sawing. Then, with a cold
chisel and hammer, remove this one side of the
nut completely by opening the saw kerf. Put an
adjustable wrench across this new flat and the
one opposite and again try to remove the frozen
nut. Since very little original metal remains

on this one side of the nut, the nut will either give or break away entirely and permit its removal.

To saw a wide kerf in the head of a cap screw or machine bolt, fit the hand hacksaw frame with two blades side by side, and with teeth lined up in the same direction. With slow, steady strokes, saw the slot approximately one-third the thickness of the head of the cap screw as shown in figure 1-34. Such a slot will permit subsequent holding or turning with a screwdriver when it is impossible, due to close quarters, to use a wrench.

Hacksaw Safety

The main danger in using hacksaws is injury to your hand if the blade breaks. The blade will break if too much pressure is applied, when the saw is twisted, when the cutting speed is too fast, or when the blade becomes loose in the frame. Additionally, if the work is not tight in the vise, it will sometimes slip, twisting the blade enough to break it.

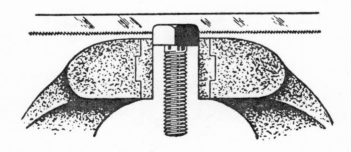

Figure 1-34.—Cutting a wide kerf in the head of a capscrew or bolt.

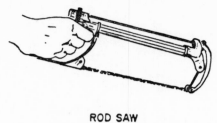

ROD SAW

ROD SAW BLADE

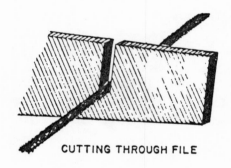

CUTTING THROUGH FILE

MAGNIFIED PORTION OF BLADE

Figure 1-35.—Rod Saw and operations.

ROD SAWS

An improvement in industrial technology provides us with a tool that can cut material an ordinary hacksaw can't even scratch. The rod saw (fig. 1-35) acts like a diamond in its capability of cutting hard metals and materials such as stainless steel, Inconel, titanium, and carbon phenolics.

The rod saw cuts through material by means of hundreds of tungsten-carbide particles permanently bonded to the rod (see magnified portion of fig. 1-35). The rod saw cuts through stainless steel and files with ease.

A unique feature of this saw is its capability of cutting on the forward and reverse strokes.

CHISELS

Chisels are tools that can be used for chipping or cutting metal. They will cut any metal that is softer than the materials of which they are made. Chisels are made from a good grade tool steel and have a hardened cutting edge and beveled head. Cold chisels are classified according to the shape of their points, and the width of the cutting edge denotes their size. The most common shapes of chisels are flat (cold chisel), cape, round nose, and diamond point (fig. 1-36).

The type chisel most commonly used is the flat cold chisel, which serves to cut rivets, split nuts, chip castings, and cut thin metal sheets. The cape chisel is used for special jobs like cutting keyways, narrow grooves and square corners. Round-nose chisels make circular grooves and chip inside corners with a fillet. Finally, the diamond-point is used for cutting V-grooves and sharp corners.

As with other tools there is a correct technique for using a chisel. Select a chisel that is large enough for the job. Be sure to use a hammer that matches the chisel; that is, the larger chisel will absorb the blows of a light hammer and will do virtually no cutting.

As a general rule, hold the chisel in the left hand with the thumb and first finger about 1 inch from the top. It should be held steadily but not tightly. The finger muscles should be relaxed, so if the hammer strikes the hand it will permit the hand to slide down the tool and lessen the effect of the blow. Keep the eyes on the cutting edge of the chisel, not on the head, and swing the hammer in the same plane as the body of the chisel. If you have a lot of chiseling to do, slide a piece of rubber hose over the chisel. This will lessen the shock to your hand.

When using a chisel for chipping, always wear goggles to protect your eyes. If other men are working close by, see that they are protected from flying chips by erecting a screen or shield to contain the chips. Remember that the time to take these precautions is before you start the job.

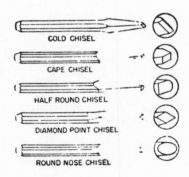

Figure 1-36.—Types of points on
metal cutting chisel.

FILES

A toolkit is not complete unless it contains an assortment of files. There are a number of different types of files in common use, and each type may range in length from 3 to 18 inches.

Grades

Files are graded according to the degree of fineness, and according to whether they have single- or double-cut teeth. The difference is apparent when you compare the files in figure 1-37A.

Single-cut files have rows of teeth cut parallel to each other. These teeth are set at an angle of about 65 degrees with the centerline. You will use single-cut files for sharpening tools, finish filing, and drawfiling. They are also the best tools for smoothing the edges of sheet metal.

Files with crisscrossed rows of teeth are double-cut files. The double cut forms teeth that are diamond-shaped and fast cutting. You will use double-cut files for quick removal of metal, and for rough work.

Files are also graded according to the spacing and size of their teeth, or their coarseness and fineness. Some of these grades are pictures in fig. 1-37B. In addition to the three grades shown, you may use some DEAD SMOOTH files, which have very fine teeth, and some ROUGH files with very coarse teeth. The fineness or coarseness of file teeth is also influenced by the length of the file. (The length of a file is the distance from the tip to the heel, and does not include the tang (fig. 1-37C).) When you have a chance, compare the actual size of the teeth of a 6-inch, single-cut smooth file and a 12-inch, single-cut smooth file; you will notice the 6-inch file has more teeth per inch than the 12-inch file.

Shapes

Files come in different shapes. Therefore, in selecting a file for a job, the shape of the finished work must be considered. Some of the cross sectional shapes are shown in figure 1-37D.

TRIANGULAR files are tapered (longitudinally) on all three sides. They are used to file acute internal angles, and to clear out square corners. Special triangular files are used to file saw teeth.

MILL files are tapered in both width and thickness. One edge has no teeth and is known as a SAFE EDGE. Mill files are used for smoothing lathe work, drawfiling, and other fine, precision work. Mill files are always single-cut.

FLAT files are general-purpose files and may be either single- or double-cut. They are tapered in width and thickness. HARD files, not shown, are somewhat thicker than flat files. They taper slightly in thickness, but their edges are parallel.

The flat or hard files most often used are the double-cut for rough work and the single-cut, smooth file for finish work.

SQUARE files are tapered on all four sides and are used to enlarge rectangular-shaped holes and slots. ROUND files serve the same purpose for round openings. Small round files are often called "rat tail" files.

The HALF ROUND file is a general-purpose tool. The rounded side is used for curved surfaces and the flat face on flat surfaces. When you file an inside curve, use a round or half-round file whose curve most nearly matches the curve of the work.

SINGLE CUT

DOUBLE CUT

A. SINGLE AND DOUBLE-CUT FILES

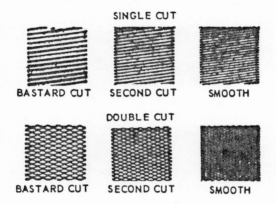

SINGLE CUT

BASTARD CUT   SECOND CUT   SMOOTH

DOUBLE CUT

BASTARD CUT   SECOND CUT   SMOOTH

B. DESIGN AND SPACING OF FILE TEETH

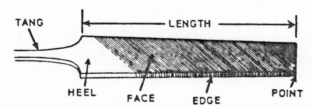

TANG   LENGTH

HEEL   FACE   EDGE   POINT

C. FILE NOMENCLATURE.

SQUARE   TRIANGULAR   ROUND

HALF ROUND   MILL   FLAT

D. CROSS-SECTIONAL SHAPES OF FILES

Figure 1-37.—File information.

Kits of small files, often called "Swiss Pattern" or "Jewelers" files, are used to fit parts of delicate mechanisms, and for filing work on instruments. Handle these small files carefully because they break easily.

FILING OPERATIONS

Using a file is an operation that is nearly indispensable when working with metal. You may be crossfiling, drawfiling, using a file card, or even polishing metal. Let's examine these operations.

When you have finished using a file it may be necessary to use an abrasive cloth or paper to finish the product. Whether this is necessary depends on how fine a finish you want on the work.

CROSSFILING.—Figure 1-38A shows a piece of mild steel being crossfiled. This means that the file is being moved across the surface of the work in approximately a crosswise direction.

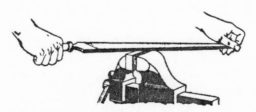

A. CROSSFILING A PIECE OF MILD STEEL

Figure 1-38.—Filing operations.

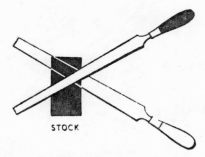

STOCK

B. ALTERNATING POSITIONS WHEN FILING

C. POLISHING ROUND METAL STOCK

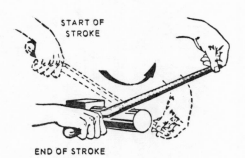

START OF STROKE

END OF STROKE

D. FILING ROUND METAL STOCK

Figure 1-38.–

51

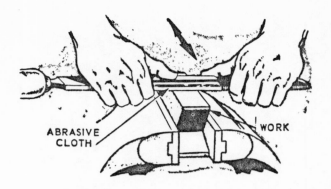

A. POLISHING METAL WITH ABRASIVE CLOTH WRAPPED AROUND A FILE

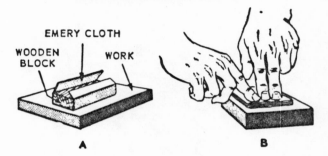

B. ALTERNATE METHODS FOR POLISHING METAL SURFACE

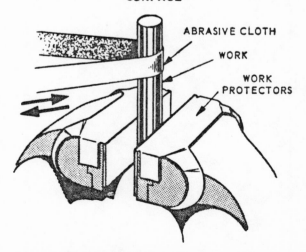

C. POLISHING ROUND METAL STOCK

Figure 1-39.—Polishing operations.

For best results, keep your feet spread apart to steady yourself as you file with slow, full-length, steady strokes. The file cuts as you push it—ease up on the return stroke to keep from dulling the teeth. Keep your file clean.

Figure 1-38B shows the alternate positions of the file when an exceptionally flat surface is required. Using either position first, file across the entire length of the stock. Then, using the other position, file across the entire length of the stock again. Because the teeth of the file pass over the surface of the stock from two directions, the high spots and low spots will readily be visible after filing in both positions. Continue filing first in one position or direction and then the other until the surface has been filed flat. Test the flatness with a straight edge or with prussian blue and a surface plate.

DRAW FILING.—Draw filing produces a finer surface finish and usually a flatter surface than crossfiling. Small parts, as shown in figure 1-38C, are best held in a vise. Hold the file as shown in the figure; notice that the arrow indicates that the cutting stroke is away from you when the handle of the file is held in the right hand. If the handle is held in the left hand, the cutting stroke will be toward you. Lift the file away from the surface of the work on the return stroke. When draw filing will no longer improve the surface texture, wrap a piece of abrasive cltoh around the file and polish the surface as shown in figure 1-39A.

USE OF FILE CARD.—As you file, the teeth of the file may "clog up" with some of the metal filings and scratch your work. This condition is known as PINNING. You can prevent pinning by keeping the file teeth clean. Rubbing chalk between the teeth will help prevent pinning, too, but the best method is to clean the file frequently with a FILE CARD or brush. A file card (fig. 1-40) has fine wire bristles. Brush with a pulling motion, holding the card parallel to the rows of teeth.

Always keep the file clean, whether you're filing mild steel or other metals. Use chalk liberally when filing nonferrous metals.

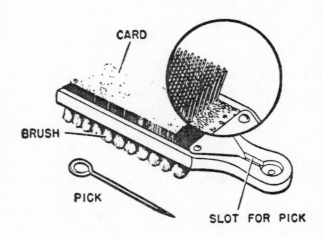

Figure 1-40.—File cleaner.

FILING ROUND METAL STOCK.—Figure 1-38D shows that, as a file is passed over the surface of round work, its angle with the work is changed. This results in a rocking motion of the file as it passes over the work. This rocking motion permits all the teeth on the file to make contact and cut as they pass over the work's surface, thus tending to keep the file much cleaner and thereby doing better work.

POLISHING A FLAT METAL SURFACE.— When polishing a flat metal surface, first draw file the surface as shown in fig. 1-38C. Then, when the best possible draw filed surface has been obtained, proceed with abrasive cloth, often called emery cloth. Select a grade of cloth suited to the draw filing. If the draw filing was well done only a fine cloth will be needed to do the polishing.

If your cloth is in a roll, and the job you are polishing is the size that would be held in a vise, tear off a 6" or 8" length of the 1" or 2" width. If you are using sheets of abrasive cloth, tear off a strip from the long edge of the 8" by 11" sheet.

Wrap the cloth around the file (fig. 1-39A) and hold the file as you would for draw filing. Hold the end of the cloth in place with your thumb. In polishing, apply a thin film of lubricating oil on the surface being polished and use a double stroke with pressure on both the forward and the backward strokes. Note that this is different from the drawfiling stroke in which you cut with the file in only one direction.

When further polishing does not appear to improve the surface, you are ready to use the next finer grade of cloth. Before changing to the finer grade, however, reverse the cloth so that its back is toward the surface being polished.

Work the reversed cloth back and forth in the abrasive-laden oil as an intermediate step between grades of abrasive cloth. Then, with the solvent available in your shop, clean the job thoroughly before proceeding with the next finer grade of cloth. Careful cleaning between grades helps to ensure freedom from scratches.

For the final polish, use a strip of crocus cloth—first the face and then the back—with plenty of oil. When polishing is complete, again carefully clean the job with a solvent and protect it, with oil or other means, from rusting.

Figure 1-39B(A) shows another way to polish in which the abrasive cloth is wrapped around a block of wood. In figure 1-39B(B), the cloth has simply been folded to form a pad from which a worn, dull surface can be removed by simply tearing it off to expose a new surface.

POLISHING ROUND METAL STOCK.—In figure 1-39C, a piece of round stock is being polished with a strip of abrasive cloth which is "seesawed" back and forth as it is guided over the surface being polished.

Remember that the selection of grades of abrasive cloth, the application of oil, and the cleaning between grades, applies to polishing regardless of how the cloth is held or used.

Care of Files

A new file should be broken in carefully by using it first on brass, bronze, or smooth cast iron. Just a few of the teeth will cut at first, so use a light pressure to prevent tooth breakage. Do not break in a new file by using it first on a narrow surface.

Protect the file teeth by hanging your files in a rack when they are not in use, or by placing them in drawers with wooden partitions. Your files should not be allowed to rust—keep them away from water and moisture. Avoid getting the files oily. Oil causes a file to slide across the work and prevents fast, clean cutting. Files that you keep in your toolbox should be wrapped in paper or cloth to protect their teeth and prevent damage to other tools.

Never use a file for prying or pounding. The tang is soft and bends easily. The body is hard and extremely brittle.

Safety

Never use a file unless it is equipped with a tight-fitting handle. If you use a file without the handle and it bumps something or jams to a sudden stop, the tang may be driven into your hand. To put a handle on a file tang, drill a hole in the handle, slightly smaller than the tang. Insert the tang end, and then tap the end of the handle to seat it firmly. Make sure you get the handle on straight.

TWIST DRILLS

Making a hole in a piece of metal is generally a simple operation, but in most cases is an important and a precise job. A large number of different tools and machines have been designed so that holes may be made speedily, economically, and accurately in all kinds of material.

In order to be able to use these tools efficiently, it is well to become acquainted with them. The most common tool for making holes in metal is the twist drill. It consists of a cylindrical piece of steel with spiral grooves. One end of the cylinder is pointed while the other end is shaped so that it may be attached to a drilling machine. The grooves, usually called FLUTES, may be cut into the steel cylinder, or the flutes may be formed by twisting a flat piece of steel into a cylindrical shape.

The principal parts of a twist drill are the body, the shank, and the point (fig. 1-41). The dead center of a drill is the sharp edge at the extreme tip end of the drill. It is formed by the intersection of the cone-shaped surfaces of the point and should always be in the exact center of the axis of the drill. The point of the drill should not be confused with the dead center. The point is the entire cone-shaped surface at the end of the drill.

The lip or cutting edge of a drill is that part of the point that actually cuts away the metal

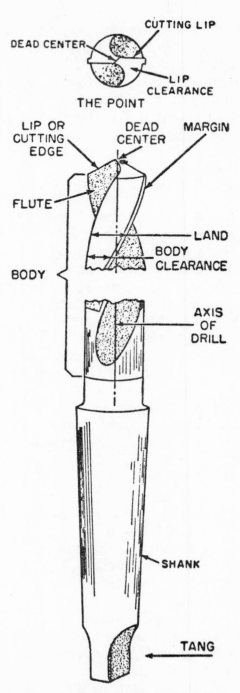

Figure 1-41.—Twist drill
nomenclature.

58

when drilling a hole. It is ordinarily as sharp as the edge of a knife. There is a cutting edge for each flute of the drill.

The lip clearance of a drill is the surface of the point that is ground away or relieved just back of the cutting edge of the drill. The strip along the inner edge of the body is called the margin. It is the greatest diameter of the drill and extends the entire length of the flute. The diameter of the margin at the shank end of the drill is smaller than the diameter at the point. This allows the drill to revolve without binding when drilling deep holes.

The shank is the part of the drill which fits into the socket, spindle, or chuck of the drill press. Several types exist (fig. 1-42).

A tang is found only on tapered-shank drills. It is designed to fit into a slot in the socket or spindle of a machine. It may bear a portion of the driving torque, but its principal use is to

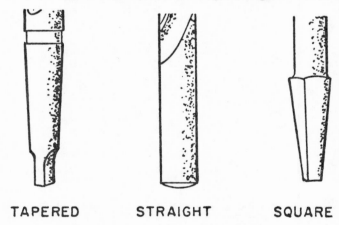

TAPERED   STRAIGHT   SQUARE

Figure 1-42.—Representative shanks.

make it easy to remove the drill from the socket of the driving machine.

Twist drills are provided in various sizes. They are sized by letters, numerals, and fractions.

Drill	Decimal	Drill	Decimal
80	0.0135	49	0.073
79	0.0145	48	0.076
78	0.016	5/64	0.078125
1/64	0.0156	47	0.0785
77	0.018	46	0.081
76	0.02	45	0.082
75	0.021	44	0.086
74	0.0225	43	0.089
73	0.024	42	0.0935
72	0.025	3/32	0.09375
71	0.026	41	0.096
70	0.028	40	0.098
69	0.0292	39	0.0995
68	0.031	38	0.1015
1/32	0.03125	37	0.104
67	0.032	36	0.1055
66	0.033	7/64	0.109375
65	0.035	35	0.11
64	0.036	34	0.111
63	0.037	33	0.113
62	0.038	32	0.116
61	0.039	31	0.12
60	0.04	1/8	0.125
59	0.041	30	0.1285
58	0.042	29	0.136
57	0.043	28	0.1405
56	0.0465	9/64	0.140625
3/64	0.046875	27	0.144
55	0.052	26	0.147
54	0.055	25	0.1495
53	0.0595	24	0.152
1/16	0.0625	23	0.154
52	0.0635	5/32	0.15625
51	0.067	22	0.157
50	0.07	21	0.159

Drill	Decimal	Drill	Decimal
20	0.161	H	0.266
19	0.166	I	0.272
18	0.1695	J	0.277
11/64	0.171875	K	0.281
17	0.173	9/32	0.28125
16	0.177	L	0.29
15	0.18	M	0.295
14	0.182	19/64	0.296875
13	0.185	N	0.302
3/16	0.1875	5/16	0.3125
12	0.189	0	0.316
11	0.191	P	0.323
10	0.1935	21/64	0.328125
9	0.196	Q	0.332
8	0.199	R	0.339
7	0.201	11/32	0.34375
13/64	0.203125	S	0.348
6	0.204	T	0.358
5	0.2055	23/64	0.359375
4	0.209	U	0.368
3	0.213	3/8	0.375
7/32	0.21875	V	0.377
2	0.221	W	0.386
1	0.228	25/64	0.390625
A	0.234	X	0.397
15/64	0.234375	Y	0.404
B	0.238	13/32	0.40625
C	0.242	Z	0.413
D	0.246	27/64	0.421875
E	0.25	7/16	0.4375
1/4	0.25	29/64	0.453125
F	0.257	15/32	0.46875
G	0.261	31/64	0.484375
17/64	0.265625	1/2	0.5

Table 1-1.—Decimal Equivalents of Drill Sizes

Table 1-1 illustrates the relationship, by decimal equivalents, of all drill sizes (letter, number, and fractional) from number 80 to 1/2 inch. Note how the decimal sizes increase as the number of the drill decreases.

Sets of drills are usually made available according to the way the sizes are stated; that is "sets of letter drills" or "sets of number drills." However, twist drills of any size (letter, number, or fraction) are available individually if desired.

The maintenance of twist drills and more about how to use them on specific jobs are discussed later.

COUNTERSINKS

Countersinking is the operation of beveling the mouth of a hole with a rotary tool called a countersink (fig. 1-43). The construction of the countersink is similar to the twist drill. There are four cutting edges, which are taper ground, to the angle marked on the body.

A countersink is used primarily to set the head of a screw or rivet flush with the material in which it is being placed. Countersinks are made in a number of sizes. One size usually takes care of holes of several different sizes. That is, the same countersink can be used for holes from 1/4 inch to 1/2 inch in diameter. Remove only enough metal to set the screw or rivet head flush with the material. If you remove too much material the hole will enlarge and weaken the work.

Select the countersink with the correct lip angle to correspond with the screw or rivet head being used. These countersinks can be turned by any machine that will turn a twist drill.

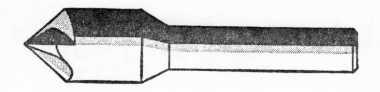

Figure 1-43.—Countersink.

REAMERS

Reamers are used to enlarge and true a hole. The reamer consists of three parts—the body, the shank, and the blades. The shank has a square tang to allow the reamer to be held with a wrench for turning. The main purpose of the body is to support the blades.

The blades on a reamer are made of steel and hardened to such an extent that they are brittle. For this reason you must be careful when using and storing the reamer to protect the blades from chipping. When you are reaming a hole, turn the reamer in the CUTTING DIRECTION ONLY. This will prevent chipping or dulling of the blades. Great care should be used to assure even, steady turning. Otherwise, the reamer will "chatter," causing the hole to become marked or scored. To prevent damage to the reamer while not in use, wrap it in an oily cloth and keep it in a box.

Reamers of the types shown in figure 1-44 are available in any standard size. They are also available in size variations of .001" for special work. A solid straight flute reamer lasts longer and is less expensive than the expansion reamer. However, the solid spiral flute reamer is preferred by craftsmen because it is less likely to chatter.

For general purposes, an expansion reamer (fig. 1-45) is the most practical. This reamer can usually be obtained in standard sizes from

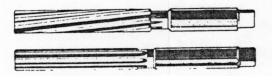

Figure 1-44.—Above—solid spiral flute reamer. Below—solid straight flute reamer.

Figure 1-45.—Expansion reamer.

1/4 of an inch to 1 inch, by 32nds. It is designed to allow the blades to expand 1/32 of an inch. For example, the 1/4-inch expansion reamer will ream a 1/4-inch to a 9/32-inch hole. A 9/32-inch reamer will enlarge the hole from 9/32 of an inch to 5/16 of an inch. This range of adjustment allows a few reamers to cover sizes up to 1 inch.

Reamers are made of carbon steel and high-speed steel. In general, the cutting blades of a high-speed reamer lose their keenness more quickly than a carbon steel reamer. However, after that keenness is gone, it will last longer than the carbon reamer.

PUNCHES

A hand punch is a tool that is held in the hand and struck on one end with a hammer. There are many kinds of punches designed to do a variety of jobs. Figure 1-46 shows several types of punches. Most punches are made of tool steel. The part held in the hand is usually octagonal shaped, or it may be knurled. This

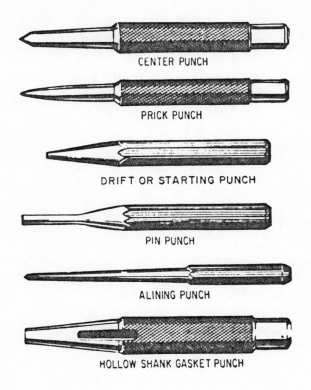

CENTER PUNCH

PRICK PUNCH

DRIFT OR STARTING PUNCH

PIN PUNCH

ALINING PUNCH

HOLLOW SHANK GASKET PUNCH

Figure 1-46.—Punches.

prevents the tool from slipping around in the hand. The other end is shaped to do a particular job.

When you use a punch, there are two things to remember:

1. When you hit the punch you do not want it to slip sideways over your work.

2. You do not want the hammer to slip off the punch and strike your fingers. You can eliminate both these troubles by holding the punch at right angles to the work, and striking the punch squarely with your hammer.

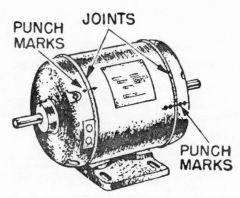

PUNCH MARKS   JOINTS

PUNCH MARKS

Figure 1-47.—Punching mating parts of a mechanism.

The center punch, as the name implies, is used for marking the center of a hole to be drilled. If you try to drill a hole without first punching the center, the drill will "wander" or "walk away" from the desired center.

Another use of the center punch is to make corresponding marks on two pieces of an assembly to permit reassembling in the original positions. Before taking a mechanism apart, make a pair of center punchmarks in one or more places to help in reassembly. To do this, select places, staggered as shown in figure 1-47, where matching pieces are joined. First clean the places selected. Then scribe a line across the joint and center punch the line on both sides of the joint, with single and double marks as shown to eliminate possible errors. In reassembly, refer first to the sets of punchmarks to determine the approximate position of the parts. Then line up the scribed lines to determine the exact position.

Automatic center punches are useful for layout work. They are operated by pressing down on the shank by hand. An inside spring is compressed and released automatically, striking a blow on the end of the punch. The impression is light, but adequate for marking, and serves to locate the point of a regular punch when a deeper impression is required.

The point of a center punch is accurately ground central with the shank, usually at a 60-90 degree angle, and is difficult to regrind by hand with any degree of accuracy. It is, therefore, advisable to take care of a center punch and not to use it on extremely hard materials. When extreme accuracy is required a prick punch is used. Compare the point angle of the center and prick punches.

To make the intersection of two layout lines, bring the point of the prick punch to the exact point of intersection and tap the punch lightly with a hammer. If inspection shows that the exact intersection and the punchmark do not coincide, as at A in figure 1-48, slant the punch as shown at B and again strike with the hammer, thus enlarging the punchmark and centering it exactly. When the intersection has been correctly punched, finish off with a light blow on the punch held in an upright position. C shows the corrected punchmark.

DRIFT punches, sometimes called "starting punches," have a long taper from the tip to the body. They are made that way to withstand the shock of heavy blows. They may be used for knocking out rivets after the heads have been chiseled off, or for freeing pins which are "frozen" in their holes.

After a pin has been loosened or partially driven out, the drift punch may be too large to finish the job. The followup tool to use is the PIN PUNCH. It is designed to follow through the hole without jamming. Always use the largest drift or pin punch that will fit the hole. These punches usually come in sets of three to five assorted sizes. Both of these punches will have flat points, never edged or rounded.

To remove a bolt or pin that is extremely tight, start with a drift punch that has a point

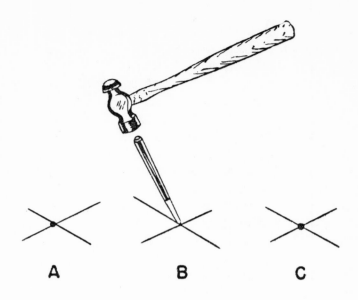

Figure 1-48.—Marking the intersection of lines with a prick
punch.

diameter that is slightly smaller than the diameter of the object you are removing. As soon
as it loosens, finish driving it out with a pin
punch. Never use a pin punch for starting a pin
because it has a slim shank and a hard blow
may cause it to bend or break.

For assembling units of a machine an
ALINEMENT (alining) punch is invaluable. It is
usually about 1 foot long and has a long gradual
taper. Its purpose is to line up holes in mating
parts.

Hollow metal cutting punches are made from
hardened tool steel. They are made in various
sizes and are used to cut holes in light gage
sheet metal.

Other punches have been designed for special
uses. One of these is the soft-faced drift. It is
made of brass or fiber and is used for such
jobs as removing shafts, bearings, and wrist
pins from engines. It is generally heavy enough

to resist damage to itself, but soft enough not to injure the finished surface on the part that is being driven.

You may have to make gaskets of rubber, cork, leather, or composition materials. For cutting holes in gasket materials a hollow shank GASKET PUNCH may be used (fig. 1-46). Gasket punches come in sets of various sizes to accommodate standard bolts and studs. The cutting end is tapered to a sharp edge to produce a clean uniform hole. To use the gasket punch, place the gasket material to be cut on a piece of hard wood or lead so that the cutting edge of the punch will not be damaged. Then strike the punch with a hammer, driving it through the gasket where holes are required.

TAPS AND DIES

Taps and dies are used to cut threads in metal, plastics, or hard rubber. The taps are used for cutting internal threads, and the dies are used to cut external threads. There are many different types of taps. However, the most common are the taper, plug, bottoming, and pipe taps (fig. 1-49).

The taper (starting) hand tap has a chamfer length of 8 to 10 threads. These taps are used when starting a tapping operation and when tapping through holes.

Plug hand taps have a chamfer length of 3 to 5 threads and are designed for use after the taper tap.

Bottoming hand taps are used for threading the bottom of a blind hole. They have a very short chamfer length of only 1 to 1 1/2 threads for this purpose. This tap is always used after the plug tap has already been used. Both the taper and plug taps should precede the use of the bottoming hand tap.

TAPER PIPE

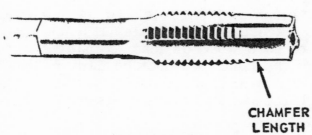

CHAMFER LENGTH

TAPER HAND

PLUG HAND—NATIONAL COARSE

BOTTOMING HAND

Figure 1-49.—Types of common taps.

Pipe taps are used for pipe fittings and other places where extremely tight fits are necessary. The tap diameter, from end to end of threaded portion, increases at the rate of 3/4 inch per foot. All the threads on this tap do the cutting, as compared to the straight taps where only the nonchamfered portion does the cutting.

Dies are made in several different shapes and are of the solid or adjustable type. The square pipe die (fig. 1-50) will cut American Standard Pipe Thread only. It comes in a variety of sizes for cutting threads on pipe with diameters of 1/8 inch to 2 inches.

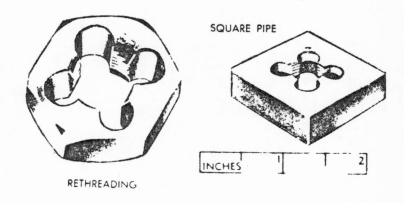

Figure 1-50.—Types of solid dies.

A rethreading die (fig. 1-50) is used principally for dressing over bruised or rusty threads on screws or bolts. It is available in a variety of sizes for rethreading American Standard Coarse and Fine threads. These dies are usually hexagon in shape and can be turned with a socket, box, open-end, or any wrench that will fit. Rethreading dies are available in sets of 6, 10, 14, and 28 assorted sizes in a case.

Round split adjustable dies (fig. 1-51) are called "Button" dies and can be used in either hand diestocks or machine holders. The adjustment in the screw adjusting type is made by a fine-pitch screw which forces the sides of the die apart or allows them to spring together. The adjustment in the open adjusting types is made by means of three screws in the holder, one for expanding and two for compressing the dies. Round split adjustable dies are available in a variety of sizes to cut American Standard Coarse and Fine threads, special form threads, and the standard sizes of threads that are used in Britain and other European countries. For hand threading, these dies are held in diestocks (fig. 1-52). One type die stock has three pointed screws that will hold round dies of any construction, although it is made specifically for open adjusting-type dies.

Two piece collet dies (fig. 1-51) are used with a collet cap (fig. 1-52) and collet guide. The die halves are placed in the cap slot and are held in place by the guide which screws into the underside of the cap. The die is adjusted by means of setscrews at both ends of the internal slot. This type of adjustable die is issued in various sizes to cover the cutting range of American Standard Coarse and Fine and special form threads. Diestocks to hold the dies come in three different sizes.

Two-piece rectangular pipe dies (fig. 1-51) are available to cut American Standard Pipe threads. They are held in ordinary or ratchet-type diestocks (fig. 1-53). The jaws of the dies are adjusted by means of setscrews. An adjustable guide serves to keep the pipe in alinement with respect to the dies. The smooth jaws of the guide are adjusted by means of a cam plate; a thumbscrew locks the jaws firmly in the desired position.

72

TWO-PIECE RECTANGULAR PIPE DIE

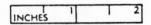

INCHES   1   2

TWO-PIECE COLLET DIE

ADJUSTING
SCREW

SCREW ADJUSTING TYPE

OPEN ADJUSTING TYPE

Figure 1-51.—Types of adjustable dies.

73

STRAIGHT HANDLED TAP WRENCH

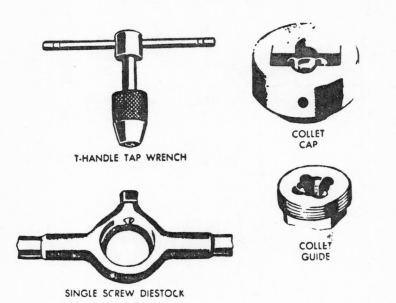

T-HANDLE TAP WRENCH

COLLET
CAP

COLLET
GUIDE

SINGLE SCREW DIESTOCK

COLLET DIESTOCK

THREE SCREW DIESTOCK

Figure 1-52.—Diestocks, diecollet,
and tap wrenches.

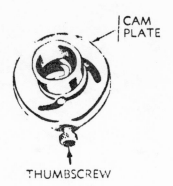

CAM PLATE

THUMBSCREW

ADJUSTABLE GUIDE

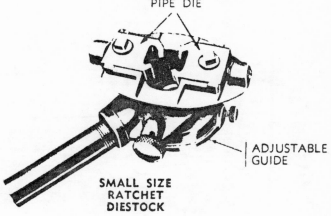

TWO PIECE RECTANGULAR PIPE DIE

ADJUSTABLE GUIDE

SMALL SIZE RATCHET DIESTOCK

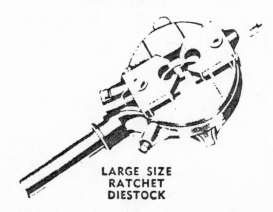

LARGE SIZE RATCHET DIESTOCK

Figure 1-53.—Adjustable die guide and ratchet diestocks.

75

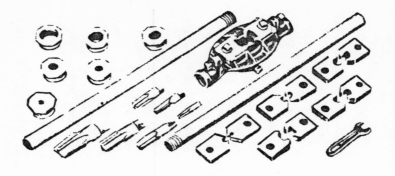

PIPE THREADING SET WITH RECTANGULAR
ADJUSTABLE DIES, DIESTOCK,
WRENCH, GUIDES AND TAPS

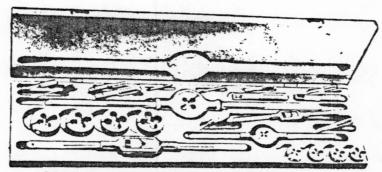

BOLT AND SCREW THREADING SET WITH
ROUND ADJUSTABLE SPLIT DIES,
DIESTOCKS, TAPS, TAP WRENCHES,
AND SCREWDRIVERS

Figure 1-54.—Threading sets.

Threading sets are available in many different combinations of taps and dies, together with diestocks, tap wrenches, guides and necessary screwdrivers and wrenches to loosen and tighten adjusting screws and bolts. Figure 1-54 illustrates typical threading set for pipe, bolts, and screws.

76

Never attempt to sharpen taps or dies. Sharpening of taps and dies involves several highly precise cutting processes which involve the thread characteristics and chamfer. These sharpening procedures must be done by experienced personnel in order to maintain the accuracy and the cutting effectiveness of taps and dies.

Keep taps and dies clean and well oiled when not in use. Store them so that they do not contact each other or other tools. For long periods of storage, coat taps and dies with a rust-preventive compound, place in individual or standard threading set boxes, and store in a dry place.

THREAD CHASERS

Thread chasers are threading tools that have several teeth and are used to rethread

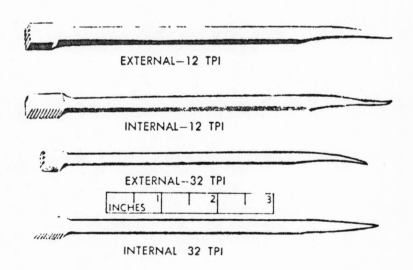

Figure 1-55.—Thread chasers.

(chase) damaged external or internal threads (fig. 1-55). These tools are available to chase standard threads. The internal thread chaser has its cutting teeth located on a side face. The external thread chaser has its cutting teeth on the end of the shaft. The handle end of the tool shaft tapers to a point.

SCREW AND TAP EXTRACTORS

Screw extractors are used to remove broken screws without damaging the surrounding material or the threaded hole. Tap extractors are used to remove broken taps.

Some screw extractors (fig. 1-56A) are straight, having flutes from end to end. These extractors are available in sizes to remove broken screws having 1/4 to 1/2 inch outside diameters. Spiral tapered extractors are sized to remove screws and bolts from 3/16 inch to 2 1/8 inches outside diameter.

Most sets of extractors include twist drills and a drill guide. Tap extractors are similar to the screw extractors and are sized to remove taps ranging from 3/16 to 2 1/8 inches outside diameter.

To remove a broken screw or tap with a spiral extractor, first drill a hole of proper size in the screw or tap. The size hole required for each screw extractor is stamped on it. The extractor is then inserted in the hole, and turned counterclockwise to remove the defective component.

If the tap has broken off at the surface of the work, or slightly below the surface of the work, the straight tap extractor shown in figure 1-56 may remove it. Apply a liberal amount of penetrating oil to the broken tap. Place the tap extractor over the broken tap and lower the upper collar to insert the four sliding prongs down into the four flutes of the tap. Then slide the

78

bottom collar down to the surface of the work so that it will hold the prongs tightly against the body of the extractor. Tighten the tap wrench on the square shank of the extractor and carefully work the extractor back and forth to loosen the tap. It may be necessary to remove the extractor and strike a few sharp blows with a small hammer and pin punch to jar the tap loose. Then reinsert the tap remover and carefully try to back the tap out of the hole.

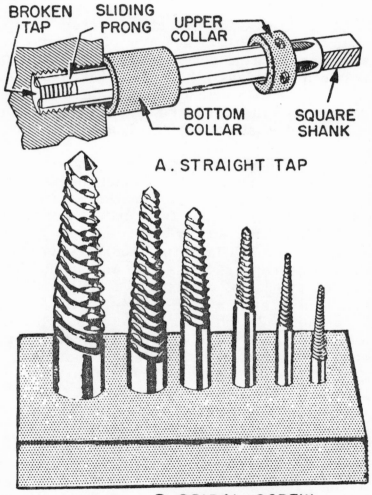

A. STRAIGHT TAP

B. SPIRAL SCREW

Figure 1-56.—Screw and tap extractors.

PIPE AND TUBING CUTTERS AND FLARING TOOLS

Pipe cutters (fig. 1-57) are used to cut pipe made of steel, brass, copper, wrought iron, and lead. Tube cutters (fig. 1-57) are used to cut tubing made of iron, steel, brass, copper, and aluminum. The essential difference between pipe and tubing is that tubing has considerably thinner walls. Flaring tools (fig. 1-58) are used to make single or double flares in the ends of tubing.

Most TUBE CUTTERS closely resemble pipe cutters, except that they are of lighter construction. A hand screw feed tubing cutter of 1/8-inch to 1 1/4-inch capacity (fig. 1-57) has two rollers with cutouts located off center so that cracked flares may be held in them and cut off without waste of tubing. It also has a retractable cutter blade that is adjusted by turning a knob. The other tube cutter shown is designed to cut tubing up to and including 3/4 and 1 inch outside diameter. Rotation of the triangular portion of the tube cutter within the tubing will eliminate any burrs.

FLARING TOOLS (fig. 1-58) are used to flare soft copper, brass, or aluminum. The single flaring tool consists of a split die block that has holes for 3/16-, 1/4-, 5/16-, 3/8-, 7/16-, and 1/2-inch outer diameter (o.d.) tubing, a clamp to lock the tube in the die block, and a yoke that slips over the die block and has a compressor screw and a cone that forms a 45° flare or a bell shape on the end of the tube. The screw has a T-handle. A double flaring tool has the additional feature of adapters that turn in the edge of the tube before a regular 45° double flare is made. It consists of a die block with holes for 3/16-, 1/4-, 5/16-, 3/8-, and 1/2-inch tubing, a yoke with a screw and a flaring cone, plus five adapters for different size tubing, all carried in a metal case.

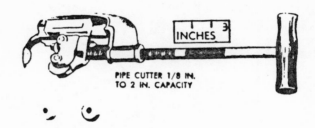

PIPE CUTTER 1/8 IN.
TO 2 IN. CAPACITY

TUBE CUTTER 1/8 IN.
TO 1 1/4 IN. CAPACITY

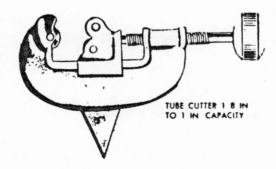

TUBE CUTTER 1 8 IN
TO 1 IN CAPACITY

TUBE CUTTER 1/8 IN.
TO 3 4 IN CAPACITY

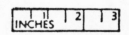

Figure 1-57.—Pipe and tubing cutters.

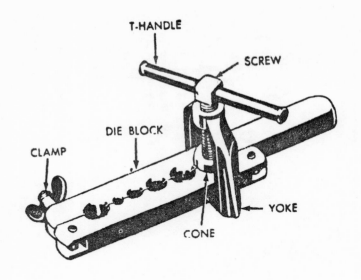

SINGLE FLARING TOOL

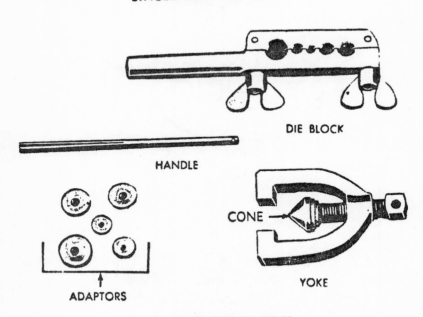

DOUBLE FLARING TOOL

Figure 1-58.—Flaring tools.

WOODCUTTING HANDTOOLS

A man working with wood uses a large variety of handtools. He should be familiar with these tools, their proper names, the purpose for which they are used, and how to keep them in good condition.

HANDSAWS

The most common carpenter's handsaw consists of a steel blade with a handle at one end. The blade is narrower at the end opposite the handle. This end of the blade is called the "point" or "toe." The end of the blade nearest the handle is called the "heel" (fig. 1-59). One edge of the blade has teeth, which act as two rows of cutters. When the saw is used, these teeth cut two parallel grooves close together. The chips (sawdust) are pushed out from between the grooves (kerf) by the beveled part of the teeth. The teeth are bent alternately to one side or the other, to make the kerf wider than the thickness of the blade. This bending is called the "set" of the teeth (fig. 1-60). The number of teeth per inch, the size and shape of the teeth, and the amount of set depend on the

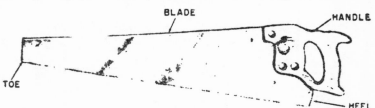

Figure 1-59.—Nomenclature of a handsaw.

Figure 1-60.—"Set" of hand saw teeth.

use to be made of the saw and the material to be cut. Carpenter's handsaws are described by the number of points per inch. By custom, there is always one more point than there are teeth per inch. A number stamped near the handle gives the number of points of the saw.

Cross-cut and Rip Saws

Woodworking handsaws designed for general cutting consist of RIPSAWS and CROSSCUT saws. Ripsaws are used for cutting with the grain and crosscut saws are for cutting across the grain.

The major difference between a ripsaw and a crosscut saw is the shape of the teeth. A tooth with a square-faced chisel-type cutting edge, like the ripsaw tooth shown in figure 1-61, does a good job of cutting with the grain (called ripping), but a poor job of cutting across the grain (called crosscutting). A tooth with a beveled, knifetype cutting edge, like the crosscut saw tooth shown in the same figure, does a good job of cutting across the grain, but a poor job of cutting with the grain.

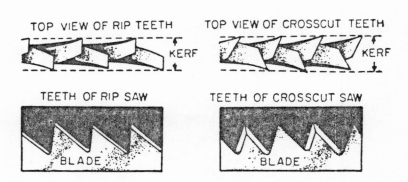

TOP VIEW OF RIP TEETH   TOP VIEW OF CROSSCUT TEETH

KERF   KERF

TEETH OF RIP SAW   TEETH OF CROSSCUT SAW

BLADE   BLADE

Figure 1-61.—Comparing rip and crosscut-saw teeth.

Special Purpose Saws

The more common types of saws used for special purposes are shown in figure 1-62. The BACKSAW is a crosscut saw designed for sawing a perfectly straight line across the face of a piece of stock. A heavy steel backing along the top of the blade keeps the blade perfectly straight.

The DOVETAIL saw is a special type of backsaw with a thin, narrow blade and a chisel-type handle.

The COMPASS saw is a long, narrow, tapering ripsaw designed for cutting out circular or other nonrectangular sections from within the margins of a board or panel. A hole is bored near the cutting line to start the saw. A KEY-HOLE saw is simply a finer, narrower compass saw.

The COPING saw is used to cut along curved lines.

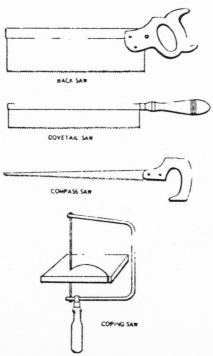

BACK SAW

DOVETAIL SAW

COMPASS SAW

COPING SAW

Figure 1-62.—Special saws.

Saw Precautions

A saw that is not being used should be hung up or stowed in a toolbox. A toolbox designed for holding saws has notches that hold them on edge, teeth up. Stowing saws loose in a toolbox may allow the saw teeth to become dulled or bent by contacting other tools. Some right and wrong methods of using and caring for a saw are shown in figure 1-63. Be sure to read the captions for each section of the illustration.

Before using a saw, be sure there are no nails or other edge-destroying objects in the line of the cut. When sawing out a strip of waste, do not break out the strip by twisting the saw blade. This dulls the saw and may spring or break the blade.

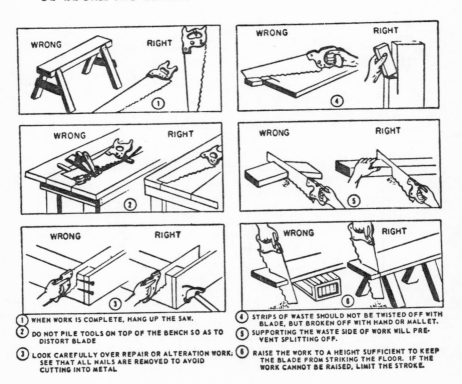

① WHEN WORK IS COMPLETE, HANG UP THE SAW.

② DO NOT PILE TOOLS ON TOP OF THE BENCH SO AS TO DISTORT BLADE

③ LOOK CAREFULLY OVER REPAIR OR ALTERATION WORK; SEE THAT ALL NAILS ARE REMOVED TO AVOID CUTTING INTO METAL

④ STRIPS OF WASTE SHOULD NOT BE TWISTED OFF WITH BLADE, BUT BROKEN OFF WITH HAND OR MALLET.

⑤ SUPPORTING THE WASTE SIDE OF WORK WILL PREVENT SPLITTING OFF.

⑥ RAISE THE WORK TO A HEIGHT SUFFICIENT TO KEEP THE BLADE FROM STRIKING THE FLOOR. IF THE WORK CANNOT BE RAISED, LIMIT THE STROKE.

Figure 1-63.—Care of handsaws.

Be sure that the saw will go through the full stroke without striking the floor or some other object. If the work cannot be raised high enough to obtain full clearance for the saw, you must carefully limit the length of each stroke.

Using A Hand Saw

To saw across the grain of the stock, use the crosscut saw, and to saw with the grain, use a ripsaw. Study the teeth in both kinds of saws so you can readily identify the saw that you need.

Place the board on a saw horse (fig. 1-64), or some other suitable object. Hold the saw in the right hand and extend the first finger along the handle as shown in the figure. Grasp the board as shown and take a position so that an

Figure 1-64.—Proper position for sawing a board to size.

imaginary line passing lengthwise of the right forearm will be at an angle of approximately 45 degrees with the face of the board. Be sure the side of the saw is plumb or at right angles with the face of the board. Place the heel of the saw on the mark. Keep the saw in line with the forearm and pull it toward you to start the cut.

To begin with, take short, light strokes, gradually increasing the strokes to the full length of the saw. Do not force or jerk the saw. Such procedure will only make sawing more difficult. The arm that does the sawing should swing clear of your body so that the handle of the saw operates at your side rather than in front of you.

Use one hand to operate the saw. You may be tempted to use both hands at times, but if your saw is sharp, one hand will serve you better. The weight of the saw is sufficient to make it cut. Should the saw stick or bind, it may be because the saw is dull and is poorly "set." The wood may have too much moisture in it, or you may have forced the saw and thus have caused it to leave the straight line.

Keep your eye on the line rather than on the saw while sawing. Watching the line enables you to see instantly any tendency to leave the line. A slight twist of the handle, and taking short strokes while sawing, will bring the saw back. Blow away the sawdust frequently so you can see the layout line.

Final strokes of the cut should be taken slowly. Hold the waste piece in your other hand so the stock will not split when taking the last stroke.

Short boards may be placed on one sawhorse when sawing. Place long boards on two sawhorses, but do not saw so your weight falls between them or your saw will bind. Place long boards so that your weight is directly on one end of the board over one sawhorse while the other end of the board rests on the other saw-horse.

Short pieces of stock are more easily cut when they are held in a vise. When ripping short stock it is important that you keep the saw from sticking, so it may be necessary to take a squatting position. The saw can then take upward direction and thus work easily. When ripping long boards it will probably be necessary to use a wedge in the saw kerf to prevent binding (fig. 1-65).

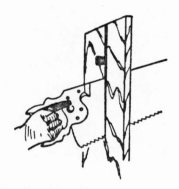

Figure 1-65.—Using a wedge in a saw kerf
to prevent binding.

PLANES

The plane is the most extensively used of the hand shaving tools. Most of the lumber handled by anyone working with wood is dressed on all four sides, but when performing jobs such as fitting doors and sash, and interior trim work, planes must be used.

Bench and block planes are designed for general surface smoothing and squaring. Other planes are designed for special types of surface work.

The principal parts of a bench plane and the manner in which they are assembled are shown in figure 1-66. The part at the rear that you grasp to push the plane ahead is called the handle; the part at the front that you grasp to guide the plane along its course is called the knob. The main body of the plane, consisting of the bottom, the sides, and the sloping part which carries the plane iron, is called the frame. The bottom of the frame is called the sole, and the opening in the sole, through which the blade emerges, is called the mouth. The front end of the sole is called the toe; the rear end, the heel.

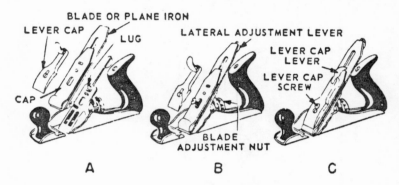

Figure 1-66.—Parts of a bench plane.

A plane iron cap, which is screwed to the upper face of the plane iron, deflects the shaving upward through the mouth, as indicated in figure 1-67C, and thus prevents the mouth from becoming choked with jammed shavings. The edge of the cap should fit the back of the iron as shown in figure 1-67A, not as shown in figure 1-67B. The lower end of the plane iron cap should be set back 1/32 in. from the edge of the plane top, as shown in figure 1-67A. The iron in a bench plane goes in bevel-down.

The edge of the plane iron is brought into correct cutting position by the manipulation of first the ADJUSTING NUT and next the LATERAL ADJUSTMENT LEVER, as shown in fig-

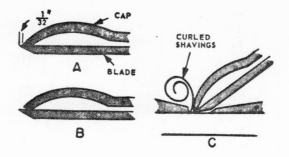

Figure 1-67.—Plane iron and plane iron cap.

ures 1-68 and 1-69. The adjusting nut moves
the edge of the iron up or down; the lateral adjustment lever cants it to the right or left. To
adjust the plane you hold it upside-down, sight
along the sole from the toe, and work the adjusting nut until the edge of the blade appears.
Then work the lateral adjustment lever until the
edge of the blade is in perfect alinement with
the sole, as shown in figures 1-68B and 1-69B.
Then use the adjusting nut to give the blade the
amount of protrusion you want. This amount
will depend, of course, upon the depth of the cut
you intend to make.

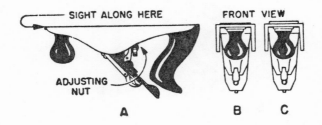

Figure 1-68.—Manipulation of the adjusting nut moves the plane iron up or
down.

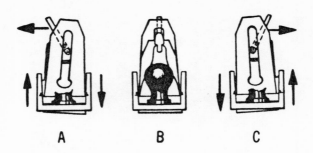

Figure 1-69.—Effect of manipulation of the
lateral adjustment lever.

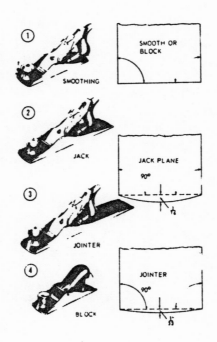

Figure 1-70.—Types of bench planes and
block plane.

There are three types of bench planes (fig. 1-70): the SMOOTH plane, the JACK plane, and the JOINTER plane (sometimes called the FORE plane or the GAGE plane). All are used primarily for shaving and smoothing with the grain; the chief difference is the length of the sole. The sole of the smooth plane is about 9 in. long, the sole of the jack plane about 14 in. long, and the sole of the jointer plane from 20 to 24 in. long.

The longer the sole of the plane is, the more uniformly flat and true the planed surface will be. Consequently, which bench plane you should use depends upon the requirements with regard to surface trueness. The smooth plane is, in general, smoother only; it will plane a smooth, but not an especially true surface in a short time. It is also used for cross-grain smoothing and squaring of end-stock.

The jack plane is the general "jack-of-all-work" of the bench plane group. It can take a deeper cut and plane a truer surface than the smooth plane. The jointer plane is used when the planed surface must meet the highest requirements with regard to trueness.

A BLOCK PLANE and the names of its parts are shown in figure 1-71. Note that the plane iron in a block plane does not have a plane iron cap, and also that, unlike the iron in a bench plane, the iron in a block plane goes in bevel-up.

The block plane, which is usually held at an angle to the work, is used chiefly for cross-grain squaring of end-stock. It is also useful, however, for smoothing all plane surfaces on very small work.

BORING TOOLS

When working with wood, you will frequently be required to bore holes. It is important, therefore, that you know the proper procedures

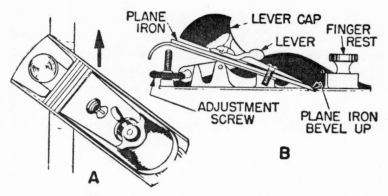

Figure 1-71.—Block plane nomenclature.

and tools used for this job. Auger bits and a variety of braces and drills are used extensively for boring purposes.

Auger Bits

Bits are used for boring holes for screws, dowels, and hardware, as an aid in mortising (cutting a cavity in wood for joining members) and in shaping curves and for many other purposes. Like saws and planes, bits vary in shape and structure with the type of job to be done. Some of the most common bits are described in this section.

AUGER bits are screw-shaped tools consisting of six parts: the cutter, screw, spur, twist, shank, and tang (fig. 1-72). The twist ends with two sharp points called the spurs, which score the circle, and two cutting edges which cut shavings within the scored circle. The screw centers the bit and draws it into the wood. The threads of the screw are made in three different pitches: steep, medium, and fine. The steep pitch makes for quick boring and thick chips, and the fine or slight pitch makes for slow boring and fine chips. For end-wood boring, a steep- or medium-pitch screw bit should be used because end wood is likely to

94

be forced in between the fine screw threads, and that will prevent the screw from taking hold. The twist carries the cuttings away from the cutters and deposits them in a mound around the hole.

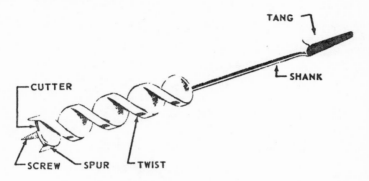

Figure 1-72.—Nomenclature of an auger bit.

The sizes of auger bits are indicated in sixteenths of an inch and are stamped on the tang (fig. 1-73). A number 10 stamped on the tang means 10/16 or 5/8 in.; number 5 means 5/16 in. and so on. The most common woodworkers auger bit set ranges in size from 1/4 to 1 in.

Ordinary auger bits up to 1 in. in diameter are from 7 to 9 inches long. Short auger bits that are about 3 1/2 inches long are called DOWEL bits.

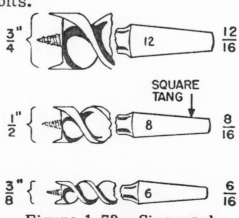

Figure 1-73.—Size markings on auger bits.

95

EXPANSIVE auger bits have adjustable cutters, for boring holes of different diameters (fig. 1-74). Expansive bits are generally made in two different sizes. The largest size has three cutters and bores holes up to 4 inches in diameter. A scale on the cutter blade indicates the diameter of the hole to be bored.

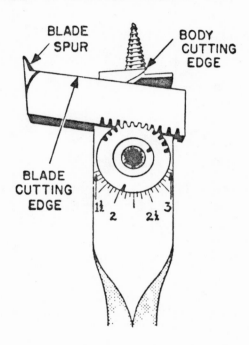

Figure 1-74.—Expansive bit.

Braces and Drills

The auger bit is the tool that actually does the cutting in the wood; however, it is necessary that another tool be used to hold the auger bit and give you enough leverage to turn the bit. The tools most often used for holding the bit are the carpenter's brace, breast drill, and push drill (fig. 1-75).

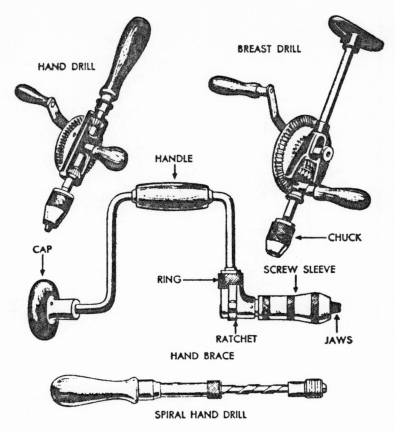

Figure 1-75.—Brace and drills.

BORING THROUGH HOLES IN WOOD.—To bore a hole in wood with an auger bit, first select the proper fit indicated on or near the square tang. Then you insert the auger bit into the chuck (fig. 1-76).

To chuck the bit, hold the shell of the chuck (fig. 1-76A), as you turn the handle to open the jaws. When the jaws are apart far enough to take the square tang of the bit, insert it (fig. 1-76B), until the end seats in the square driving socket at the bottom of the chuck. Then tighten the chuck by turning the handle to close the jaws and hold the bit in place.

With a chuck having no driving socket (a square hole which is visible if you look directly into the chuck), additional care must be taken to seat and center the corners of the tapered shank in the V grooves of the chuck jaws. (See figure 1-76C.) In this type of chuck the

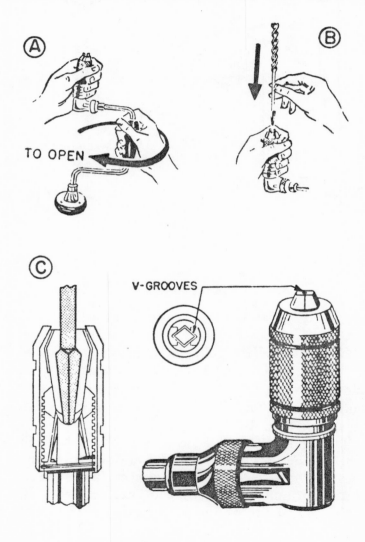

Figure 1-76.—Placing an auger bit in a chuck.

jaws serve to hold the bit in the center and to prevent it from coming out of the chuck.

After placing the point of the feed screw at the location of the center of the hole you will bore, steady the brace against your body, if possible, with the auger bit square with the surface of the work.

To bore a horizontal hole in the stock held in the bench vise, hold the head of the brace with one hand, steadying it against your body, while turning the handle with the other hand. Scrap stock behind the job will prevent splintering (fig. 1-77).

When it is not possible to make a full turn with the handle of the bit brace, turn the cam ring, shown in figure 1-75, clockwise until it stops. This will raise one of the two ratchet pawls affording clockwise ratchet action for rotating the bit. For counterclockwise ratchet action, turn the cam ring counterclockwise as far as it will go.

To bore a vertical hole in stock held in a bench vise, hold the brace and bit perpendicular to the surface of the work. Placing a trysquare

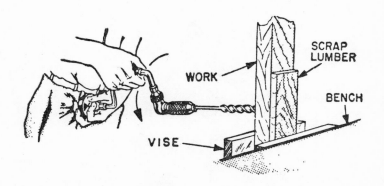

Figure 1-77.—Using scrap lumber to prevent splintering when boring.

near the bit, alternately in the two positions shown in figure 1-78, will help you sight it in.

Another way to bore a through hole without splitting out on the opposite face is to reverse the bit one or two turns when the feed screw just becomes visible through this opposite face (fig. 1-79A). This will release the bit. Remove the bit while pulling it up and turning it clockwise. This will remove the loose chips from the hole. Finish the hole by boring from the opposite face. This will remove the remaining material which is usually in the form of a wooden disk held fast to the feed screw (fig. 1-79B).

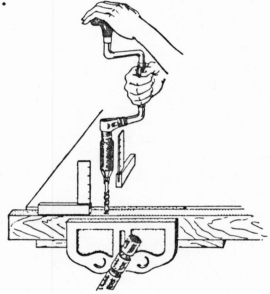

Figure 1-78.—Method of sighting in for perpendicular hole.

Figure 1-79.—Boring a through hole by reversing direction.

DRILLING HOLES WITH A TWIST DRILL.—
An ordinary twist drill may be used to drill
holes in wood. Select a twist drill of the size
required (fig. 1-80) and secure it in the chuck
of a drill.

In figure 1-81, the twist drill has been
chucked. Notice that the job is secured to the
table with a pair of C-clamps. Beneath the job
is a block of wood. In drilling through wood, a
backup block is used to ensure a clean hole at
the bottom of the job.

Figure 1-82 shows a hole being drilled with
a breast drill. Turn the crank handle with one
hand as you hold the side handle with the other
hand. This will steady the breast drill while
feed pressure is applied by resting your chest
on the breast plate shown in figure 1-82. Notice,
too, that the breast drill has a high or a low

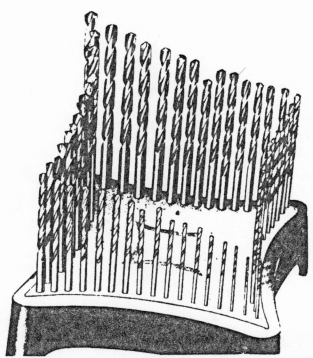

Figure 1-80.—Twist drills (Sizes
No. 1 to No. 60).

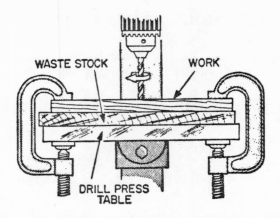

Figure 1-81.—Drilling a hole in wood
with a twist drill.

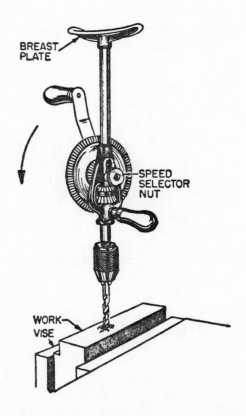

Figure 1-82.—Drilling a hole with
a breast drill.

speed available, according to the setting of the speed selector nut. When drilling a horizontal hole, apply feed pressure by resting your body against the breast plate.

In drilling a horizontal hole with the hand drill shown in figure 1-83, operate the crank with the right hand and with the left hand guide the drill by holding the handle which is opposite the chuck end of the drill.

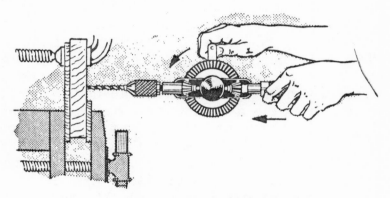

Figure 1-83.—Drilling a hole with a hand drill.

DRILLING HOLES WITH A "PUSH" DRILL.— Figure 1-84A shows the Stanley "Yankee" automatic drill which is often called a "push" drill.

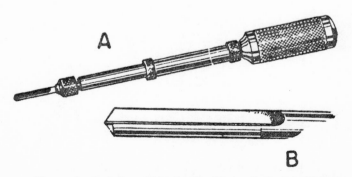

Figure 1-84.—Push drill and drill point.

This drill can be used to drill either horizontal or vertical holes when the accuracy of the right angle with the work is not critical.

The drill point used in push drills (fig. 1-84B) is a straight flute drill. Sharpen its point on the grinder and provide only slight clearance behind the cutting edge. It will drill holes in wood and other soft materials.

To select a drill for use in a push drill, hold the handle of the drill in one hand and release the magazine by turning the knurled screw as shown in figure 1-85A. This will permit you to drop the magazine. Figure 1-85B shows the drill magazine lowered to expose the drills from which the proper size can be selected.

To chuck the drill, loosen the chuck several turns and insert the drill as far as it will go. Turn the drill until it seats in the driving socket in the bottom of the chuck. Then tighten the chuck to hold the drill in place. (fig. 1-85C).

To drill a vertical hole with this drill (fig. 1-86A), place the job on a flat surface and operate the push drill with alternate strokes up

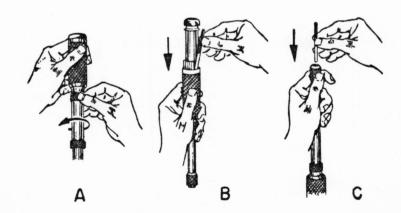

A   B   C

Figure 1-85.—Selecting a drill for use in a push drill.

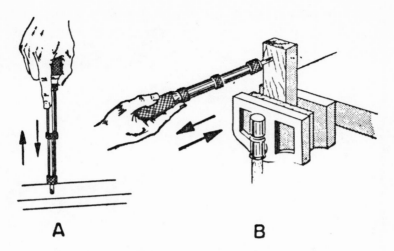

Figure 1-86.—Drilling horizontal and
vertical holes with a push drill.

and down. If it is necessary to hold the work in
place while it is being drilled, use some mechanical means if you can. If you must hold the
job with your hand, grasp the material as far as
possible from where the drill is drilling.

In drilling horizontal holes with the push
drill, as in figure 1-86B, secure the job in a
vise. The back-and-forth strokes rotate the
drill, advancing it into the work on the forward
stroke as the drilling proceeds. The index
finger, extended along the body of the tool, will
help guide the drilling at right angles to the
work.

WOOD CHISELS

A wood chisel is a steel tool fitted with a
wooden or plastic handle. It has a single beveled cutting edge on the end of the steel part, or
blade. According to their construction, chisels
may be divided into two general classes: TANG
chisels, in which part of the chisel enters the
handle, and SOCKET chisels, in which the handle
enters into a part of the chisel (fig. 1-87).

TANG CHISEL

THE SHANK OF THE CHISEL HAS A POINT THAT IS
STUCK INTO THE HANDLE. THE POINT IS CALLED A TANG
AND THE CHISEL IS CALLED A TANG CHISEL

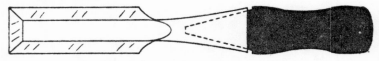

SOCKET CHISEL

IF THE SHANK OF THE CHISEL IS MADE LIKE A CUP, THE
HANDLE WILL FIT INTO IT. THIS IS CALLED A SOCKET CHISEL

Figure 1-87.—Tang and socket
wood chisels.

A socket chisel is designed for striking with a wooden mallet (never a steel hammer), while a tang chisel is designed for hand manipulation only.

Wood chisels are also divided into types, depending upon their weights and thicknesses, the shape or design of the blade, and the work they are intended to do.

The shapes of the more common types of wood chisels are shown in figure 1-88. The FIRMER chisel has a strong, rectangular-cross-section blade, designed for both heavy and light work. The blade of the PARING chisel is relatively thin, and is beveled along the sides for the fine paring work. The BUTT chisel has a short blade, designed for work in hard-to-get-at places.

The butt chisel is commonly used for chiseling the GAINS (rectangular depressions) for the BUTT hinges on doors; hence the name. The MORTISING chisel is similar to a socket firmer but has a narrow blade, designed for chiseling

SOCKET FIRMER CHISEL

TANG PARING CHISEL

MORTISING CHISEL

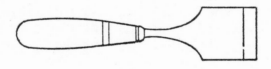

BUTT CHISEL

Figure 1-88.—Shapes of common types
of wood chisels.

out the deep, narrow MORTISES for mortise-and-tenon joints. This work requires a good deal of levering out of chips; consequently, the mortising chisel is made extra thick in the shaft to prevent breaking.

A FRAMING chisel is shaped like a firmer chisel, but has a very heavy, strong blade designed for work in rough carpentry.

A wood chisel should always be held with the flat side or back of the chisel against the work for smoothing and finishing cuts. Whenever possible, it should not be pushed straight through an opening, but should be moved laterally at the same time that it is pushed forward. This method ensures a shearing cut, which with care, will produce a smooth and even surface even when the work is cross-grained. On rough work, use a hammer or mallet to drive the socket-type chisel.

On fine work, use your hand as the driving power on tang-type chisels. For rough cuts, the bevel edge of the chisel is held against the work. Whenever possible, other tools such as saws and planes should be used to remove as much of the waste as possible, and the chisel used for finishing purposes only.

These are a few basic precautions that you should observe at all times when using a chisel.

a. Secure work so that it cannot move.

b. Keep both hands back of the cutting edge at all times.

c. Do not start a cut on a guideline. Start slightly away from it, so that there is a small amount of material to be removed by the finishing cuts.

d. When starting a cut, always chisel away from the guideline toward the waste wood, so that no splitting will occur at the edge.

e. Never cut towards yourself with a chisel.

f. Make the shavings thin, especially when finishing.

g. Examine the grain of the wood to see which way it runs. Cut with the grain. This severs the fibers and leaves the wood smooth. Cutting against the grain splits the wood and leaves it rough. This type of cut cannot be controlled.

SCREWDRIVERS

A screwdriver is one of the most basic of basic handtools. It is also the most frequently abused of all handtools. It is designed for one function only—to drive and remove screws. A screwdriver should not be used as a pry bar, a scraper, a chisel, or a punch.

STANDARD

There are three main parts to a standard screwdriver. The portion you grip is called the handle, the steel portion extending from the handle is the shank, and the end which fits into the screw is called the blade (fig. 1-89).

The steel shank is designed to withstand considerable twisting force in proportion to its size, and the tip of the blade is hardened to keep it from wearing.

Standard screwdrivers are classified by size, according to the combined length of the shank and blade. The most common sizes range in length from 2 1/2 in. to 12 in. There are many screwdrivers smaller and some larger for special purposes. The diameter of the shank, and the width and thickness of the blade are generally proportionate to the length, but again there are special screwdrivers with long thin shanks, short thick shanks, and extra wide or extra narrow blades.

Screwdriver handles may be wood, plastic, or metal. When metal handles are used, there is usually a wooden hand grip placed on each side of the handle. In some types of wood- or plastic-handled screwdrivers the shank extends through the handle, while in others the shank enters the handle only a short way and is pinned to the handle. For heavy work, special types of screwdrivers are made with a square shank. They are designed this way so that they may be

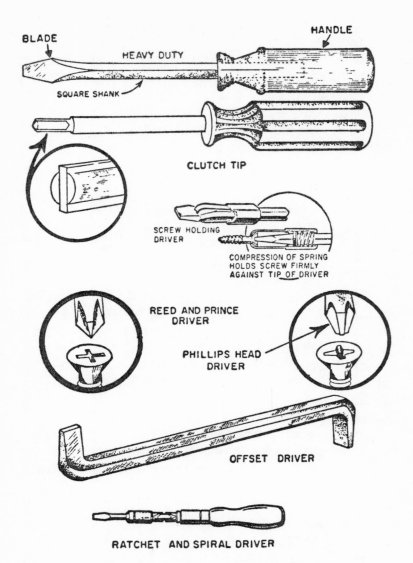

BLADE

HANDLE

HEAVY DUTY

SQUARE SHANK

CLUTCH TIP

SCREW HOLDING
DRIVER

COMPRESSION OF SPRING
HOLDS SCREW FIRMLY
AGAINST TIP OF DRIVER

REED AND PRINCE
DRIVER

PHILLIPS HEAD
DRIVER

OFFSET DRIVER

RATCHET AND SPIRAL DRIVER

Figure 1-89.—Screwdrivers.

gripped with a wrench, but this is the only kind
on which a wrench should be used.

When using a screwdriver it is important to
select the proper size so that the blade fits the
screw slot properly. This prevents burring the
slot and reduces the force required to hold the
driver in the slot. Keep the shank perpendicular to the screw head (fig. 1-90).

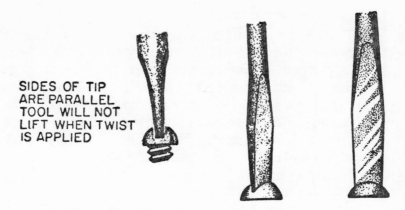

SIDES OF TIP
ARE PARALLEL
TOOL WILL NOT
LIFT WHEN TWIST
IS APPLIED

Figure 1-90.—Positioning screwdrivers.

RECESSED

Recessed screws are now available in various shapes. They have a cavity formed in the head and require a specially shaped screwdriver. The clutch tip (fig. 1-89) is one shape, but the more common include the Phillips, Reed and Prince, and newer Torq-Set types (fig. 1-91). The most common type found is the Phillips head screw. This requires a Phillips-type screwdriver (fig. 1-89).

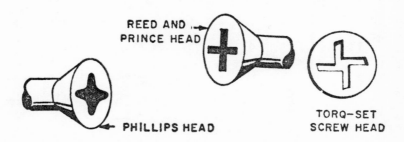

REED AND
PRINCE HEAD

PHILLIPS HEAD

TORQ-SET
SCREW HEAD

Figure 1-91.—Comparison of Phillips, Reed, and Prince and Torq-Set screwheads.

Phillips Screwdriver

The head of a Phillips-type screw has a four-way slot into which the screwdriver fits. This prevents the screwdriver from slipping. Three standard sized Phillips screwdrivers handle a wide range of screw sizes. Their ability to hold helps to prevent damaging the slots or the work surrounding the screw. It is a poor practice to try to use a standard screwdriver on a Phillips screw because both the tool and screw slot will be damaged.

Reed and Prince Screwdriver

Reed and Prince screwdrivers are not interchangeable with Phillips screwdrivers. Therefore, always use a Reed and Prince screwdriver with Reed and Prince screws and a Phillips screwdriver with Phillips screws, or a ruined tool or ruined screwhead will result.

How do you distinguish between these similar screwdrivers? Refer to figure 1-92.

The Phillips screwdriver has about 30-degree flukes and a blunt end, while the Reed and Prince has 45-degree flukes and a sharper, pointed end. The Phillips screw has beveled walls between the slots; the Reed and Prince, straight, pointed walls. In addition, the Phillips screw slot is not as deep as the Reed and Prince slot.

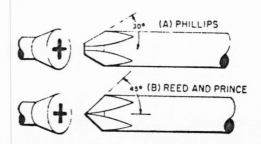

Figure 1-92.—Matching cross-slot screws and drivers.

"Torq-Set" Screws

"Torq-Set" machine screws (offset cross-slot drive) have recently begun to appear in new equipment. The main advantage of the newer type is that more torque can be applied to its head while tightening or loosening than any other screw of comparable size and material without damaging the head of the screw.

Torq-Set machine screws are similar in appearance to the more familiar Phillips machine screws.

OFFSET SCREWDRIVERS.—An offset screwdriver (fig. 1-89) may be used where there is not sufficient vertical space for a standard or recessed screwdriver. Offset screwdrivers are constructed with one blade forged in line and another blade forged at right angles to the shank handle. Both blades are bent 90 degrees to the shank handle. By alternating ends, most screws can be seated or loosened even when the swinging space is very restricted. Offset screwdrivers are made for both standard and recessed head screws.

RATCHET SCREWDRIVER

For fast easy work the ratchet screwdriver (fig. 1-89), is extremely convenient, as it can be used one-handed and does not require the bit to be lifted out of the slot after each turn. It may be fitted with either a standard type bit or a special bit for recessed heads. The ratchet screwdriver is most commonly used by the woodworker for driving screws in soft wood.

SAFETY

● Never use a screwdriver to check an electrical circuit.

● Never try to turn a screwdriver with a pair of pliers.

● Do not hold work in your hand while using a screwdriver—if the point slips it can cause a bad cut. Hold the work in a vise, with a clamp, or on a solid surface. If that is impossible, you will always be safe if you follow this rule: NEVER GET ANY PART OF YOUR BODY IN FRONT OF THE SCREWDRIVER BLADE TIP. That is a good safety rule for any sharp or pointed tool.

PLIERS

Pliers are made in many styles and sizes and are used to perform many different operations. Pliers are used for cutting purposes as well as holding and gripping small articles in situations where it may be inconvenient or impossible to use hands. Figure 1-93 shows several different kinds.

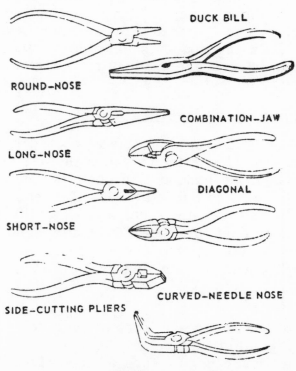

DUCK BILL

ROUND-NOSE

COMBINATION-JAW

LONG-NOSE

DIAGONAL

SHORT-NOSE

CURVED-NEEDLE NOSE

SIDE-CUTTING PLIERS

Figure 1-93.—Pliers.

The combination pliers are handy for holding or bending flat or round stock. The long-nosed pliers are less rugged, and break easily if you use them on heavy jobs. Long-nosed pliers, commonly called needle-nose pliers, are especially useful for holding small objects in tight places and for making delicate adjustments. The round-nosed kind are handy when you need to crimp sheet metal or form a loop in a wire, The diagonal cutting pliers, commonly called "diagonals" or "dikes," are designed for cutting wire and cotter pins close to a flat surface and are especially useful in the electronic and electrical fields. The duckbill pliers are used extensively in aviation areas.

Here are two important rules for using pliers:

1. Do not make pliers work beyond their capacity. The long-nosed kind are especially delicate. It is easy to spring or break them, or nick their edges. After that, they are practically useless.

2. Do not use pliers to turn nuts. In just a few seconds, a pair of pliers can damage a nut. Pliers must <u>not</u> be substituted for wrenches.

SLIP-JOINT PLIERS

Slip-joint pliers (fig. 1-94) are pliers with straight, serrated (grooved) jaws, and the screw or pivot with which the jaws are fastened together may be moved to either of two positions, in order to grasp small- or large-sized objects better.

To spread the jaws of slip-joint pliers, first spread the ends of the handles apart as far as possible. The slip-joint, or pivot, will now move to the open position. To close, again spread the handles as far as possible, then push the joint back into the closed position.

Figure 1-94.—Slipjoint pliers.

Slip-joint combination pliers (fig. 1-95) are pliers similar to the slip-joint pliers just described, but with the additional feature of a side cutter at the junction of the jaws. This cutter consists of a pair of square cut notches, one on each jaw, which act like a pair of shears when an object is placed between them and the jaws are closed.

The cutter is designed to cut material such as soft wire and nails. To use the cutter, open the jaws until the cutter on either jaw lines up with the other. Place the material to be cut as far back as possible into the opening formed by the cutter and squeeze the handles of the pliers together. Do not attempt to cut hard material such as spring wire or hard rivets with the combination pliers. To do so will spring the

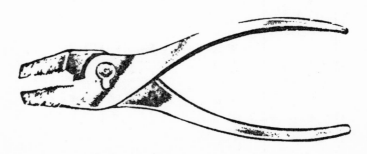

Figure 1-95.—Slipjoint combination pliers.

jaws; and if the jaws are sprung, it will be difficult thereafter to cut small wire with the cutters.

WRENCH (VISE-GRIP) PLIERS

Vise-grip pliers (fig. 1-96), can be used for holding objects regardless of their shape. A screw adjustment in one of the handles makes them suitable for several different sizes. The jaws of vise-grips may have standard serrations such as the pliers just described or may have a clamp-type jaw. The clamp-type jaws are generally wide and smooth and are used primarily when working with sheet metal.

Vise-grip pliers have an advantage over other types of pliers in that you can clamp them on an object and they will stay. This will leave your hands free for other work.

A craftsman uses this tool a number of ways. It may be used as a clamp, speed wrench, portable vise, and for many other uses where a locking, plier type jaw may be employed. These pliers can be adjusted to various jaw openings by turning the knurled adjusting screw at the end of the handle (fig. 1-96). Vise-grips can be clamped and locked in position by pulling the lever toward the handle.

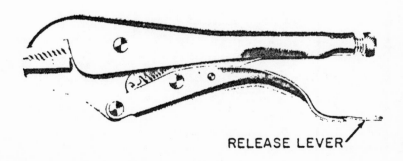

RELEASE LEVER

Figure 1-96.—Vise grip pliers.

CAUTION: Vise-grip pliers should be used with care since the teeth in the jaws tend to damage the object on which they are clamped. They should not be used on nuts, bolts, tube fittings, or other objects which must be reused.

WATER-PUMP PLIERS

Water-pump pliers were originally designed for tightening or removing water pump packing nuts. They were excellent for this job because they have a jaw adjustable to seven different positions. Water-pump pliers (fig. 1-97) are easily identified by their size, jaw teeth, and adjustable slip joint. The inner surface of the jaws consists of a series of coarse teeth formed by deep grooves, a surface adapted to grasping cylindrical objects.

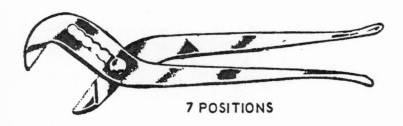

7 POSITIONS

Figure 1-97.—Water pump pliers.

CHANNEL-LOCK PLIERS

Channel-lock pliers (fig. 1-98) are another version of water-pump pliers easily identified by the extra long handles, which make them a very powerful gripping tool. They are shaped approximately the same as the pliers just described, but the jaw opening adjustment is effected differently. Channel-lock pliers have grooves on one jaw and lands on the other. The adjustment is effected by changing the position of the grooves and lands. The Channel-lock pliers are less likely to slip from the adjustment setting when gripping an object. The channel-lock pliers will only be used where it is impossible to use a more adapted wrench or holding device. Many nuts and bolts and surrounding parts have been damaged by improper use of channel-lock pliers.

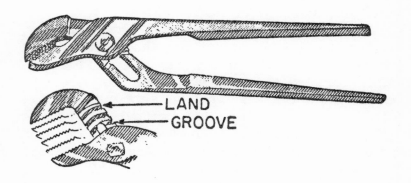

Figure 1-98.—Channel-lock pliers.

DIAGONAL PLIERS

Diagonal cutting pliers (fig. 1-93) are used for cutting small, light material, such as wire and cotter pins in areas which are inaccessible to the larger cutting tools. Also, since they are designed for cutting only, larger objects can be cut than with the slip-joint pliers.

As the cutting edges are diagonally offset approximately 15 degrees, diagonal pliers are adapted to cutting small objects flush with a surface. The inner jaw surface is a diagonal straight cutting edge. Diagonal pliers should never be used to hold objects, because they exert a greater shearing force than other types of pliers of a similar size. The sizes of the diagonal cutting pliers are designated by the overall length of the pliers.

SIDE-CUTTING PLIERS

Side-cutting pliers (sidecutters) are principally used for holding, bending, and cutting thin materials or small gage wire. Sidecutters vary in size and are designated by their overall length. The jaws are hollowed out on one side just forward of the pivot point of the pliers. Opposite the hollowed out portion of the jaws are the cutting edges (fig. 1-93).

When holding or bending light metal surfaces, the jaw tips are used to grasp the object. When holding wire grasp it as near one end as possible because the jaws will mar the wire. To cut small diameter wire the side cutting edge of the jaws near the pivot is used. Never use sidecutters to grasp large objects, tighten nuts, or bend heavy gage metal, since such operations will spring the jaws.

Sidecutters are often called electrician or lineman pliers. They are used extensively for stripping insulation from wire and for twisting wire when making a splice.

DUCKBILL PLIERS

Duckbill pliers (fig. 1-99A), have long wide jaws and slender handles. Duckbills are used in confined areas where the fingers cannot be used. The jaw faces of the pliers are scored to aid in holding an item securely. Duckbills are ideal for twisting the safety wire used in securing nuts, bolts, and screws.

Figure 1-99.—Pliers. (A) Duckbills (B) needle nose; and (C) wire twister.

NEEDLE-NOSE PLIERS

Needle-nose pliers (fig. 1-99B), are used in the same manner as duckbill pliers. However, there is a difference in the design of the jaws. Needle-nose jaws are tapered to a point which makes them adapted to installing and removing small cotter pins. They have serrations at the nose end and a side cutter near the throat. Needle-nose pliers may be used to hold small items steady, to cut and bend safety wire, or to do numerous other jobs which are too intricate or too difficult to be done by hand alone.

NOTE: Duckbill and needle-nose pliers are especially delicate. Care should be exercised when using these pliers to prevent springing, breaking, or chipping the jaws. Once these pliers are damaged, they are practically useless.

WIRE-TWISTER PLIERS

Wire-twister pliers (fig. 1-99C), are three-way pliers, which hold, twist, and cut. They are designed to reduce the time used in twisting safety wire on nuts and bolts. To operate, grasp the wire between the two diagonal jaws, and the thumb will bring the locking sleeve into place. A pull on the knob twirls the twister, making uniform twists in the wire. The spiral rod may be pushed back into the twister without unlocking it, and another pull on the knob will give a tighter twist to the wire. A squeeze on the handle unlocks the twister, and the wire can be cut to the desired length with the side cutter. The spiral of the twister should be lubricated occasionally.

MAINTENANCE OF PLIERS

Nearly all sidecutting pliers and diagonals are designed so that the cutting edges can be reground. Some older models of pliers will not close if material is ground from the cutting edges. When grinding the cutting edges never take any more material from the jaws than is necessary to remove the nicks. Grind the same amount of stock from both jaws.

NOTE: When jaws on pliers do not open enough to permit grinding, remove the pin that attaches the two halves of the pliers so that the jaws can be separated.

The serrations on the jaws of pliers must be sharp. When they become dull, the pliers should be held in a vise and the serrations recut by using a small 3-corner file.

Pliers should be coated with light oil when they are not in use. They should be stored in a toolbox in such a manner that the jaws cannot be injured by striking hard objects. Keep the pin or bolt at the hinge just tight enough to hold the two parts of the pliers in contact and always keep the pivot pin lubricated with a few drops of light oil.

VISES AND CLAMPS

Vises are used for holding work when it is being planed, sawed, drilled, shaped, sharpened, or riveted, or when wood is being glued. Clamps are used for holding work which cannot be satisfactorily held in a vise because of its shape and size, or when a vise is not available. Clamps are generally used for light work.

A MACHINIST'S BENCH VISE is a large steel vise with rough jaws that prevent the work from slipping. Most of these vises have a swivel base with jaws that can be rotated, while others cannot be rotated. A similar light duty model is equipped with a cutoff. These vises are usually bolt-mounted onto a bench.

THE BENCH AND PIPE VISE has integral pipe jaws for holding pipe from 3/4 inch to 3 inches in diameter. The maximum working main jaw opening is usually 5 inches, with a jaw

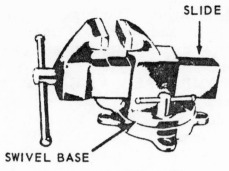

SLIDE

SWIVEL BASE

MACHINIST'S
BENCH

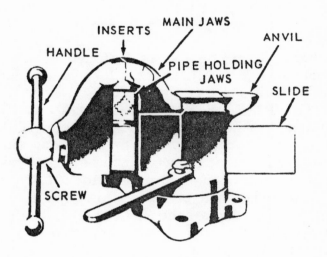

INSERTS

MAIN JAWS

HANDLE

ANVIL

PIPE HOLDING
JAWS

SLIDE

SCREW

BENCH AND PIPE

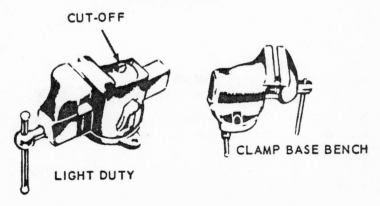

CUT-OFF

LIGHT DUTY

CLAMP BASE BENCH

Figure 1-100.—Common types of bench vises.

width of 4 to 5 inches. The base can be swiveled to any position and locked. These vises are equipped with an anvil and are also bolted onto a workbench.

The CLAMP BASE VISE usually has a smaller holding capacity than the machinist's or the bench and pipe vise and is usually clamped to the edge of a bench with a thumb-screw. These type vises can be obtained with a maximum holding capacity varying between 1 1/2 in. and 3 in. These vises normally do not have pipe holding jaws.

The BLACKSMITH'S VISE (fig. 1-101) is used for holding work that must be pounded with a heavy hammer. It is fastened to a sturdy workbench or wall, and the long leg is secured into a solid base on the floor.

The PIPE VISE (fig. 1-101) is specifically designed to hold round stock or pipe. The vise shown has a capacity of 1 to 3 inches. One jaw is hinged so that the work can be positioned and then the jaw brought down and locked. This vise is also used on a bench. Some pipe vises are designed to use a section of chain to hold down the work. Chain pipe vises range in size from 1/8- to 2 1/2 inch pipe capacity up to 1/2- to 8-inch pipe capacity.

A C-CLAMP (fig. 1-102) is shaped like the letter C. It consists of a steel frame threaded to receive an operating screw with a swivel head. It is made for light, medium, and heavy service in a variety of sizes.

A HAND SCREW CLAMP (fig. 1-102) consists of two hard maple jaws connected with two operating screws. Each jaw has two metal inserts into which the screws are threaded. The hand screw clamp is also issued from supply in a variety of sizes.

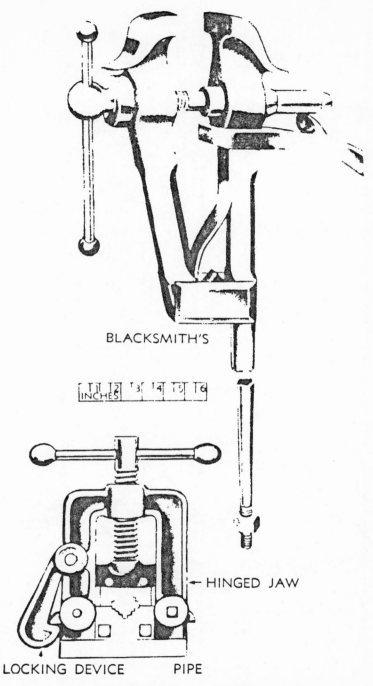

BLACKSMITH'S

INCHES 1 2 3 4 5 6

HINGED JAW

LOCKING DEVICE   PIPE

Figure 1-101.—Blacksmith's and pipe vises.

HAND SCREW

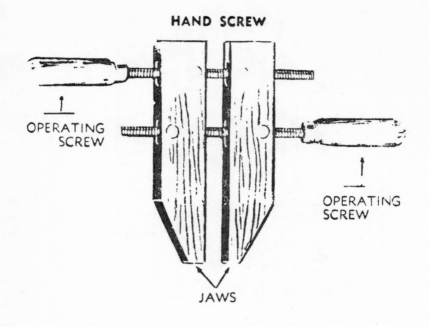

OPERATING
SCREW

OPERATING
SCREW

JAWS

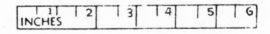

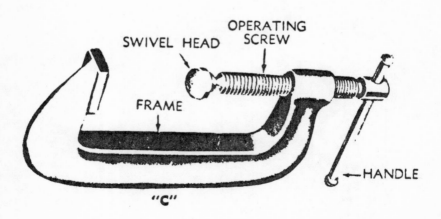

SWIVEL HEAD

OPERATING
SCREW

FRAME

HANDLE

"C"

Figure 1-102.—C-Clamp and handscrew clamp.

CARE

Keep vises clean at all times. They should be cleaned and wiped with light oil after using. Never strike a vise with a heavy object and never hold large work in a small vise, since these practices will cause the jaws to become sprung or otherwise damage the vise. Keep jaws in good condition and oil the screws and the slide frequently. Never oil the swivel base of swivel jaw joint: its holding power will be impaired. When the vise is not in use, bring the jaws lightly together or leave a very small gap. (The movable jaw of a tightly closed vise may break due to the expansion of the metal in heat.) Leave the handle in a vertical position.

Threads of C-clamps must be clean and free from rust. The swivel head must also be clean, smooth, and grit free. If the swivel head becomes damaged, replace it as follows: pry open the crimped portion of the head and remove the head from the ball end of the screw. Replace with a new head and crimp.

SAFETY PRECAUTIONS

When closing the jaw of a vise or clamp, avoid getting any portion of your hands or body between the jaws or between one jaw and the work.

When holding heavy work in a vise, place a block of wood under the work as a prop to prevent it from sliding down and falling on your foot.

Do not open the jaws of a vise beyond their capacity, as the movable jaw will drop off, causing personal injury and possible damage to the jaw.

SHARPENING STONES

Sharpening stones are divided into two groups, natural and artificial. Some of the natural stones are oil treated during and after the manufacturing processes. The stones that are oil treated are sometimes called oilstones. Artificial stones are normally made of silicone carbide or aluminum oxide. Natural stones have very fine grains and are excellent for putting razorlike edges on fine cutting tools. Most sharpening stones have one coarse and one fine face. Some of these stones are mounted, and the working face of some of the sharpening stones is a combination of coarse and fine grains. Stones are available in a vareity of shapes, as shown in figure 1-103.

A fine cutting oil is generally used with most artificial sharpening stones; however, other lubricants such as kerosene may be used. When a tool has been sharpened on a grinder or grindstone, there is usually a wire edge or a feather edge left by the coarse wheel. The sharpening stones are used to hone this wire or feather edge off the cutting edge of the tool. Do not attempt to do a honing job with the wrong stone. Use a coarse stone to sharpen large and very dull or nicked tools. Use a medium grain stone to sharpen tools not requiring a finished edge, such as tools for working soft wood, cloth, leather, and rubber. Use a fine stone and an oilstone to sharpen and hone tools requiring a razorlike edge.

Prevent glazing of sharpening stones by applying a light oil during the use of the stone. Wipe the stone clean with wiping cloth or cotton waste after each use. If stone becomes glazed or gummed up, clean with aqueous ammonia or drycleaning solvent. If necessary, scour with aluminum oxide abrasive cloth or flint paper attached to a flat block.

At times, stones will become uneven from improper use. True the uneven surfaces on an old grinding wheel or on a grindstone. Another method of truing the surface is to lap it with a

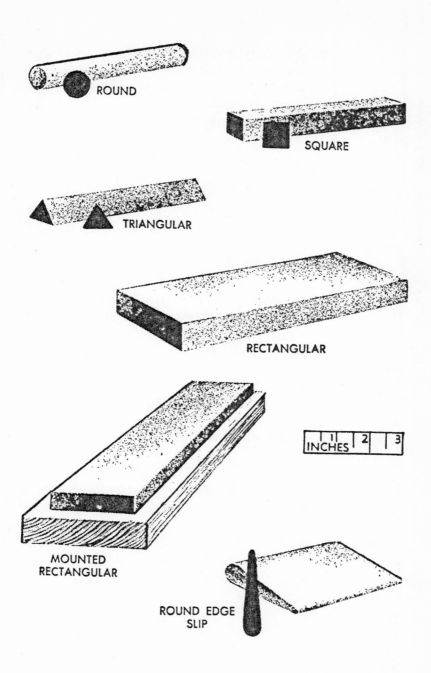

ROUND

SQUARE

TRIANGULAR

RECTANGULAR

INCHES 1 2 3

MOUNTED
RECTANGULAR

ROUND EDGE
SLIP

Figure 1-103.—Shapes of sharpening stones
and oilstones.

block of cast iron or other hard material covered with a waterproof abrasive paper, dipping the stone in water at regular intervals and continuing the lapping until the stone is true.

Stones must be carefully stored in boxes or on special racks when not in use. Never lay them down on uneven surfaces or place them where they may be knocked off a table or bench, or where heavy objects can fall on them. Do not store in a hot place.

SHARPENING A WOOD CHISEL

To sharpen a wood chisel with a sharpening stone, use a common oilstone that has coarse grit on one side and fine grit on the other (fig. 1-104). Make sure the stone is firmly held so that it cannot move. Cover the stone with a light machine oil so that the fine particles of steel ground off will float and thus prevent the stone from clogging.

Hold the chisel in one hand with the bevel flat against the coarse side of the stone. Use the fingers of your other hand to steady the chisel and hold it down against the stone. Using smooth even strokes, rub the chisel back and forth parallel to the surface of the stone (fig.1-104). The entire surface of the stone should be used to avoid wearing a hollow in the center of the stone. Do not rock the blade. The angle of the blade with the stone must remain constant during the whetting process.

After a few strokes, a burr, wire edge, or feather edge is produced. To remove the burr, first take a few strokes with the flat side of the chisel held flat on the fine grit side of the stone. Be careful not to raise the chisel even slightly; avoid putting the slightest bevel on the flat side, for then the chisel must be ground until the bevel is removed.

After whetting the flat side on the fine grit

130

side of the stone, turn the chisel over and place the bevel side down and hold it at the same angle as used when whetting on the coarse side of the stone. Take two or three light strokes to remove the burr.

To test the sharpness of the cutting edge, hold the chisel where a good light will shine on the cutting edge. A keen edge does not reflect light in any position. If there are no shiny or white spots it is a good edge.

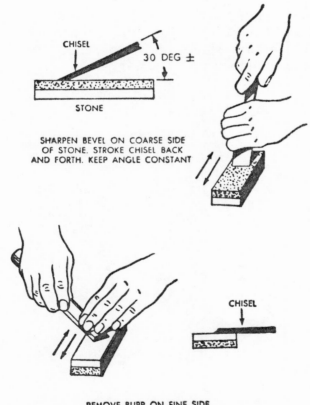

Figure 1-104.—Sharpening a woodworker's chisel.

SHARPENING A POCKET KNIFE

Pocket knives may be sharpened on a medium or fine grade sharpening stone with a few drops of oil spread on the surface. Hold the handle of the knife in one hand and place the blade across the stone. Press down with the fingers of the other hand and stroke the blade following a circular motion as shown in figure 1-105. After several strokes, reverse the blade and stroke the opposite side, following the same type of motion. Use a light even pressure. A thin blade overheats quickly and can lose its temper. The wire edge or burr that may be left on a knife blade after whetting may be removed by stropping both sides on a soft wood block, canvas or leather.

Figure 1-105.—Sharpening a pocket knife.

MISCELLANEOUS TOOLS

KNIVES

Most knives are used to cut, pare, and trim wood, leather, rubber and other similar materials. The types you will probably encounter

132

most frequently are the shop knife, pocket knife, and the putty knife (fig. 1-106).

The shop knife can be used to cut cardboard, linoleum, and paper. It has an aluminum handle and is furnished with interchangeable blades stored in the 5-inch handle.

Pocket knives are used for light cutting, sharpening pencils, cutting strings, etc. They are unsuited for heavy work. Multi-purpose knives have an assortment of blades designed for forcing holes, driving screws and opening cans, as well as cutting. The blades are hinged and should be contained within the case when not in use. They are spring loaded to keep them firmly in place when open or closed.

A putty knife is used for applying putty to window sash when setting in panes of glass. The blade has a wide square point available in different lengths and widths.

Safety with knives is essential. Do not use knives larger than can be safely handled. Use knives only for the purpose for which they were designed. Always cut away from your body. Do not carry open knives in your pocket or leave them where they may come into contact with or cause injury to others. Put knives away carefully after use to protect sharp cutting edges from contacting other hard objects.

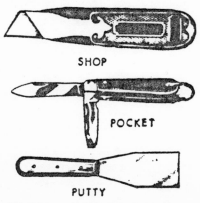

SHOP

POCKET

PUTTY

Figure 1-106.—Knives.

MECHANICAL FINGERS

Small articles which have fallen into places where they cannot be reached by hand may be retrieved with the mechanical fingers. This tool is also used when starting nuts or bolts in difficult areas. The mechanical fingers, shown in figure 1-107 have a tube containing flat springs which extend from the end of the tube to form clawlike fingers, much like the screw holder. The springs are attached to a rod that extends from the outer end of the tube. A plate is attached to the end of the tube, and a similar plate to be pressed by the thumb is attached to the end of the rod. A coil spring placed around the rod between the two plates holds them apart and retracts the fingers into the tube. With the bottom plate grasped between the fingers and enough thumb pressure applied to the top plate to compress the spring, the tool fingers extend from the tube in a grasping position. When the thumb pressure is released, the tool fingers retract into the tube as far as the object they hold will allow. Thus, enough pressure is applied on the object to hold it securely. Some mechanical fingers have a flexible end on the tube to permit their use in close quarters or around obstructions (fig. 1-107).

NOTE: Mechanical fingers should not be used as a substitute for wrenches or pliers. The fingers are made of thin sheet metal or spring wire and can be easily damaged by overloading.

INSPECTION MIRROR

The inspection mirror aids in making detailed inspection where the human eye cannot directly see the inspection area. By angling the mirror, and with the aid of a flashlight, it is possible to inspect most required areas. A late

134

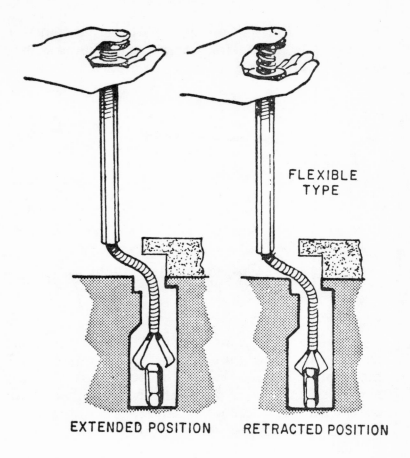

FLEXIBLE TYPE

EXTENDED POSITION   RETRACTED POSITION

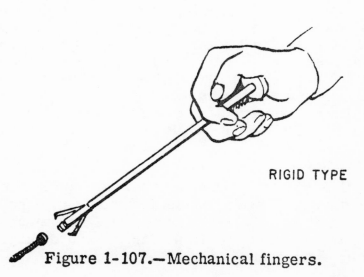

RIGID TYPE

Figure 1-107.—Mechanical fingers.

model inspection mirror features a built-in
light to aid in viewing those dark places where
use of a flashlight is not convenient.

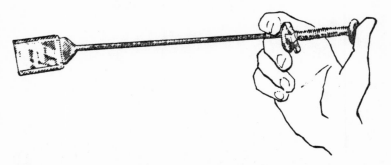

Figure 1-108.—Adjustable inspection
mirror.

SAFETY SHOES

Some safety shoes are designed to limit
damage to your toes from falling objects. A
steel plate is placed in the toe area of such
shoes so that your toes are not crushed if an
object impacts there.

GOGGLES

Appropriate use of goggles will limit eye
hazards. Some goggles have plastic windows
which resist shattering upon impact. Others
are designed to limit harmful infrared and ul-
traviolet radiation from arcs or flames by appropriate filter lenses.

Remember, eye damage can be excruciatingly
painful. **PROTECT YOUR EYES.**

GLOVES

Use gloves whenever you are required to
handle rough, scaly, or splintery objects. Special flameproof gloves are designed for gas and
electric welding, to limit danger and damage
from sparks and other hot flying objects (fig.
1-110).

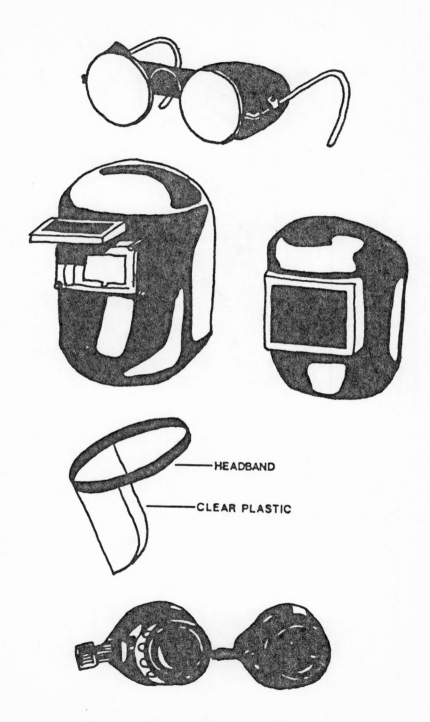

HEADBAND

CLEAR PLASTIC

Figure 1-109.—Eye protection devices.

137

Figure 1-110.—Gas and electric-arc
welding gauntlet gloves.

BODY BELT   SAFETY STRAP

Figure 1-111.—Safety equipment.

PROTECTIVE HELMETS

Protective helmets (hard hats) come in a variety of shapes. They may be made of tough polyethylene or polycarbonate, one of the toughest hat materials yet developed. Many a man has had his life saved because he wore a protective hat (fig. 1-112). When a falling object struck the hat the shock-absorbing suspension capabilities minimized damage to the man's head.

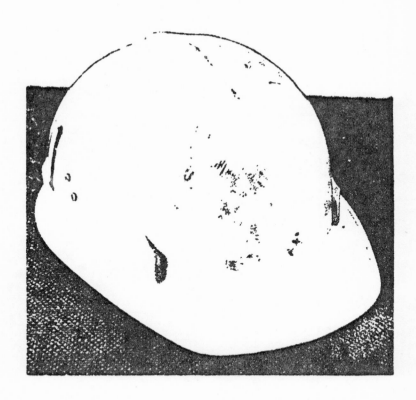

Figure 1-112.—Hard hat.

CHAPTER 2

COMMON POWER TOOLS

SAFETY

Safe practices in the use of power tools cannot be overemphasized. There are several general safety measures to observe in operating or maintaining power equipment.

● First of all, never operate power equipment unless you are thoroughly familiar with its controls and operating procedures. When in doubt, consult the appropriate operating instruction or ask someone who knows.

● All portable tools should be inspected before use to see that they are clean and in a proper state of repair.

● Have ample illumination. If extension lights are required, ensure that a light guard is provided (fig. 2-1).

● Before a power tool is connected to a source of power (electricity, air, etc.), BE SURE that the switch on the tool is in the "OFF" position.

● When operating a power tool, give it your FULL and UNDIVIDED ATTENTION.

● Keep all safety guards in position and use safety shields or goggles when necessary.

● Fasten all loose sleeves and aprons.

● Never try to clear jammed machinery unless you remove the source of power first.

● After using a power tool, turn off the power, remove the power source, wait for all rotation of the tool to stop, and then clean the tool.

● Never plug the power cord of a portable electric tool into an electrical power source before ensuring that the source has the voltage and type of current (alternating or direct) called for on the nameplate of the tool.

● If an extension cord is required, always connect the cord of a portable electric power tool into the extension cord before the extension cord is inserted into a convenience outlet

NEVER USE AN EXTENSION LIGHT WITHOUT A GUARD.

Figure 2-1.—Safety poster.

(fig. 2-2). Always unplug the extension cord from the receptacle before the cord of the portable power tool is unplugged from the extension cord.

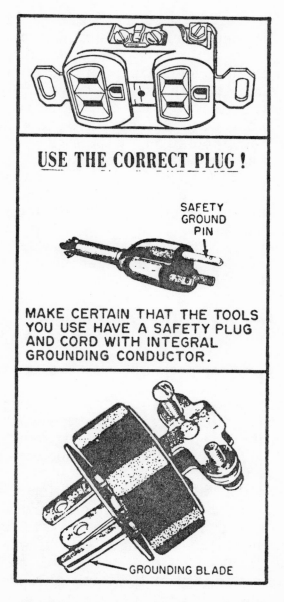

USE THE CORRECT PLUG !

SAFETY
GROUND
PIN

MAKE CERTAIN THAT THE TOOLS YOU USE HAVE A SAFETY PLUG AND CORD WITH INTEGRAL GROUNDING CONDUCTOR.

GROUNDING BLADE

Figure 2-2.—Grounding plugs and convenience outlet.

● Be sure to use a grounded plug and 3-conductor cord. Figure 2-2 shows a permanently molded type of grounded plug and also one used for replacement purposes.

One exception to the use of 3-conductor grounded cord concerns plastic-cased tools (drills, sanders, grinders, etc.) that have been developed to eliminate the risk of electric shock. In these tools the shafts and chucks are isolated electrically from the drive motors. DO NOT replace the two-conductor cable on plastic-cased tools with 3-conductor cable IF the plastic-cased tool has an information plate on it stating that "grounding is not required"!

● Be sure that power cords do not come in contact with sharp objects. The cords should not be allowed to kink, nor should they be allowed to come in contact with oil, grease, hot surfaces, or chemicals.

● When cords are damaged, they should be replaced.

● Portable cables should be of sufficient length that they will not be subjected to longitudinal stresses or need to be pulled taut to make connections.

● Electrical portable cables should be checked frequently while in service to detect unusual heating. Any cable which feels more than comfortably warm to the bare hand placed outside the insulation should be checked immediately for overloading by competent electrical personnel.

● See that all cables are positioned so that they will not constitute tripping hazards.

● Electricity must be treated with respect and handled properly (fig. 2-3). If water exists anywhere in the vicinity of energized equipment—be especially cautious, and wherever possible, deenergize the equipment.

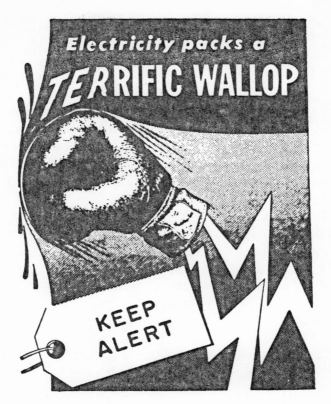

Figure 2-3.—Know what you are doing.

- Always remember:

    1. ELECTRICITY strikes without warning.
    2. Every electrical circuit is a POTENTIAL SOURCE OF DANGER and MUST BE TREATED AS SUCH.
    3. Make no electrical repairs yourself unless you are qualified to do so.
    4. Sparking electric tools should never be used in places where flammable gases or liquids or exposed explosives are present. Pneumatic tools are used in these areas.
    5. The power should always be disconnected before accessories on tools are changed.

DRILLS

The revolutions per minute (rpm) and power the drill will deliver are most important when choosing a drill for a job. You will find that the speed of the drill motor decreases with an increase in size, primarily because the larger units are designed to turn larger cutting tools or to drill in heavy materials, and both these factors require slower speed.

If you are going to do heavy work, such as drilling in masonry or steel, then you would probably need to use a drill with a 3/8 or 1/2 inch capacity. If most of your drilling will be forming holes in wood or small holes in sheet metal, then a 1/4-inch drill will probably be adequate.

The chuck is the clamping device into which the drill is inserted. Nearly all electric drills are equipped with a three-jaw chuck. Some of the drill motors have a hand-type chuck that you tighten or loosen by hand but most of the drills used are tightened and loosened by

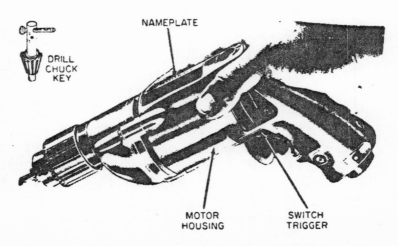

Figure 2-4.—1/4-inch portable electric drill.

means of a chuck key, shown in figure 2-5. Do not apply further pressure with pliers or wrenches after you hand tighten the chuck with the chuck key.

Always remove the key IMMEDIATELY after you use it. Otherwise the key will fly loose when the drill motor is started and may cause serious injury.

The trigger latch is a button in the bottom of the drill handle. It is pushed in, while the switch trigger is held down, to lock the trigger switch in the "ON" position. The trigger latch is released by squeezing and then releasing the switch trigger.

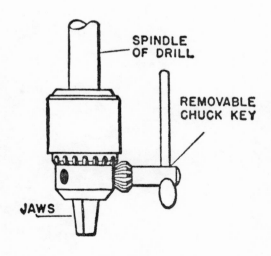

Figure 2-5.—Three jaw chuck
and chuck key.

SANDERS

Portable sanders are tools designed to hold and operate abrasives for sanding wood, plastics and metals.

Disk Sander

Electric disk sanders (fig. 2-6) are especially useful on work where a large amount of material is to be removed quickly such as scaling surfaces in preparation for painting. This machine, however, must not be used where a mirror smooth finish is required.

The disk should be moved smoothly and lightly over the surface. Never allow the disk to stay in one place too long because it will cut into the metal and leave a large depression.

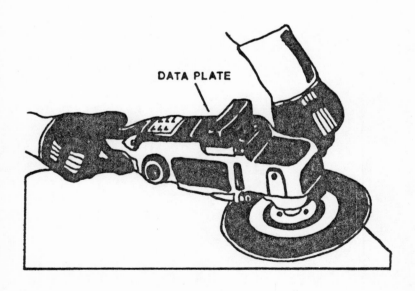

DATA PLATE

Figure 2-6.—Portable electric sander.

Belt Sander

The belt sander (fig. 2-7) is commonly used for surfacing lumber used for interior trim, furniture, or cabinets. Wood floors are almost always made ready for final finishing by using a belt sander. Whereas these types of sanding operations were once laborious and time-consuming, it is now possible to perform the operations quickly and accurately with less effort.

The portable belt sanders use endless sanding belts that can be obtained in many different grades (grits). The belts are usually 2, 3, or 4 inches wide and can be easily changed when they become worn or when you want to use a different grade of sanding paper.

The first thing to do when preparing to use the sander is to be sure that the object to be sanded is firmly secured. Then, after the motor has been started verify that the belt is tracking on center. Any adjustment to make it track centrally is usually made by aligning screws.

The moving belt is then placed on the surface of the object to be sanded with the rear part of the belt touching first. The machine is then leveled as it is moved forward. When you use the sander, don't press down or "ride" it, because the weight of the machine exerts enough pressure for proper cutting. (Excessive pressure also causes the abrasive belt to clog and the motor to overheat). Adjust the machine over the surface with overlapping strokes, always in a direction parallel to the grain.

By working over a fairly wide area, and avoiding any machine tilting or pausing in any one spot, an even surface will result. Upon completion of the sanding process, lift the machine off the work and then stop the motor.

Some types of sanders are provided with a

bag that takes up the dust that is produced. Use it if available.

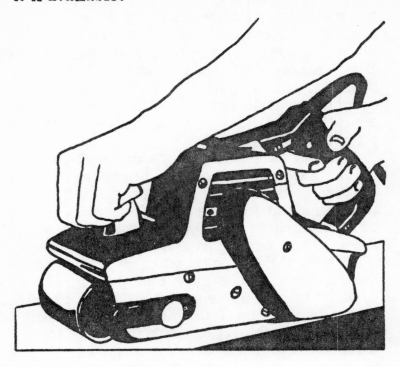

Figure 2-7.—Portable belt sander.

Orbital Sander

The orbital sander (fig. 2-8) is so named because of the action of the sanding pad. The pad moves in a tiny orbit, with a motion that is hardly discernible, so that it actually sands in all directions. This motion is so small and so fast that, with fine paper mounted on the pad, it is nearly impossible to see any scratches on the finished surface.

The pad, around which the abrasive sheet is wrapped, usually extends beyond the frame of the machine so it is possible to work in tight corners and against vertical surfaces.

Some models of the orbital sanders have a bag attached to catch all dust that is made from the sanding operation. Orbital sanders (pad sanders) do not remove as much material as fast as the belt sander or disk sander but do a better job on smoothing a surface for finishing. If both a belt or disk sander and an orbital sander are available you should use the belt or disk sander for rough, preliminary work and the orbital sander for finishing. The sandpaper used on the sander may be cut to size from a bulk sheet of paper or may be available in the correct size for the sander you have. The paper is wrapped around a pad on the sander and is fastened to the pad by means of levers on the front and rear of the sander. The lever action fasteners make changing the paper easy and quick.

Figure 2-8.—Orbital sander.

PORTABLE GRINDERS

Portable grinders are power tools that are used for rough grinding and finishing of metallic surfaces.

The abrasive wheels are easily replaceable so that different grain size and grades of abrasives can be used for the varying types of surfaces to be ground and the different degrees of finish desired.

A flexible shaft attachment is available for most portable grinders. This shaft is attached by removing the grinding wheel then attaching the shaft to the grinding wheel drive spindle. The grinding wheel can then be attached to the end of the flexible shaft. This attachment is invaluable for grinding surfaces in hard to reach places.

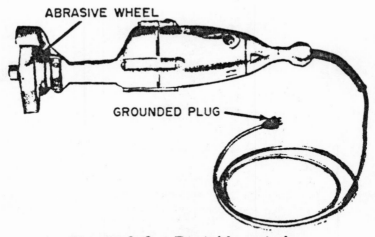

Figure 2-9.—Portable grinder.

The wheel guard on the grinder should be positioned so that abrasive dust and metal particles will be deflected away from your face.

Before you turn the grinder on, make sure the abrasive grinding wheel is properly secured to the grinder spindle and not cracked or damaged.

152

PORTABLE CIRCULAR SAW

The portable circular saw is becoming more and more popular as a woodworking tool because of the time and labor it saves, the precision with which it works, and its ease of handling and maneuverability.

The sizes of portable electric saws range from one-sixth horsepower with a 4-inch blade to one-and-one half horsepower with a 14-inch blade. They are so constructed that they may be used as a carpenter's handsaw, both at the job site or on a bench in the woodworking shop.

The portable electric saw (fig. 2-10) is started by pressing a trigger inserted in the handle and stopped by releasing it. The saw will run only when the trigger is held.

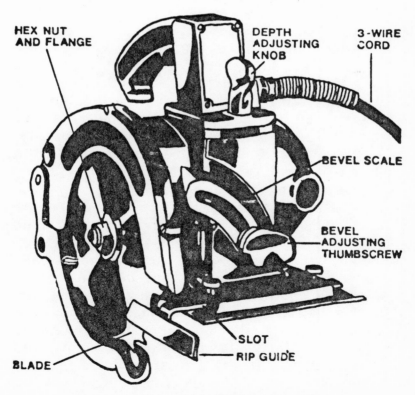

HEX NUT AND FLANGE

DEPTH ADJUSTING KNOB

3-WIRE CORD

BEVEL SCALE

BEVEL ADJUSTING THUMBSCREW

SLOT

RIP GUIDE

BLADE

Figure 2-10.—Portable electric circular saw.

Most saws may be adjusted for cross-cutting or for ripping. The ripsaw guide shown in figure 2-10 is adjusted by the two small knurled nuts at the base of the saw. When the guide is inserted in the rip guide slot to the desired dimensions, the nuts are then tightened to hold it firmly in place.

In crosscutting, a guideline is generally marked across the board to be cut. Place the front of the saw base on the work so that the guide mark on the front plate and the guide line on the work are aligned. Be sure the blade is clear of the work. Start the saw and allow the cutting blade to attain full speed. Then advance the saw, keeping the guide mark and guide line aligned. If the saw stalls, back the saw out. DO NOT RELEASE the starting trigger. When the saw resumes cutting speed, start cutting again.

Additional adjustments include a depth knob and a bevel thumbscrew. The depth of the cut is regulated by adjusting the depth knob. The bevel adjusting thumbscrew is used for adjusting the angle of the cut. This permits the base to be tilted in relation to the saw. The graduated scale marked in degrees on the quadrant (fig. 2-10) enables the operator to measure his adjustments and angles of cut.

The bottom plate of the saw is wide enough to provide the saw with a firm support on the lumber being cut. The blade of the saw is protected by a spring guard which opens when lumber is being cut but snaps back into place when the cut is finished. Many different saw blades may be placed on the machine for special kinds of sawing. By changing blades almost any building material from slate and corrugated metal sheets to fiberglass can be cut.

To change saw blades, first disconnect the power. Remove the blade by taking off the saw clamp screw and flange, using the wrench provided for this purpose. Attach the new saw blade making certain the teeth are in the proper cutting direction (pointing upward toward the front of the saw) and tighten the flange and clamp screw with the wrench.

CAUTION: Do not put the saw blade on backwards; most blades have instructions stamped on them with the words "This Side Out."

THE PORTABLE ELECTRIC SAW IS ONE OF THE MOST DANGEROUS POWER TOOLS IN EXISTENCE WHEN IT IS NOT PROPERLY USED. Make sure the board you are sawing is properly secured so it will not slip or turn. After making a cut be sure the saw blade has come to a standstill before laying the saw down.

When using an electric saw remember that all the blade you can normally see is covered; the portion of the blade that projects under the board being cut is not covered. The exposed teeth under the work are dangerous and can cause serious injury if any part of your body should come into contact with them.

Make sure the blade of a portable circular saw is kept sharp at all times. The saw blade will function most efficiently when the rate of feed matches the blade's capacity to cut. You will not have to figure this out—you will be able to feel it. With a little practice you will know when the cut is smooth and you will know when you are forcing it. Let the blade do its own cutting. The tool will last longer and you will work easier because it is less fatiguing.

SABER SAW

The saber saw (fig. 2-11) is a power driven jigsaw that will let you cut smooth and decorative curves in wood and light metal. Most saber saws are light duty machines and are not designed for extremely fast cutting.

There are several different blades designed

to operate in the saber saw and they are easily interchangeable. For fast cutting of wood, a blade with coarse teeth may be used. A blade with fine teeth is designed for cutting metal.

The best way to learn how to handle this type of tool is to use it. Before trying to do a finished job with the saber saw, clamp down a piece of scrap plywood and draw some curved as well as straight lines to follow. You will develop your own way of gripping the tool, and this will be affected somewhat by the particular tool you are using. On some tools, for example, you will find guiding easier if you apply some downward pressure on the tool as you move it forward. If you are not firm with your grip, the tool will tend to vibrate excessively and this will roughen the cut. Do not force the cutting faster than the design of the blade allows or you will break the blade.

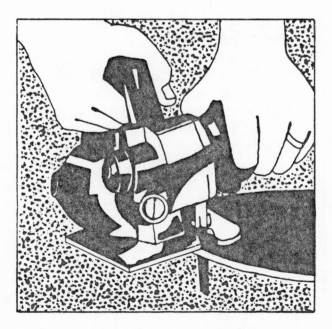

Figure 2-11.—Saber or bayonet
saw operations.

ELECTRIC IMPACT WRENCH

The electric impact wrench (fig. 2-12) is a portable hand-type reversible wrench. The one shown has a 1/2-inch square impact driving anvil over which 1/2-inch square drive sockets can be fitted. Wrenches also can be obtained that have impact driving anvils ranging from 3/8 inch to 1 inch. The driving anvils are not interchangeable, however, from one wrench to another.

The electric wrench with its accompanying equipment is primarily intended for applying and removing nuts, bolts, and screws. It may also be used to drill and tap metal, wood, plastics, etc., and drive and remove socket-head, Phillips-head, or slotted-head wood, machine, or self-tapping screws.

Before you use an electric impact wrench depress the on-and-off trigger switch and allow the electric wrench to operate a few seconds, noting carefully the direction of rotation.

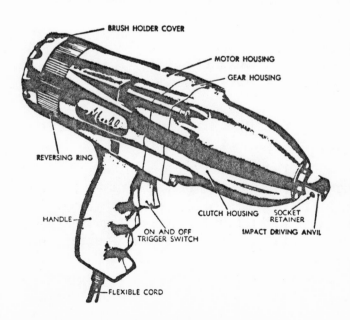

Figure 2-12.—Reversible electric impact wrench.

157

Release the trigger switch to stop the wrench. Turn the reversing ring located at the rear of the tool; it should move easily in one direction (which is determined by the current direction of rotation). Depress the on-and-off trigger again to start the electric wrench. The direction of rotation should now be reversed. Continue to operate for a few seconds in each direction to be sure that the wrench and its reversible features are functioning correctly. When you are sure the wrench operates properly, place the suitable equipment on the impact driving anvil and go ahead with the job at hand.

PORTABLE PNEUMATIC POWER TOOLS

Portable pneumatic power tools are tools that look much the same as electric power tools but use the energy of compressed air instead of electricity.

SAFETY

In operating or maintaining air-driven tools, take the following precautionary measures to protect yourself and others from the damaging effects of compressed air.

● Inspect the air hose for cracks or other defects; replace the hose if found defective.

● Before connecting an air hose to the compressed air outlet, open the control valve momentarily. Then, make sure the hose is clear of water and other foreign material by connecting it to the outlet and again opening the valve momentarily.

● Stop the flow of air to a pneumatic tool by closing the control valve at the compressed air outlet before connecting, disconnecting, adjusting, or repairing a pneumatic tool.

158

PNEUMATIC CHIPPING HAMMER

The pneumatic chipping hammer (fig. 2-13) consists basically of a steel piston which is reciprocated (moved backward and forward alternately) in a steel barrel by compressed air. On its forward stroke the piston strikes the end of the chisel, which is a sliding fit in a nozzle pressed into the barrel. The rearward stroke is cushioned by compressed air to prevent any metal-to-metal contact. Reciprocation of the piston is automatically controlled by a valve located on the rear end of the barrel. Located on the rear end of the barrel is a grip handle, containing a throttle valve.

The throttle valve is actuated by a throttle lever which protrudes from the upper rear of the grip handle for thumb operation. Projecting from the butt of the handle is an air inlet. The handle is threaded onto the barrel and is prevented from unscrewing by a locking ring. Surrounding and retaining the locking ring is an exhaust deflector. This deflector may be located in any of four positions around the barrel in order to throw the stream of exhaust air in the desired direction.

The pneumatic hammer may be used for beveling, calking or beading operations, and for drilling in brick, concrete, and other masonry.

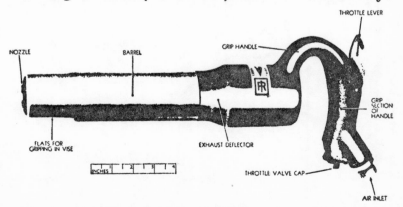

Figure 2-13.—Pneumatic chipping hammer.

When nearing the end of a cut, ease off on the throttle lever to reduce the intensity of the blows. This will avoid any possibility of the chip or tool flying.

If for any reason you have to lay the chipping hammer down, always remove the attachment tool from the nozzle.

NEEDLE AND ROTARY IMPACT SCALERS

Needle and rotary scalers (figs. 2-14 and 2-15) are used to remove rust, scale, and old paint from metallic and masonry surfaces. You must be especially careful when using these tools since they will "chew" up anything in their path. Avoid getting the power line or any part of your body in their way.

Figure 2-14.—Needle impact scaler.

Figure 2-15.—Rotary impact scaler.

Needle scalers accomplish their task with an assembly of individual needles impacting on a surface hundreds of times a minute. The advantage of using individual needles is that irregular surfaces can be cleaned readily. See the operations and how the needle scaler self-adjusts to the contour of various surfaces in figure 2-16.

The rotary scaling and chipping tool, sometimes called a "jitterbug," has a bundle of cutters or chippers for scaling or chipping (fig. 2-15). In use, the tool is pushed along the surface to be scaled and the rotating chippers do the work. Replacement bundles of cutters are available when the old ones are worn.

BE SURE YOU ARE NOT DAYDREAMING when you use the rotary scaler.

Figure 2-16.—Needle scaler operations.

PORTABLE PNEUMATIC
IMPACT WRENCH

The portable pneumatic impact wrench (fig. 2-17) is designed for installing or removing nuts and bolts. The wrench comes in different sizes and is classified by the size of the square anvil on the drive end. The anvil is equipped with a socket lock which provides positive locking of the socket wrenches or attachments. The wrench has a built-in oil reservoir and an adjustable air valve regulator which adjusts the torque output of the wrench. The torque regulator reduces the possibility of shearing or damaging threads when installing nuts and bolts to their required tension.

Nearly all pneumatic wrenches operate most efficiently on an air pressure range of 80 to 90 psi. A variation in excess of plus or minus 5 pounds is serious. Lower pressure causes a decrease in the driving speeds while higher pressure causes the wrench to overspeed with subsequent abnormal wear of the motor impact mechanisms.

The throttle lever located at the rear of the pneumatic wrench provides the means for starting and stopping the wrench. Depressing the throttle lever starts the wrench in operation. Upon release, the lever raises to its original position stopping the wrench.

The valve stem is seated beneath the pivot end of the throttle lever. Most wrenches have a window cut in the throttle lever so that the markings on the upper surface of the valve stem will be visible. Two letters, "F" and "R," have been engraved on the head of the valve stem to indicate the forward (clockwise) and reverse (counterclockwise) rotation of the anvil. To change from forward to reverse rotation, or vice versa, turn the valve stem 180°

until the desired marking is visible through the window in the throttle lever. When the valve stem is in proper position, the valve stem pin engages a recess on the under side of the valve stem, preventing accidental turning of the stem.

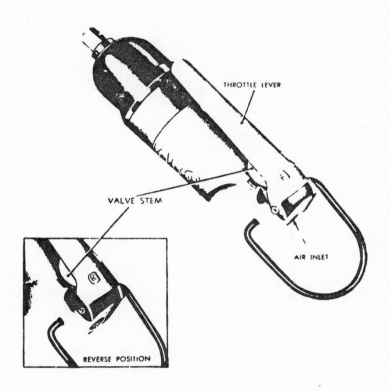

Figure 2-17.—Portable pneumatic impact wrench.

The air valve regulator is located at the bottom and towards the rear of the wrench. Using a screwdriver and altering the setting of the air regulator up to 90°, either to the right or left, reduces the torque from full power to zero power.

Before operating the pneumatic impact wrench make sure the socket or other attachment you are using is properly secured to the anvil. It is always a good idea to operate the wrench free of load in both forward and reverse directions to see that it operates properly. Check the installation of the air hose to make sure it is in accordance with the manufacturer's recommendation.

COMMON POWER MACHINE TOOLS

Small power machine tools are, generally speaking, not portable. All work that is to be done must be brought to the shop where the machine is set up. Only the most common types of power machine tools will be discussed in this chapter.

DRILL PRESS

The drill press (fig. 2-18) is an electrically operated power machine that was originally designed as a metal-working tool. Available accessories, plus jigs and special techniques, now make it a versatile wood-working tool as well.

The motor is mounted to a bracket at the rear of the head assembly and designed to permit V-belt changing for desired spindle speed without removing the motor from its mounting bracket. Four spindle speeds are obtained by locating the V-belt on any one of the four steps of the spindle-driven and motor-driven pulleys.

The controls of drill presses are all similar. The terms "right" and "left" are relative to the operator's position standing in front of and facing the drill press. Forward applies to movement toward the operator. Rearward applies to movement away from the operator.

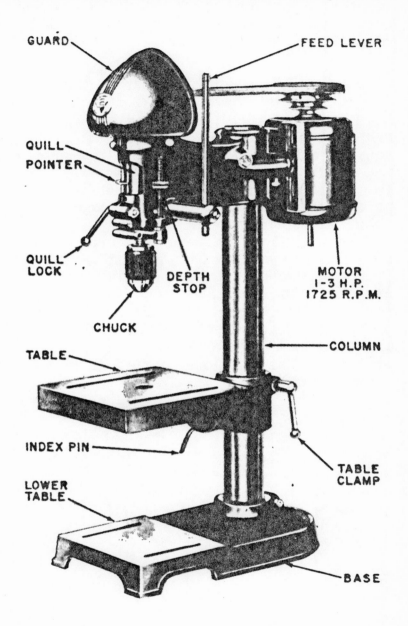

Figure 2-18.—Drill press.

The power switch (fig. 2-19) is located on the right side of the head assembly. The power cord is placed in the power receptacle and the motor started by placing the switch in the "ON" position.

The spindle and quill feed handle (fig. 2-19) is located on the lower right-front side of the head assembly. Pulling forward and down on any one of the three spindle and quill feed handles, which point upward at the time, moves the spindle and quill assembly downward. Release the feed handle and the spindle and quill assembly will return to the retracted or upper position by spring action.

The quill lock handle (fig. 2-20) enables the drill press to be used as a milling tool and is located at the lower left-front side of the head assembly. Turn the quill lock handle clockwise to lock the quill at a desired operating position. Release the quill by turning the quill lock handle counterclockwise. However, in most cases, the quill lock handle will be in the released position.

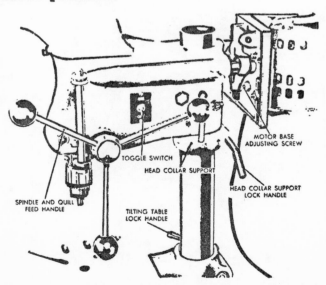

Figure 2-19.—Drill press controls—right side view.

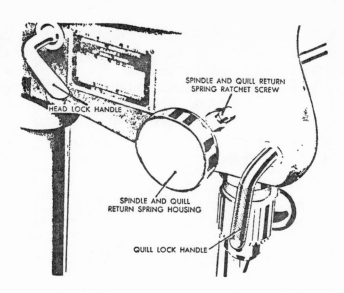

Figure 2-20.—Drill press controls—left side view.

The head lock handle (fig. 2-20) is located at the left-rear side of the head assembly. Turn the head lock handle clockwise to lock the head assembly at a desired vertical height on the bench column. Turn the headlock handle counterclockwise to release the head assembly. When operating the drill press, the head lock handle must be tight at all times.

The head collar support lock handle (fig. 2-19)· is located at the right side of the head collar support and below the head assembly. The handle locks the head collar support, which secures the head vertically on the bench column, and prevents the head from dropping when the head lock handle is released. Turn the head collar support lock handle clockwise to lock the support to the bench column and counterclockwise to release the support. When operating the drill press, the head collar support lock handle must be tight at all times.

The tilting table lock handle (fig. 2-19) is located at the left-rear side of the tilting table bracket. Turn the tilting table lock handle counterclockwise to release the tilting table bracket so it can be moved up and down or around the bench column. Lock the tilting table assembly at desired height by turning the lock handle clockwise. When operating the drill press, the tilting table lock handle must be tight at all times.

A	SPINDLE DRIVEN PULLEY
B	V-BELT
C	MOTOR DRIVE PULLEY
D	1/8 SQ x 1 SQ-END KEY
E	NO 10-24 x 5/8 HDLS SET SCREW
F	MOTOR BRACKET STUD THUMBSCREW
G	MOTOR
H	MOTOR BASE AND BRACKET ASSEMBLY
J	1/4-20NC 2 x 1 SQ-NECK RD-HD CAR-RIAGE BOLT AND 1/4-20NC-2 SQ NUT
K	DRILL CHUCK KEY
L	DRILL CHUCK KEY BRACKET
M	TOGGLE SWITCH PLATE
N	HEAD COLLAR SUPPORT
P	BENCH COLUMN
Q	CORD
R	BENCH BASE
S	TILTING TABLE LOCKPIN
T	TILTING TABLE ASSEMBLY
U	DEPTH GAGE ROD BRACKET
V	HEX NUT
W	DRILL CHUCK
X	CHUCK KNOCKOUT COLLAR
Y	SPINDLE AND QUILL ASSEMBLY
Z	DEPTH GAGE ROD
AA	HEAD ASSEMBLY
BB	DEPTH GAGE ROD ADJUSTING NUT
CC	DEPTH GAGE ROD LOCKNUT
DD	SPINDLE DRIVEN PULLEY GUARD

Figure 2-21. Drill press nomenclature.

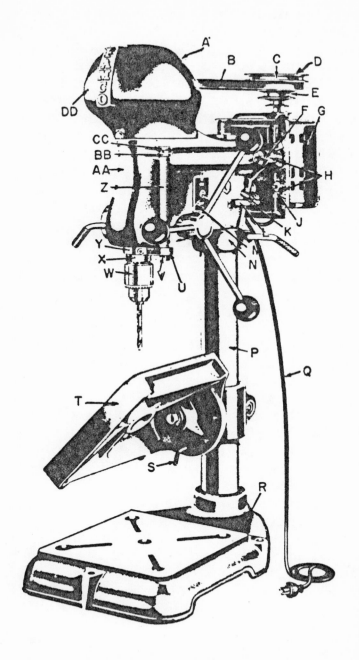

Figure 2-21.

The tilting table lockpin (S, fig. 2-21) is located below the tilting table assembly (T, fig. 2-21). The lockpin secures the table at a horizontal or 45° left or right from the horizontal position. To tilt the table left or right from its horizontal position, remove the lockpin and turn the table to align the lockpin holes. Insert the lockpin through the table and bracket holes after desired position is obtained.

The depth gage rod adjusting and locknuts (BB and CC, fig. 2-21) are located on the depth gage rod (Z, fig. 2-21). The purpose of the adjusting and locknuts is to regulate depth drilling. Turn the adjusting and locknut clockwise to decrease the downward travel of the spindle. The locknut must be secured against the adjusting nut when operating the drill press.

When operating a drill press make sure the drill is properly secured in the chuck and that the work you are drilling is properly secured in position. Do not remove the work from the tilting table or mounting device until the drill press has stopped.

Operate the spindle and quill and feed handles with a slow, steady pressure. If too much pressure is applied, the V-belt may slip in the pulleys, the twist drill may break, or the starting switch in the motor may open and stop the drill press. If the motor should stop because of overheating, the contacts of the starting switch will remain open long enough for the motor to cool, then automatically close to resume normal operation. Always turn the toggle switch to "OFF" position while the motor is cooling.

Check occasionally to make sure all locking handles are tight, and that the V-belt is not slipping and adjust as necessary in accordance with the manufacturer's manual.

Before operating any drill press, visually inspect the drill press to determine if all parts are in the proper place, secure, and in good

170

operating condition. Check all assemblies, such as the motor, head, pulleys, and bench for loose mountings.

While the drill press is operating, be alert for any sounds that may be signs of trouble, such as squeaks or unusual noise.

After operating a drill press, wipe off all dirt, oil, and metal particles. Inspect the V-belt to make sure no metal chips are imbedded in the driving surfaces.

BENCH GRINDER

The electric bench grinder (fig. 2-22) is designed for hand grinding operations, such as sharpening chisels or screw drivers, grinding drills, removing excess metal from work, and smoothing metal surfaces. It is usually fitted with both a medium grain and fine grain abrasive wheel; the medium wheel is satisfactory for rough grinding where a considerable quantity of metal has to be removed, or where a smooth finish is not important. For sharpening tools or grinding to close limits of size, the fine wheel should be used as it removes metal slower, gives the work a smooth finish and does not generate enough heat to anneal the cutting edges.

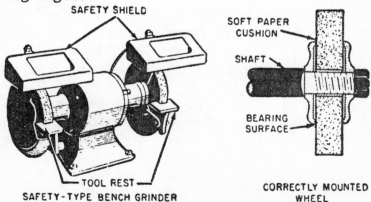

Figure 2-22.—Bench grinder and wheel.

When a deep cut is to be taken on work or a considerable quantity of metal removed, it is often practical to grind with the medium wheel first and finish up with the fine wheel. Most bench grinders are so made that wire brushes, polishing wheels, or buffing wheels can be substituted for the removable grinding wheels.

To protect the operator during the grinding operation, an eye shield and wheel guard are provided for each grinding wheel. A tool rest is provided in front of each wheel to rest and guide the work during the grinding procedure. The rests are removable, if necessary, for grinding odd-shaped or large work.

When starting a grinder, turn it on and stand to one side until the machine comes up to full speed. There is always a possibility that a wheel may fly to pieces when coming up to full speed. Never force work against a cold wheel; apply work gradually to give the wheel an opportunity to warm. You thereby minimize the possibility of breakage.

Handle grinding wheels carefully. Before replacing a wheel always check it for cracks. Make sure that a fiber or rubber gasket is in place between each side of the wheel and its retaining washer. Tighten the spindle nut just enough to hold the wheel firmly; if the nut is tightened too much the clamping strain may damage the wheel. When selecting a replacement wheel, ascertain that the grinder will not exceed the manufacturer's recommended speed for the wheel.

When grinding, always keep the work moving across the face of the wheel; grinding against the same spot on the wheel will cause grooves to be worn into the face of the wheel. Keep all wheel guards tight and in place. Always keep the tool rest adjusted so that it just clears the wheel and is at or just below the center line of the wheel, to prevent accidental jamming of work between tool rest and wheel.

Wear goggles, even if eye shields are attached to the grinder. Keep your thumbs and fingers out of the wheel.

CHAPTER 3

MEASURING TOOLS AND TECHNIQUES

RULES AND TAPES

There are many different types of measuring tools ordinarily in use. Where exact measurements are required, a micrometer caliper (mike) is used. Such a caliper, when properly used, gives measurements to within .001 of an inch accuracy. On the other hand, where accuracy is not extremely critical, the common rule or tape will suffice for most measurements.

Figure 3-1 shows some of the types of rules and tapes commonly used for a job. Of all measuring tools, the simplest and most common is the steel rule. This rule is usually 6 or 12 inches in length, although other lengths are available. Steel rules may be flexible or nonflexible, but the thinner the rule, the easier it is to measure accurately because the division marks are closer to the work.

Generally a rule has four sets of graduations, one on each edge of each side. The longest lines represent the inch marks. On one edge, each inch is divided into 8 equal spaces; so each space represents 1/8 in. The other edge of this side is divided into sixteenths. The 1/4-in. and 1/2-in. marks are commonly made longer than the smaller division marks to facilitate counting, but the graduations are not, as a rule, numbered individually, as they are sufficiently far apart to be counted without difficulty. The opposite side is similarly divided into 32 and 64 spaces per inch, and it is common practice to number every fourth division for easier reading.

There are many variations of the common rule. Sometimes the graduations are on one side only, sometimes a set of graduations is added across one end for measuring in narrow spaces, and sometimes only the first inch is divided into 64ths, with the remaining inches divided into 32nds and 16ths.

A metal or wood folding rule may be used for measuring purposes. These folding rules are usually 2 to 6 feet long. The folding rules cannot be relied on for extremely accurate measurements because a certain amount of play develops at the joints after they have been used for a while.

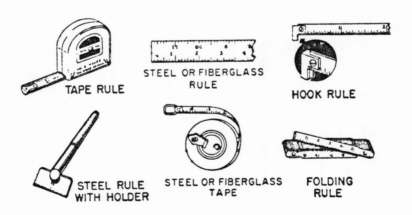

Figure 3-1.—Some common types of rules.

Steel tapes are made from 6 to about 300 ft. in length. The shorter lengths are frequently made with a curved cross section so that they are flexible enough to roll up, but remain rigid when extended. Long, flat tapes require support over their full length when measuring, or the natural sag will cause an error in reading.

The flexible-rigid tapes are usually contained in metal cases into which they wind themselves when a button is pressed, or into which they can be easily pushed. A hook is provided at one end to hook over the object being measured so one man can handle it without assistance. On some models, the outside of the case can be used as one end of the tape when measuring inside dimensions.

MEASURING PROCEDURES

To take a measurement with a common rule, hold the rule with its edge on the surface of the object being measured. This will eliminate parallax and other errors which might result due to the thickness of the rule. Read the measurement at the graduation which coincides with the distance to be measured, and state it as being so many inches and fractions of an inch. (Fig. 3-2.) Always reduce fractions to their lowest terms, for example, 6/8 inch would be called 3/4 inch. A hook or eye at the end of a tape or rule is normally part of the first measured inch.

Bolts or Screws

The length of bolts or screws is best measured by holding them up against a rigid rule or tape. Hold both the bolt or screw to be measured and the rule up to your eye level so that your line of sight will not be in error in reading the measurement. As shown in figure 3-3, the

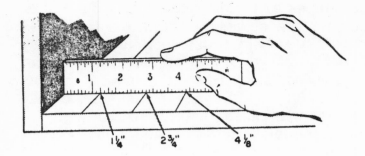

Figure 3-2.—Measuring with and reading
a common rule.

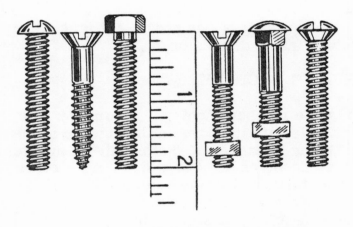

Figure 3-3.—Measuring the length
of a bolt or screw.

bolts or screws with countersink type heads are
measured from the top of the head to the opposite end, while those with other type heads
are measured from the bottom of the head.

Outside Pipe Diameters

To measure the outside diameter of a pipe,
it is best to use some kind of rigid rule. A
folding wooden rule or a steel rule is satisfactory for this purpose. As shown in figure

178

3-4, line up the end of the rule with one side of the pipe, using your thumb as a stop. Then with the one end held in place with your thumb, swing the rule through an arc and take the maximum reading at the other side of the pipe. For most practical purposes, the measurement obtained by using this method is satisfactory. It is necessary that you know how to take this measurement as the outside diameter of pipe is sometimes the only dimension given on pipe specifications.

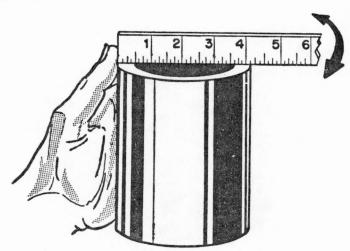

Figure 3-4.—Measuring the outside
diameter of a pipe.

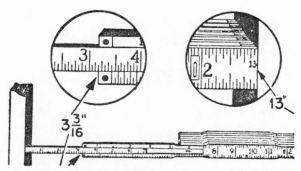

Figure 3-5.—Measuring the inside
diameter of a pipe.

Inside Pipe Diameters

To measure the inside diameter of a pipe with a rule, as shown in figure 3-5, hold the rule so that one corner of the rule just rests on the inside of one side of the pipe. Then, with one end thus held in place, swing the rule through an arc and read the diameter across the maximum inside distance. This method is satisfactory for an approximate inside measurement.

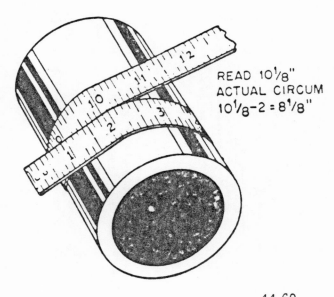

READ 10⅛"
ACTUAL CIRCUM
10⅛-2 = 8⅛"

44.69

Figure 3-6.—Measuring the circumference of a pipe with a tape.

Pipe Circumferences

To measure the circumference of a pipe, a flexible type rule that will conform to the cylindrical shape of the pipe must be used. A tape rule or a steel tape is adaptable for this job. When measuring pipe, make sure the tape has been wrapped squarely around the axis of the

180

pipe (i.e., measurement should be taken in a plane perpendicular to the axis) to ensure that the reading will not be more than the actual circumference of the pipe. This is extremely important when measuring large diameter pipe.

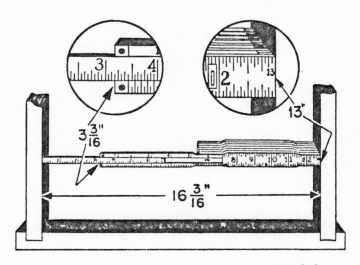

44.26.6

Figure 3-7.—Using a folding rule to measure an inside dimension.

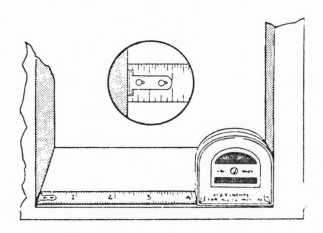

Figure 3-8.—Measuring an inside dimension with a tape rule.

181

Hold the rule or tape as shown in figure 3-6. Take the reading, using the 2-inch graduation, for example, as the reference point. In this case the correct reading is found by subtracting 2 inches from the actual reading. In this way the first 2 inches of the tape, serving as a handle, will enable you to hold the tape securely.

Inside Dimensions

To take an inside measurement, such as the inside of a box, a folding rule that incorporates a 6- or 7-inch sliding extension is one of the best measuring tools for this job. To take the inside measurement, first unfold the folding rule to the approximate dimension. Then extend the end of the rule and read the length that it extends, adding the length of the extension to the length on the main body of the rule. (Fig. 3-7.) In this illustration the length of the main body of the rule is 13 inches and the extension is pulled out 3 3/16 inches. In this case the total inside dimension being measured is 16 3/16 inches.

In figure 3-8 notice in the circled insert that the hook at the end of the particular rule shown is attached to the rule so that it is free to move slightly. When an outside dimension is taken by hooking the end of the rule over an edge, the hook will locate the end of the rule even with the surface from which the measurement is being taken. By being free to move, the hook will retract away from the end of the rule when an inside dimension is taken. To measure an inside dimension using a tape rule, extend the rule between the surfaces as shown, take a reading at the point on the scale where the rule enters the case, and add 2 inches. The 2 inches are the width of the case. The total is the inside dimension being taken.

To measure the thickness of stock through a hole with a hook rule, insert the rule through the hole, hold the hook against one face of the stock, and read the thickness at the other face. (Fig. 3-9.)

Outside Dimensions

To measure an outside dimension using a tape rule, hook the rule over the edge of the

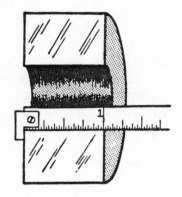

Figure 3-9.—Measuring the thickness of stock through a hole.

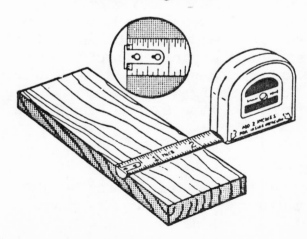

Figure 3-10.—Measuring an outside dimension using a tape rule.

stock. Pull the tape out until it projects far enough from the case to permit measuring the required distance. The hook at the end of the rule is designed so that it will locate the end of the rule at the surface from which the measurement is being taken. (Fig. 3-10.) When taking a measurement of length, the tape is held parallel to the lengthwise edge. For measuring widths, the tape should be at right angles to the lengthwise edge. Read the dimension of the rule exactly at the edge of the piece being measured.

It may not always be possible to hook the end of the tape over the edge of stock being measured. In this case it may be necessary to butt the end of the tape against another surface or to hold the rule at a starting point from which a measurement is to be taken.

Distance Measurements

Steel or fiberglass tapes are generally used for making long measurements. Secure the hook end of the tape. Hold the tape reel in the hand and allow it to unwind while walking in the direction in which the measurement is to be taken. Stretch the tape with sufficient tension to overcome sagging. At the same time make sure the tape is parallel to an edge or the surface being measured. Read the graduation on the tape by noting which line on the tape coincides with the measurement being taken.

CARE

Rules and tapes should be handled carefully and kept lightly oiled to prevent rust. Never allow the edges of measuring devices to become nicked by striking them with hard objects. They should preferably be kept in a wooden box when not in use.

To avoid kinking tapes, pull them straight out

from their cases—do not bend them backward. With the windup type, always turn the crank clockwise—turning it backward will kink or break the tape. With the spring-wind type, guide the tape by hand. If it is allowed to snap back, it may be kinked, twisted, or otherwise damaged. Do not use the hook as a stop. Slow down as you reach the end.

SIMPLE CALIPERS

Outside calipers for measuring outside diameters are bow-legged; those used for inside diameters have straight legs with the feet turned outward. Calipers are adjusted by pulling or pushing the legs to open or close them. Fine adjustment is made by tapping one leg lightly on a hard surface to close them, or by turning them upside down and tapping on the joint end to open them.

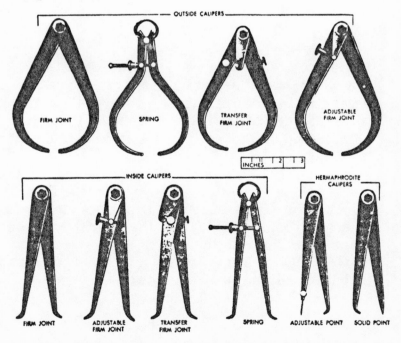

Figure 3-11.—Simple calipers—noncalibrated.

Spring-joint calipers have the legs joined by a strong spring hinge and linked together by a screw and adjusting nut. For measuring chamfered cavities (grooves), or for use over flanges, transfer calipers are available. They are equipped with a small auxiliary leaf attached to one of the legs by a screw. (Fig. 3-11.) The measurement is made as with ordinary calipers; then the leaf is locked to the leg. The legs may then be opened or closed as needed to clear the obstruction, then brought back and locked to the leaf again, thus restoring them to the original setting.

A different type of caliper is the hermaphrodite, sometimes called odd-leg caliper. This caliper has one straight leg ending in a sharp point, sometimes removable, and one bow leg. The hermaphrodite caliper is used chiefly for locating the center of a shaft, or for locating a shoulder.

USING CALIPERS

A caliper is usually used in one of two ways. Either the caliper is set to the dimension of the work and the dimension transferred to a scale, or the caliper is set on a scale and the work machined until it checks with the dimension set up on the caliper. To adjust a caliper to a scale dimension, one leg of the caliper should be held firmly against one end of the scale and the other leg adjusted to the desired dimension. To adjust a caliper to the work, open the legs wider than the work and then bring them down to the work.

CAUTION: Never place a caliper on work that is revolving in a machine.

Measuring The Diameter of Round or The Thickness of Flat Stock

To measure the diameter of round stock, or the thickness of flat stock, adjust the outside caliper so that you feel a slight drag as you pass it over the stock. (See fig. 3-12.) After the proper "feel" has been attained, measure the setting of the caliper with a rule. In reading the measurement, sight over the leg of the caliper after making sure the caliper is set squarely with the face of the rule.

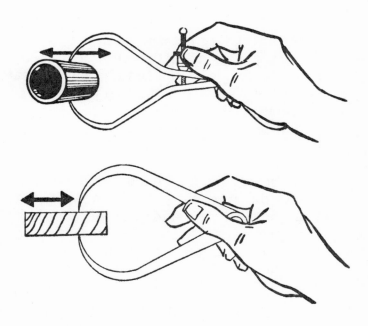

Figure 3-12.—Using an outside caliper.

Measuring Hard to Reach Dimensions

To measure an almost inaccessible outside dimension, such as the thickness of the bottom of a cup, use an outside transfer firm-joint caliper as shown in figure 3-13. When the proper "feel" is obtained, tighten the lock joint.

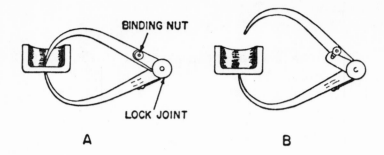

Figure 3-13.—Measuring the thickness
of the bottom of a cup.

Then loosen the binding nut and open the caliper enough to remove it from the cup. Close the caliper again and tighten the binding nut to seat in the slot at the end of the auxiliary arm. The caliper is now at the original setting, representing the thickness of the bottom of the cup. The caliper setting can now be measured with a rule.

To measure a hard to reach inside dimension, such as the internal groove shown in figure 3-14, a lock-joint inside caliper should be used. The procedure followed for measuring a hard to reach outside dimension is used.

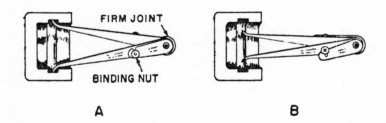

Figure 3-14.—Measuring a hard to reach
inside dimension with an inside caliper.

Measuring The Distance
Between Two Surfaces

To measure the distance between two surfaces with an inside caliper, first set the caliper
to the approximate distance being measured.
Hold the caliper with one leg in contact with one
of the surfaces being measured. (See fig. 3-15.)
Then as you increase the setting of the caliper,
move the other leg from left to right. Feel for
the slight drag indicating the proper setting of
the caliper. Then remove the caliper and
measure the setting with a rule.

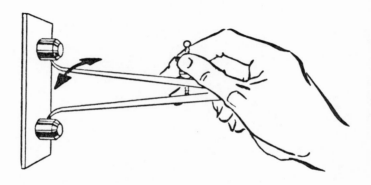

Figure 3-15.—Measuring the distance
between two surfaces with an
inside caliper.

Measuring Hole Diameters

To measure the diameter of a hole with an
inside caliper, hold the caliper with one leg in
contact with one side of the hole (fig. 3-16) and,
as you increase the setting, move the other leg
from left to right, and in and out of the hole.
When you have found the point of largest diameter, remove the caliper and measure the caliper setting with a rule.

Figure 3-16.—Measuring an inside
diameter with an inside caliper.

Setting A Combination
Firm Joint Caliper

To set a combination firm joint caliper with
a rule, when the legs are in position for outside
measurements, grasp the caliper with both
hands, as shown in figure 3-17A, and adjust
both legs to the approximate setting. By adjusting both legs, the shape of the tool will be approximately symmetrical. Thus it will maintain
its balance and be easier to handle.

Check this approximate setting as shown in
figure 3-17B. Sight squarely across the leg at
the graduations on the rule to get the exact setting required.

If it is necessary to decrease or increase the
setting, tap one leg of the caliper, as shown in
figure 3-18. The arrow indicates the change in
setting that will take place.

When the caliper is set for inside measurements, the same directions for adjusting the

setting apply. Figure 3-19 shows how the end of the rule and one leg of the caliper are rested on the bench top so that they are exactly even with each other when the reading is taken.

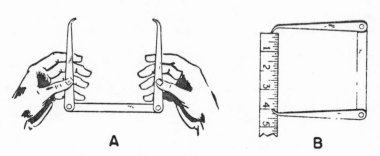

A   B

Figure 3-17.—Setting a combination firm joint caliper.

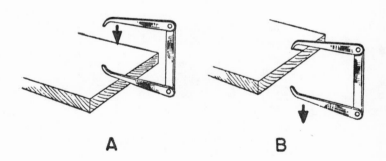

A   B

Figure 3-18.—Decreasing and increasing the setting of a firm joint caliper.

Setting Outside And Inside
Spring Calipers

To set a particular reading on an outside spring caliper, first open the caliper to the approximate setting. Then, as shown in figure 3-20, place one leg over the end of the rule, steadying it with index finger. Make the final setting by sighting over the other leg of the caliper, squarely with the face of the rule at the reading, and turning the knurled adjusting nut until the desired setting is obtained.

To set an inside spring caliper to a particular reading, place both caliper and rule on a flat surface as shown in figure 3-21. The rule must be held squarely or normal (90° in both directions) to the surface to ensure accuracy. Adjust the knurled adjusting nut, reading the setting on the rule with line of sight normal to the face of the rule at the reading.

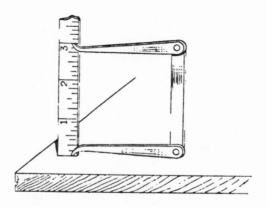

Figure 3-19.—Setting a combination firm joint caliper for inside measurements.

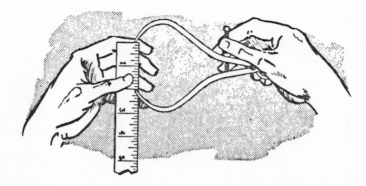

Figure 3-20.—Setting an outside spring caliper.

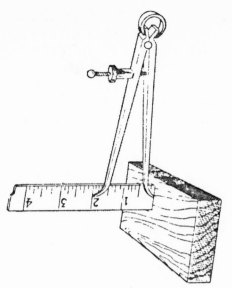

Figure 3-21.—Setting an inside
spring caliper.

Transferring Measurements From One Caliper To Another

To transfer a measurement from one spring caliper to another, hold the calipers as shown in figure 3-22. Note that one of the man's fingers is extended to steady the point of con-

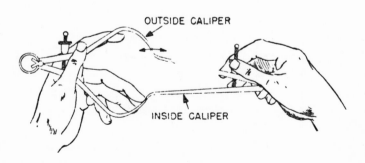

OUTSIDE CALIPER

INSIDE CALIPER

Figure 3-22.—Transferring a measurement from an outside to an inside caliper.

tact of the two lower caliper legs. In this figure the inside caliper is being adjusted to the size of the outside caliper. As careful measurements with calipers depend on one's sense of touch, which is spoken of as "feel," calipers are best held lightly. When you notice a slight drag, the caliper is at the proper setting.

CARE

Keep calipers clean and lightly oiled, but do not overoil the joint of firm joint calipers or you may have difficulty in keeping them tight. Do not throw them around or use them for screwdrivers or pry bars. Even a slight force may spring the legs of a caliper so that other measurements made with it are never accurate. Remember they are measuring instruments and must be used only for the purpose for which they are intended.

SLIDE CALIPER

The main disadvantage of using ordinary calipers is that they do not give a direct reading of a caliper setting. As explained earlier, you must measure a caliper setting with a rule. To overcome this disadvantage, use slide calipers (fig. 3-23). This instrument is occasionally called a caliper rule.

Slide calipers can be used for measuring outside, inside, and other dimensions. One side of the caliper is used as a measuring rule, while the scale on the opposite side is used in measuring outside and inside dimensions. Graduations on both scales are in inches and fractions thereof. A locking screw is incorporated to hold the slide caliper jaws in position during use. Stamped on the frame are two words, "IN" and "OUT." These are used in reading the scale while making inside and outside measurements, respectively.

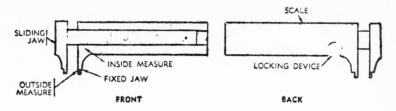

SLIDING JAW

INSIDE MEASURE

OUTSIDE MEASURE

FIXED JAW

FRONT

SCALE

LOCKING DEVICE

BACK

Figure 3-23.—Caliper square
(slide caliper).

To measure the outside diameter of round stock, or the thickness of flat stock, move the jaws of the caliper into firm contact with the surface of the stock. Read the measurement at the reference line stamped OUT. (See fig. 3-24.)

When measuring the inside diameter of a hole, or the distance between two surfaces, insert only the rounded tips of the caliper jaws into the hole or between the two surfaces. (See fig. 3-25.) Read the measurement on the reference line stamped IN.

Note that two reference lines are needed if the caliper is to measure both outside and inside dimensions, and that they are separated

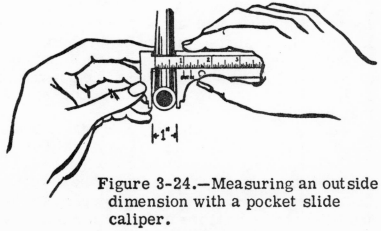

Figure 3-24.—Measuring an outside dimension with a pocket slide caliper.

195

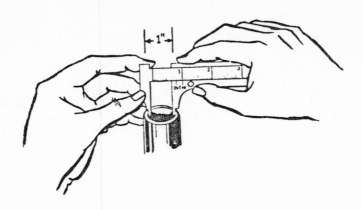

Figure 3-25.—Measuring an inside
dimension with a slide caliper.

by an amount equal to the outside dimension of
the rounded tips when the caliper is closed.

Pocket models of slide calipers are commonly made in 3-in. and 5-in. sizes and are
graduated to read in 32nds and 64ths. Pocket
slide calipers are valuable when extreme precision is not required. They are frequently used
for duplicating work when the expense of fixed
gages is not warranted.

VERNIER CALIPER

A vernier caliper (fig. 3-26) consists of an
L-shaped member with a scale engraved on the
long shank. A sliding member is free to move
on the bar and carries a jaw which matches the
arm of the L. The vernier scale is engraved on
a small plate that is attached to the sliding
member.

Perhaps the most distinct advantage of the
vernier caliper, over other types of caliper, is
the ability to provide very accurate measurements over a large range. It can be used for
both internal and external surfaces. Pocket
models usually measure from zero to 3 in., but

sizes are available all the way to 4 ft. In using
the vernier caliper, you must be able to measure with a slide caliper and be able to read a
vernier scale.

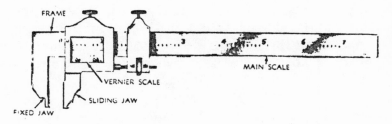

Figure 3-26.—Vernier caliper.

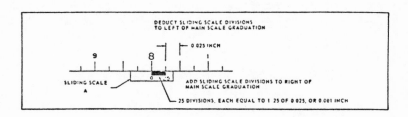

Figure 3-27.—Vernier scale principle.

PRINCIPLES OF THE
VERNIER SCALE

It would be possible to etch graduations
1/1000 inch (0.001) in. apart on a steel rule or
sliding caliper as shown in figure 3-27. This
enlarged illustration shows two graduated
scales. The top scale has divisions which are
0.025 inches apart. The small sliding lower
scale has 25 0.001 inch graduations which can
divide any of the main scale divisions of 0.025
inch into 25 parts. When the first graduation
marked "O" on this small scale aligns with a
graduation on the main scale, the last, or 25th
will also align with a graduation on the main
scale as shown. Consequently, the small 0.00

197

graduations are not significant in this position. But when the zero graduation does not align with a graduation on the main scale, it can be readily determined how many thousandths the zero missed the 0.025 inch graduation by counting the misaligned graduation at either end of the small scale. When the zero or index line on the sliding scale does not quite reach the graduation, the amount of misalignment must be subtracted, but when it passes the 0.025 graduation from which the reading is made, it must be added. This illustrates the simple arrangement to increase the accuracy of a common scale. Unfortunately, the 0.001 inch graduations are not too legible and so the system is not practical. A vernier arrangement overcomes this problem.

VERNIER SCALE ARRANGEMENT

The main difference between the vernier scale and the arrangement shown in fig. 3-27 is the spacing of the 25 divisions. Instead of 25 graduations crowded within the space of one main scale division, the vernier graduations are arranged at intervals exactly 0.001 inch less than the main scale graduations, as shown

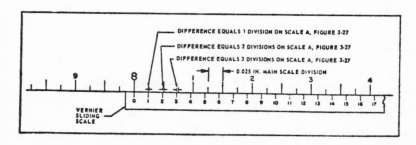

Figure 3-28.—Expanded view
of the vernier scale.

in fig. 3-28. This arrangement results in an accumulation of misalignments starting with the first vernier graduation past the zero so that each may be marked as shown with a number representing the space in thousandths to the next upper scale graduation. For example, if the zero index line would be moved past the 8 inch graduation until the vernier graduation number 5 aligned with the next main scale graduation, the exact reading would be 8 inches plus 0.005 or 8.005 inches.

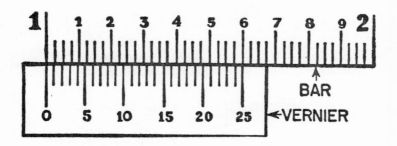

Figure 3-29.—English-measure vernier scale.

READING A VERNIER CALIPER

Figure 3-29 shows a bar 1 inch long divided by graduations into 40 parts so that each graduation indicates one-fortieth of an inch (0.025 inch). Every fourth graduation is numbered; each number indicates tenths of an inch (4 x 0.025 inch). The vernier, which slides along the bar, is graduated into 25 divisions which together, are as long as 24 divisions on the bar. Each division of the vernier is 0.001 inch smaller than each division on the bar. Verniers that are calibrated as just explained are known as English-measure verniers. The metric-measure vernier is read the same, except that the units of measurement are in millimeters.

199

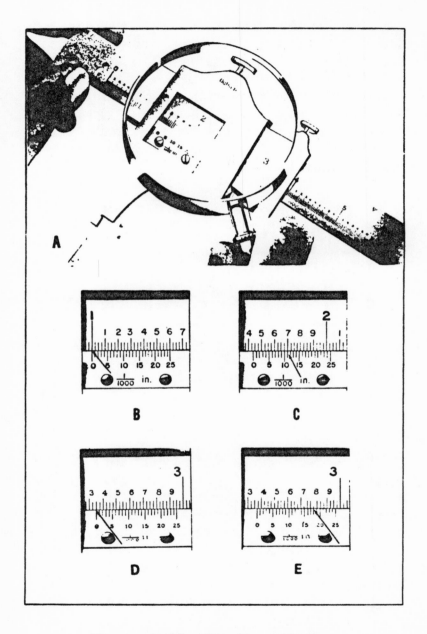

Figure 3-30.—Vernier caliper.

In figure 3-30, insert A illustrates the English measure vernier caliper. Insert B shows an enlarged view of the vernier section. As you can see in this figure, when the zero on the vernier coincides with the 1-inch mark, no other lines coincide until the 25th mark on the vernier.

To read the caliper in insert C, write down in a column the number of inches (1.000 in.), of tenths of an inch (0.400 in.), and of thousandths of an inch that the zero mark on the vernier is from the zero mark on the rule. Because the zero mark on the vernier is a little past a 0.025 in. mark, write down the 0.025 in. and then note the highest number on the vernier where a line on the vernier coincides with one on the rule. In this case it is at the 0.011 in. line on the vernier, so you also write the 0.011 in. in the column which will then look like this:

$$
\begin{array}{r}
1.000 \text{ in.} \\
.400 \text{ in.} \\
.025 \text{ in.} \\
\underline{.011 \text{ in.}} \\
1.436 \text{ in.}
\end{array}
$$

The reading on the caliper shown in insert C is 1.436 in. and was obtained by adding four separate "readings." After a little practice you will be able to make these calculations mentally.

Now try to read the settings of the two verniers shown in inserts D and E. Follow the above procedure. You should read 2.350 in. on D and 2.368 in. on E.

To read a metric-measure vernier, note the number of millimeters, and the 0.25 millimeter if the setting permits, that the zero on the vernier has moved from the zero on the scale. Then add the number of hundredths of a millimeter indicated by the line on the vernier that coincides with a line on the scale.

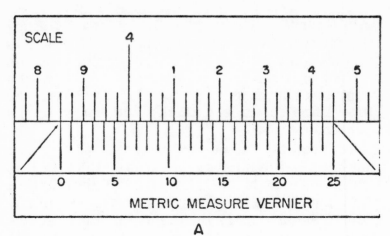

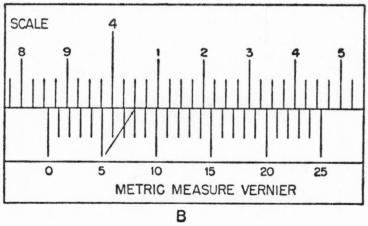

Figure 3-31.—Metric-measure
vernier scales.

For example, figure 3-31A shows the zero
graduation on the vernier coinciding with a
0.5-mm graduation on the scale resulting in a
38.50 mm reading. The reading in figure 3-31B
indicates that 0.08 mm should be added to the
scale reading and results in 38.00 mm + 0.50
mm + 0.08 mm = 38.58 mm.

If a vernier caliper is calibrated in either
English measure or in metric measure, usually

one side will be calibrated to take outside measurements and the other to take inside measurements directly. The vernier plate for inside measurements is set to compensate for the thickness of the measuring points of the tools. But if a vernier caliper is calibrated for both English and metric measure, one of the scales will appear on one side and one on the other. Then it will be necessary, when taking inside measurements over the measuring points, to add certain amounts to allow for their thickness. For example, table 3-1 shows the amounts to be added for various sizes of vernier calipers.

Table 3-1.—Measuring Point Allowances

Size of Caliper	English Measure	Metric Measure
6" or 150 mm .	Add 0.250"...	Add 6.35 mm.
12" or 300 mm .	.300"...	7.62 mm.
24" or 600 mm .	.300"...	7.62 mm.
36" or 600 mm .	.500"...	12.70 mm.

Outside Surface Measurements

To measure the distance between outside surfaces or the outside diameter of round stock with a vernier caliper, steady the stock with one hand and hold the caliper in the other as shown in figure 3-32. In the figure, the clamping screws are at A and B; the horizontal adjusting screw nut is at C. With A and B loose, slide the movable jaw toward the piece being measured until it is almost in contact. Then tighten A to make C operative. With C, adjust the movable jaw to the proper feel and secure the setting with B. The reading can then be taken as explained previously.

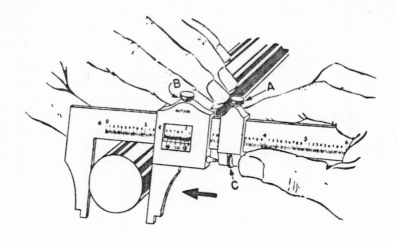

Figure 3-32.—Measuring an outside diameter with a vernier caliper.

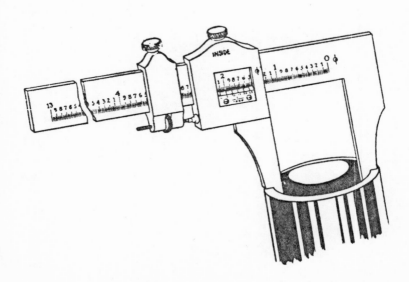

Figure 3-33.—Measuring an inside diameter with a vernier caliper.

Inside Surface Measurements

To measure the distance between inside surfaces, or the inside diameter of a hole, with a vernier caliper, use the scale marked "inside." Figure 3-33 shows the measuring points in place. Remember that if you are using a vernier caliper with both metric and English scales, the scales appear on opposite sides of the caliper and apply only to outside measurements. Then, to get correct inside measurements, you add to the actual reading the measuring point allowance for the size of caliper you are using. Take this allowance from table 3-1 or the manufacturer's instructions. The actual measurement in this case is made in the same manner as taking an outside measurement.

CARE OF THE VERNIER CALIPER

The inside faces of the jaws and the outside of the tips must be treated with great care. If they become worn, or the jaws bent, the tool will no longer give accurate readings. The accuracy of vernier calipers should be checked periodically by measuring an object of known dimension. Vernier calipers can be adjusted when they are not accurate, but the manufacturer's recommendations for this adjustment must be followed. Keep vernier calipers lightly oiled to prevent rust and keep them stored away from heavy tools.

MICROMETER

In much wider use than the vernier caliper is the micrometer commonly called the "mike." It is important that a person who is working with machinery or in a machine shop thoroughly understand the mechanical principles, construction, use, and care of the micrometer. Figure

205

3-34 shows an outside micrometer caliper with the various parts clearly indicated. Micrometers are used to measure distances to the nearest one thousandth of an inch. The measurement is usually expressed or written as a decimal; so you must know the method of writing and reading decimals.

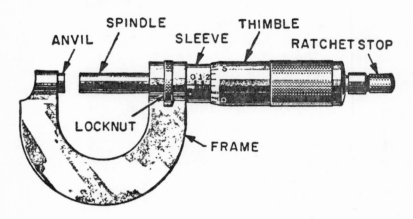

Figure 3-34.—Nomenclature of an outside micrometer caliper.

SELECTING THE PROPER MICROMETER

The types of micrometers commonly used are made so that the longest movement possible between the spindle and the anvil is 1 inch. This movement is called the "range." The frames of micrometers, however, are available in a wide variety of sizes, from 1 inch up to as large as 24 inches. The range of a 1-inch micrometer is from 0 to 1 inch; in other words, it can be used on work where the part to be measured is 1 inch or less. A 2-inch micrometer has a range from 1 inch to 2 inches, and will measure only work between 1 and 2 inches thick; a 6-inch micrometer has a range from 5 to 6 inches, and will measure only work between 5 and 6 inches thick. It is necessary, therefore, that the mechanic in selecting a micrometer first find the approximate size of the work to the nearest inch, and then select a micrometer that will fit it. For example, to find the exact diameter of a piece of round stock; use a rule and find the approximate diameter of the stock. If it is found to be approximately 3 1/4 inches, a micrometer with a 3- to 4-inch range would be required to measure the exact diameter. Similarly, with inside and depth micrometers, rods of suitable lengths must be fitted into the tool to get the approximate dimension within an inch, after which the exact measurement is read by turning the thimble. The size of a micrometer indicates the size of the largest work it will measure.

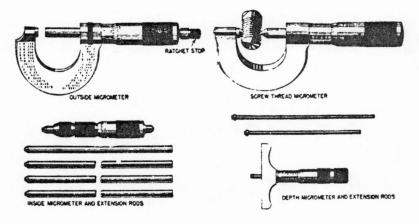

Figure 3-35.—Common types of micrometers.

READING A MICROMETER CALIPER

The sleeve and thimble scales of the micrometer caliper have been enlarged in figure 3-36. To understand these scales, you need to know that the threaded section on the spindle, which revolves, has 40 threads per inch. Therefore, every time the thimble completes a revolution, the spindle advances or recedes 1/40" (0.025").

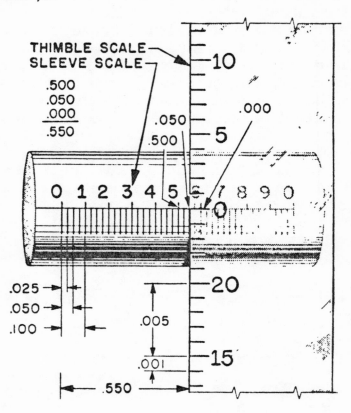

THIMBLE SCALE
SLEEVE SCALE

```
 .500
 .050
 .000
─────
 .550
```

.050
.500

.000

10

5

0 1 2 3 4 5

7 8 9 0

0

.025
.050
.100

.005

20

.001

15

── .550 ──

Figure 3-36.—Sleeve and thimble scales of a micrometer (enlarged).

Notice that the horizontal line on the sleeve is divided into 40 equal parts per inch. Every fourth graduation is numbered 1, 2, 3, 4, etc., representing 0.100", 0.200", etc. When you turn the thimble so that its edge is over the first sleeve line past the "0" on the thimble scale, the spindle has opened 0.025". If you turn the spindle to the second mark, it has moved 0.025" plus 0.025" or 0.050". You use the scale on the thimble to complete your reading when the edge

208

of the thimble stops between graduated lines. This scale is divided into 25 equal parts, each part representing 1/25 of a turn. And 1/25 of 0.025" is 0.001". As you can see, every fifth line on the thimble scale is marked 5, 10, 15, etc. The thimble scale, therefore, permits you to take very accurate readings to the thousandths of an inch, and, since you can estimate between the divisions on the thimble scale, fairly accurate readings to the ten thousandth of an inch are possible.

The closeup in figure 3-37 will help you understand how to take a complete micrometer reading. Count the units on the thimble scale and add them to the reading on the sleeve scale. The reading in the figure shows a sleeve reading of 0.250" (the thimble having stopped slightly more than halfway between 2 and 3 on the sleeve) with the 10th line on the thimble scale coinciding with the horizontal sleeve line. Number 10 on this scale means that the spindle has

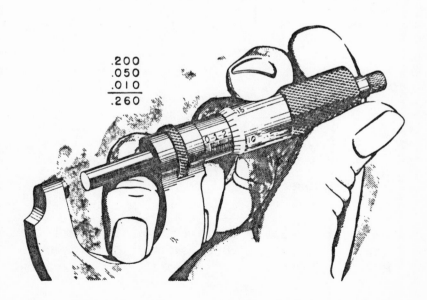

Figure 3-37.—Read a micrometer caliper.

moved away from the anvil an additional 10 x 0.001" or 0.010". Add this amount to the 0.250" sleeve reading, and the total distance is 0.260".

Read each of the micrometer settings in figure 3-38 so that you can be sure of yourself when you begin to use this tool on the job. The correct readings are given following the figure so that you can check yourself.

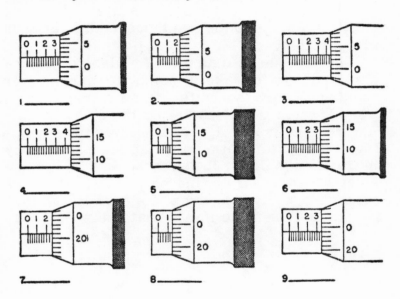

Answers for checking—

1. = 0.327	4. = 0.438	7. = 0.246
2. = 0.229	5. = 0.137	8. = 0.148
3. = 0.428	6. = 0.336	9. = 0.349

Figure 3-38.—Micrometer-reading exercises.

Figure 3-39 shows a reading in which the horizontal line falls between two graduations on the thimble scale and is closer to the 15 graduation than it is to the 14. To read this to THREE decimal places, refer to figure 3-39 and calculation A. To read it to FOUR decimal places, estimate the number of tenths of the distance between thimble-scale graduations the horizontal line has fallen. Each tenth of this distance equals one ten-thousandth (0.0001) of an inch. Add the ten-thousandths to the reading as shown in the calculations of figure 3-39B.

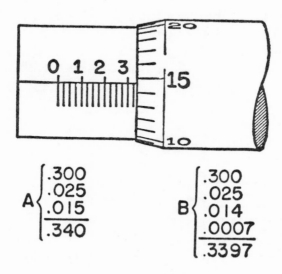

A $\begin{cases} .300 \\ .025 \\ .015 \\ \overline{.340} \end{cases}$ B $\begin{cases} .300 \\ .025 \\ .014 \\ .0007 \\ \overline{.3397} \end{cases}$

Figure 3-39.—Interpolating a
micrometer reading.

READING A VERNIER
MICROMETER CALIPER

Many times you may be required to work to exceptionally precise dimensions. Under these conditions it is better to use a micrometer that is accurate to ten-thousandths of an inch. This degree of accuracy is obtained by the addition of a vernier scale. This scale, shown in figure 3-40, furnishes the fine readings between the lines on the thimble rather than making you estimate. The 10 spaces on the vernier are equivalent to 9 spaces on the thimble. Therefore, each unit on the vernier scale is equal to 0.0009" and the difference between the sizes of

211

the units on each scale is 0.0001".

When a line on the thimble scale does not coincide with the horizontal sleeve line, you can determine the additional space beyond the readable thimble mark by finding which vernier mark coincides with a line on the thimble scale. Add this number, as that many ten-thousandths of an inch, to the original reading. In figure 3-41 see how the second line on the vernier scale coincides with a line on the thimble scale.

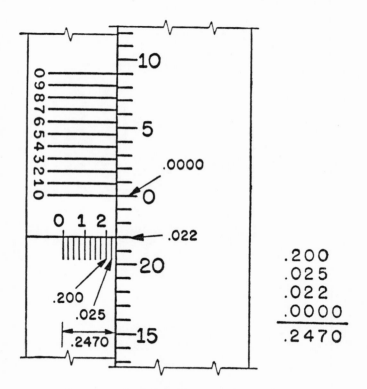

Figure 3-40.—Vernier scale on
a micrometer.

This means that the 0.011 mark on the thimble scale has been advanced an additional 0.0002" beyond the horizontal sleeve line. When you add this to the other readings, the reading will be 0.200 + 0.075 + 0.011 + 0.0002 or 0.2862", as shown.

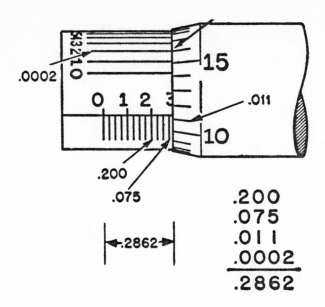

.200
.075
.011
.0002
―――――
.2862

Figure 3-41.—Read a vernier
micrometer caliper.

MEASURING HOLE DIAMETERS
WITH AN INSIDE MICROMETER
CALIPER

To measure the diameter of small holes
from 0.2" to 1" in diameter, an inside micrometer caliper of the jaw type as shown in figure
3-42A may be used. Note that the figures on
both the thimble and the barrel are reversed,
increasing in the opposite direction from those
on an outside micrometer caliper. This is because this micrometer reads inside measurements. Thus as you turn the thimble clockwise on this micrometer, the measuring
surfaces move farther apart and the reading
increases. (On an outside micrometer caliper,
as you turn the thimble clockwise, the measuring surfaces move closer together and the
reading decreases.)

213

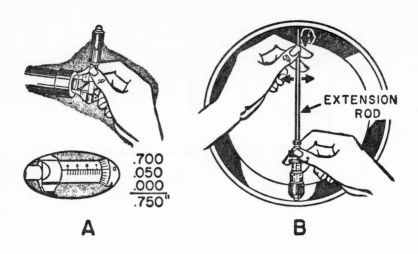

A   **B**

Figure 3-42.—Measuring an inside
diameter with an inside caliper.

For holes from 2" up to several feet in
diameter, select the inside micrometer having
extension rods whose range includes the required dimension. The extension rod marked
"6-7," for example, when inserted into the
head of the micrometer, will measure inside
diameters from 6" to 7". The shoulder on the
rod must seat properly to ensure a correct
reading. Figure 3-42B shows that, for large
measurements, both hands are used to set the
micrometer for checking a diameter. Hole one
end in place with one hand as you "feel" for the
maximum possible setting by moving the other
end from left to right, and in and out of the
hole with the other hand. When no left-to-right
movement is possible, and a slight drag is noticed on the in-and-out swing, take the reading.

MEASURING ROUND STOCK

When measuring the diameter of a small
piece of round stock, hold the stock to be measured in one hand. Hold the micrometer in the

other hand so that the thimble rests between the thumb and the forefinger. (See fig. 3-43.) The third finger is then in a position to hold the frame against the palm of the hand. The frame is supported in this manner and makes it easy to guide the work over the anvil. The thumb and forefinger are in position to turn the thimble either directly or through the ratchet and bring the spindle over against the surface being measured.

Turn the spindle down to contact by "feel," or else use the ratchet stop. Your feel should produce the same contact pressure and therefore the same reading as that produced when the ratchet stop is used. Develop your "feel" by measuring a certain dimension both with and without the aid of the ratchet stop. When you have the correct feel, you will get the same readings by both methods.

In measuring round stock the feel must be very light because there is only a line contact between the spindle and the stock and the anvil and the stock. Therefore the contact area is exceptionally small, causing a proportionally high contact pressure per unit of area. This tends to give a reading smaller than the true reading unless the light feel is used. Moreover, in measuring a ball from a ball bearing, the contact is at only two points, so the contact area is again very small, which results in a tremendous pressure per unit of area. This condition requires only the lightest possible contact pressure to give a true reading.

Hold the micrometer lightly and for only as long as is necessary to make the measurement. Wrapping the hand around it or holding it for too long a time will cause expansion of the metal and will introduce errors in measurement. Read the setting on the thimble scale (if the object is small) without removing the micrometer caliper from the object.

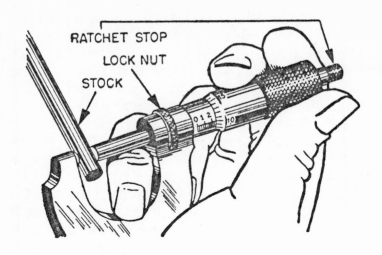

RATCHET STOP
LOCK NUT
STOCK

Figure 3-43.—Measuring round stock
with a micrometer caliper.

MEASURING A FLAT SURFACE

When measuring a flat surface with a micrometer caliper, the entire area of both the anvil and the spindle is in contact with the surface being measured. This causes a proportionally low contact pressure per unit of area. Therefore the "feel" should be slightly heavier than when measuring round stock.

On large flat work, it is necessary to have the work stationary and positioned to permit access for the micrometer. The proper method of holding a micrometer when checking a part too large to be held in one hand is shown in figure 3-44. The frame is held by one hand to position it and to locate it square to the measured surface. The other hand operates the thimble either directly or through the ratchet. A large flat surface should be measured in several places to determine the amount of variation. It is good practice to lock the spindle in place with the locknut before removing the micrometer from the part being measured. After removal of the micrometer the measurement indicated on the thimble scale can then be read.

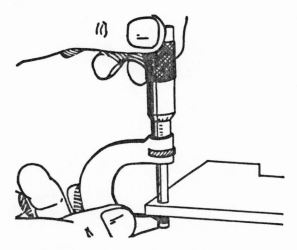

Figure 3-44.—Measuring flat stock with a micrometer caliper.

To retain a particular setting, in cases where several pieces are to be gaged, lock the spindle in place with the locknut. When a piece is "gaged" with a micrometer whose spindle is locked to a particular setting, the piece can quickly be identified as oversize, correct size, or undersize.

CARE OF MICROMETERS

Keep micrometers clean and lightly oiled. Make sure they are placed in a case or box when they are not in use. Anvil faces must be protected from damage and must not be cleaned with emery cloth or other abrasive.

SQUARES

Squares are primarily used for testing and

checking trueness of an angle or for laying out lines on materials. Most squares have a rule marked on their edge. As a result they may also be used for measuring.

CARPENTER'S SQUARE

The size of a carpenter's steel square (fig. 3-45) is usually 12 inches x 8 inches, 24 inches x 16 inches, or 24 inches x 18 inches. The flat sides of the blade and the tongue are graduated in inches and fractions of an inch. (The square also contains information that helps to simplify or eliminate the need for computations in many woodworking tasks.) The most common uses for this square are laying out and squaring up large patterns, and for testing the flatness and squareness of large surfaces. Squaring is accomplished by placing the square at right angles to adjacent surfaces and observing if light shows between the work and the square.

One type of carpenter's square (framing) has additional tables engraved on the square. With the framing square, the craftsman can perform calculations rapidly and layout rafters, oblique joints and stairs.

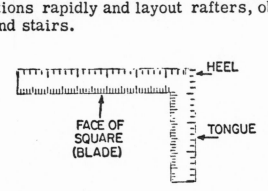

Figure 3-45.—Carpenter's square.

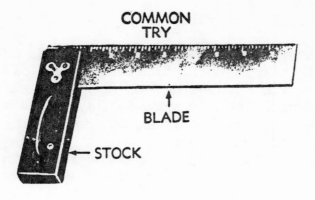

Figure 3-46.—Common try square.

TRY SQUARE

The try square (fig. 3-46) consists of two parts at right angles to each other; a thick wood or iron stock and a thin, steel blade. Most try squares are made with the blades graduated in inches and fractions of an inch. The blade length varies from 2 inches to 12 inches. This square is used for setting or checking lines or surfaces which have to be at right angles to each other.

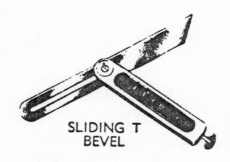

Figure 3-47.—Sliding T-bevel.

SLIDING T BEVEL

The sliding T-bevel (fig. 3-47) is an adjustable try square with a slotted beveled blade. Blades are normally 6 or 8 inches long. The sliding T-bevel is used for laying out angles other than right angles, and for testing constructed angles such as bevels. These squares are made with either wood or metal handles.

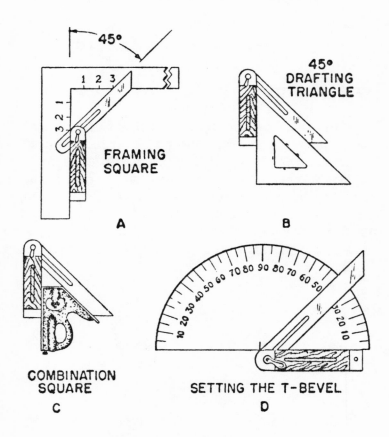

Figure 3-48.—Adjusting a sliding T-bevel to a desired setting.

Adjustments

To adjust a sliding T-bevel to a desired setting, loosen the blade screw, at the round end of the handle, just enough to permit the blade to slide along its slot and to rotate with slight friction.

To set the blade at a 45° angle, hold the handle against a framing square, as shown in figure 3-48A, with the blade intersecting equal graduations on the tongue and blade of the square. Or: hold the bevel against the edges of a 45° drafting triangle as shown in figure 3-48B. When using drafting triangles for setting a sliding T-bevel, different size triangles must be used for each different setting. A 45° angle can also be set by using the squaring head of a combination set as shown in figure 3-48C.

A sliding T-bevel can be set to any desired angle by using a protractor. Loosen the blade screw as before, and hold the bevel with its blade passing through the graduation selected, and the center of the protractor as shown at (D) in figure 3-48.

Constructed Angle Verification

To test a chamfer or bevel for trueness, set the T-bevel to the required angle, and hold the handle to the working face of the stock being tested. Face a source of light, and with the blade brought into contact with the surface to be tested, pass the blade along the length of the surface. (See fig. 3-49.) The appearance of light between the blade and the surface of the stock indicates where the angle is not correct. Figure 3-49 indicates the checking of a bevel, but testing the trueness of a chamfer is accomplished in the same way.

221

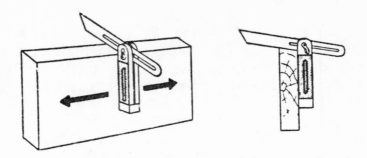

Figure 3-49.—Testing the trueness
of a bevel.

COMBINATION SQUARE

A combination square is equipped with movable heads called a SQUARE HEAD, PROTRACTOR HEAD, and a CENTER HEAD. These combine the functions of several tools, and serve a wide variety of purposes. (See figs. 3-50 and 3-51.) Normally, only one head is used at a time.

The SQUARE HEAD may be adjusted to any position along the scale and clamped securely in place. The combination square can thus serve as a depth gage, height gage, or scribing gage. Two of the faces of the head are ground at right angles to each other, and a third face at 45 degrees. A small spirit level is built into the head for checking whether surfaces are plumb, and a small scriber is housed in a hole in the end of the head for marking layout lines.

The CENTER HEAD can be slid on to the blade in place of the square head. This is a V-shaped member so designed that the center of the 90 degree V will lie exactly along one edge of the blade. This attachment is useful when locating the exact center of round stock.

The PROTRACTOR HEAD, commonly called a bevel protractor, can be attached to the scale,

222

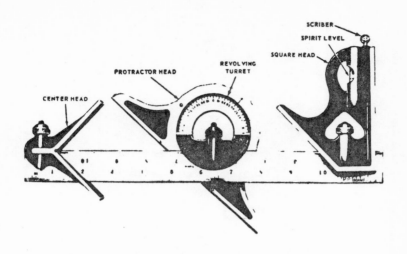

Figure 3-50.—Combination square set.

adjusted to any position on it, and turned and locked at any desired angle. Angular graduations usually read from 0 to 180 degrees both ways, permitting the supplement of the angle to be read. A spirit level may be included on some models forming, in effect, an adjustable level to show any required degree.

Care of Squares

Make certain the blades, heads, dials, and all accessories are clean. Apply a light coat of oil on all metal surfaces to prevent rusting when not in use. Do not use squares for purposes other than those intended. When storing squares or bevels for long periods of time, apply a liberal amount of oil or rust-preventive compound to all surfaces, wrap in oiled paper or cloth, and place in containers or on racks away from other tools.

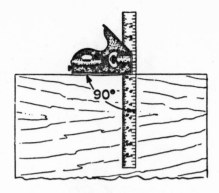

A—SQUARING A LINE ON STOCK.

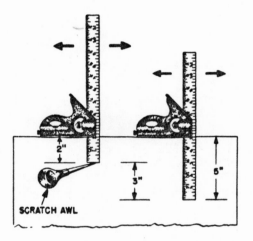

SCRATCH AWL

C—DRAWING PARALLEL LINES.

E—LOCATING A SHAFT CENTER.

Figure 3-51.—Combination square applications.

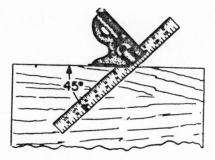

B—LAYING OUT A 45° ANGLE.

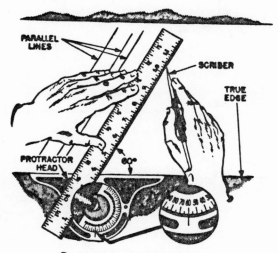

D—DRAWING ANGULAR LINES.

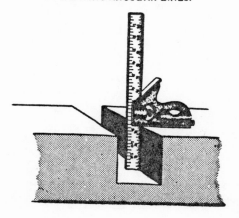

F—MEASURING THE DEPTH OF A SLOT.

Figure 3-51.—Combination square applications.

225

MISCELLANEOUS GAGES

There are a number of miscellaneous gages. The depth gage, feeler gage, thread gage, telescoping gage, dividers, and plumb bob are among some of the gages that will be discussed here.

DEPTH GAGE

A depth gage is an instrument for measuring the depth of holes, slots, counterbores, recesses, and the distance from a surface to some recessed part. (See fig. 3-52.)

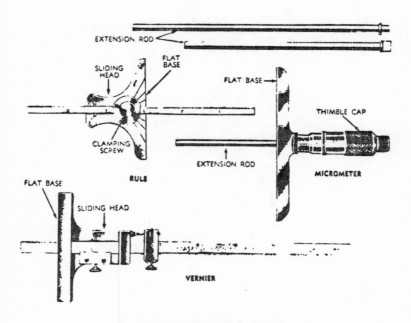

Figure 3-52.—Types of depth gages.

The rule depth gage is a graduated rule with a sliding head designed to bridge a hole or slot, and to hold the rule perpendicular to the surface on which the measurement is taken. This type has a measuring range of 0 to 5 inches. The sliding head has a clamping screw so that it

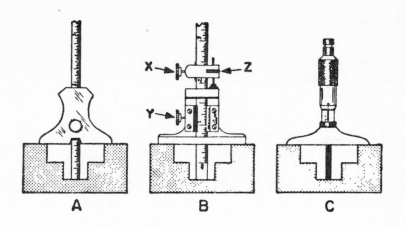

Figure 3-53.—Using depth gages.

may be clamped in any position. The sliding head has a flat base which is perpendicular to the axis of the rule and ranges in size from 2 to 2 5/8 inches in width and from 1/8 to 1/4 inch in thickness.

The micrometer depth gage consists of a flat base attached to the barrel (sleeve) of a micrometer head. These gages have a range from 0 to 9 inches, depending on the length of extension rod used. The hollow micrometer screw (the threads on which the thimble rotates) itself has a range of either 1/2 or 1 inch. Some are provided with a ratchet stop. The flat base ranges in size from 2 to 6 inches. Several extension rods are normally supplied with this type of gage.

To measure the depth of a hole or slot with reasonable accuracy, use a depth gage as shown in figure 3-53A. Hold the body of the depth gage against the surface from which the depth is to be measured and extend the scale into the hole or slot. Tighten the setscrew to maintain the setting. Withdraw the tool from the work and read the depth on the scale.

To measure the depth of a hole or slot with more accuracy than is possible with an ordinary depth gage, place a vernier depth gage over the slot as shown in figure 3-53B. Notice the clamping screws are at X and Y; the horizontal adjusting screw nut is at Z. With X and Y loose, slide the scale down into the slot being measured until it is almost in contact. Then tighten X to make Z operative. With Z, adjust the scale to the "proper feel" and secure the setting with Y. By proper feel we mean the adjustment at which you first notice contact between the end of the scale and the bottom of the slot. Then read the setting as described under "Reading a vernier scale."

To set the vernier depth gage to a particular setting, loosen both setscrews at X and at Y and slide the scale through the gage to the approximate setting. Tighten the setscrew at X, turn the knurled nut at Z until the desired setting is made, and tighten the setscrew at Y to hold the setting.

To measure the depth of a hole or slot, as shown in figure 3-53C, with more accuracy than is possible with either an ordinary depth gage or a vernier depth gage, place a micrometer depth gage over the slot and adjust the thimble until the contact of the spindle causes the ratchet stop to slip. Remove the micrometer from the work and read the micrometer. Remember, if extension rods are used, the total depth reading will be the sum of the length of the rods plus the reading on the micrometer.

SURFACE GAGE

A surface gage is a measuring tool generally used to transfer measurements to work by scribing a line, and to indicate the accuracy or parallelism of surfaces.

The surface gage (fig. 3-54) consists of a

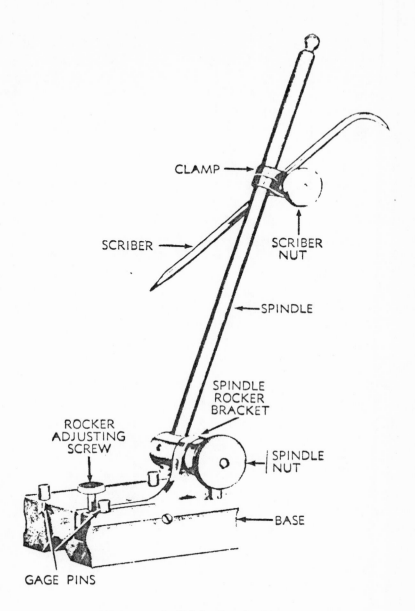

CLAMP

SCRIBER

SCRIBER NUT

SPINDLE

SPINDLE ROCKER BRACKET

ROCKER ADJUSTING SCREW

SPINDLE NUT

BASE

GAGE PINS

Figure 3-54.—Surface gage.

base with an adjustable spindle to which may be clamped a scriber or an indicator. Surface gages are made in several sizes and are classified by the length of the spindle, the smallest spindle being 4 inches long, the average 9 or 12 inches long and the largest 18 inches. The scriber is fastened to the spindle with a clamp. The bottom and the front end of the base of the surface gage have deep V-grooves cut in them, which allow the gage to be seated on a cylindrical surface.

The spindle of a surface gage may be adjusted to any position with respect to the base and tightened in place with the spindle nut. The rocket adjusting screw provides for the finer adjustment of the spindle by pivoting the spindle rocker bracket. The scriber can be positioned at any height and in any desired direction on the spindle by tightening the scriber nut. The scriber may also be mounted directly in the spindle nut mounting, in place of the spindle, and used where the working space is limited and the height of the work is within range of the scriber.

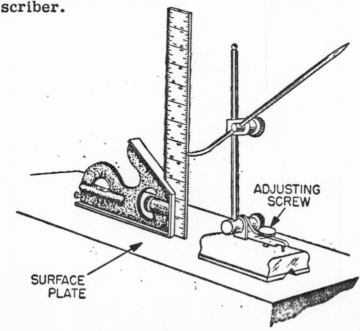

ADJUSTING
SCREW

SURFACE
PLATE

Figure 3-55.—Setting a surface gage
to height.

To set a surface gage for height, first wipe off the top of a layout table or surface plate and the bottom of the surface gage. Use either a combination square or a rule with rule holder to get the measurement. A rule alone cannot be held securely without wobbling and consequently an error in setting generally results. Because a combination square is generally available, its use for setting a surface gage is explained in this section.

Place the squaring head of a combination square on a flat surface as shown in figure 3-55, and secure the scale so that the end is in contact with the surface. Move the surface gage into position and set the scriber to the approximate height required, using the adjusting clamp that holds the scriber onto the spindle. Make the final adjustment for the exact height required (4 1/2 inches in this case) with the adjusting screw on the base of the gage.

SURFACE PLATE

A surface plate provides a true, smooth, plane surface. It is a flat-topped steel or cast iron plate that is heavily ribbed and reinforced on the under side. (See fig. 3-56.) It is often used in conjunction with a surface gage as a level base on which the gage and part to be measured are placed to obtain accurate measurements. The surface plate can also be used for testing parts that must have flat surfaces.

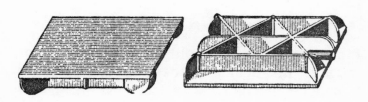

Figure 3-56.—Surface plate.

To test a surface for flatness, carefully clean it and remove all burrs. Then place the surface of the object on a flat area such as the surface plate in figure 3-57.

Figure 3-57.—Testing a surface for flatness.

For very fine work, lightly coat the surface plate with prussian blue (bearing blue) and move the piece being tested across the blue surface. (See fig. 3-58.) The low spots on the surface being tested will not take the blue; the high spots will. See insert in figure 3-58.

To determine how much variation there is from flatness—and where it is—you can insert leaves of a thickness gage to determine the amount of variation of flatness. Remember to add the thickness of all leaves together to get the total variation. (See fig. 3-59.)

A surface also may be tested for flatness with a straightedge. To do this, clean the surface thoroughly and hold the straightedge on the surface in several places as you look toward a source of light. The light showing between the surface being tested and the straightedge will reveal the low spots.

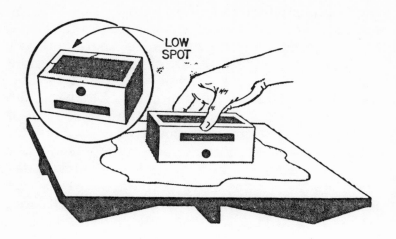

Figure 3-58.—Using prussian blue
to aid in testing a flat surface.

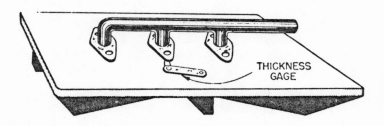

Figure 3-59.—Checking the conformity
of a flat surface.

Care of Surface Plates

The surface plate should be covered when
not in use to prevent scratching, nicking, and
denting. It must be handled carefully to prevent
warping (twisting). Never use the surface plate
as an anvil or workbench—except for precision
layout work (marking and measuring).

THICKNESS (FEELER) GAGE

Thickness (feeler) gages are used for check-

233

ing and measuring small openings such as contact point clearances, narrow slots, etc. These gages are made in many shapes and sizes and, as shown in figure 3-60, thickness gages can be made with multiple blades (usually 2 to 26). Each blade is a specific number of thousandths of an inch thick. This enables the application of one tool to the measurement of a variety of thicknesses. Some thickness gage blades are straight, while others are bent at 45 and 90 degree angles at the end. Thickness gages can also be grouped so that there are several short and several long blades together. Before using a feeler gage, remove any foreign matter from the blades. You cannot get a correct measurement unless the blades are clean.

When using a feeler gage consisting of a number of blades, insert various blades or combinations of blades between two surfaces until a snug fit is obtained. The thickness of the individual blade or the total thickness of ALL THE BLADES USED is the measurement between the surfaces.

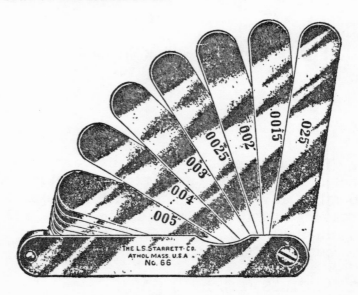

Figure 3-60.—Thickness gages.

Care of Thickness Gages

Handle the blades with care at all times. Keep from forcing the blades into openings that are too small for them. Some blades are very thin and can be bent or kinked easily. Blade edges and polished surfaces are also easy to damage. When not using a thickness gage, keep it closed.

THREAD GAGE

Thread gages (screw-pitch gages) are used to determine the pitch and number of threads per inch of threaded fasteners. (See fig. 3-61.) They consist of thin leaves whose edges are toothed to correspond to standard thread sections.

To measure the unknown pitch of a thread, compare it with the standards of the screw pitch gage. Hold a gage leaf to the thread being measured (fig. 3-62), substituting various sizes until you find an exact fit. Look at the fit toward a source of light for best results.

The number of threads per inch is indicated by the numerical value on the blade which is found to fit the unknown threads. Using this

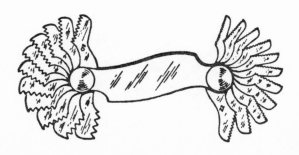

Figure 3-61.—Screw pitch gage.

value as a basis, correct sizes of nuts, bolts, tap cutters, and die cutters are selected for use.

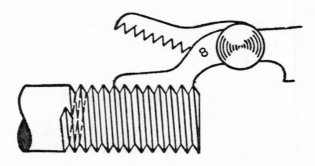

GAGING SINGLE
PITCH EXTERNAL
THREAD

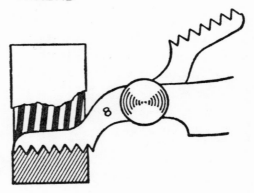

GAGING INTERNAL
THREAD

Figure 3-62.—Using a screw
pitch gage.

WIRE GAGE

The wire gage shown in fig. 3-63, is used for measuring the diameters of wires or the thickness of sheet metal. This gage is circular in shape with cutouts in the outer perimeter. Each cutout gages a different size from No. 0 to No. 36. Examination of the gage will show that the larger the gage number, the smaller the diameter or thickness.

Gages similar to the one shown in figure 3-63 are available for measuring a variety of wires and sheet metals. The names of some common standard wire gages and their uses are given in the column headings of table 3-2. The body of this table contains gage numbers and their corresponding equivalents in decimal fractions of an inch.

Wire diameters may also be expressed in mils as well as by gage numbers. One mil equals one thousandth of an inch. Each decimal equivalent in table 3-2 can be converted to mils by multiplying by 1,000. For example, the circled decimal in the table is equivalent to .0640 x 1000 or 64 mils.

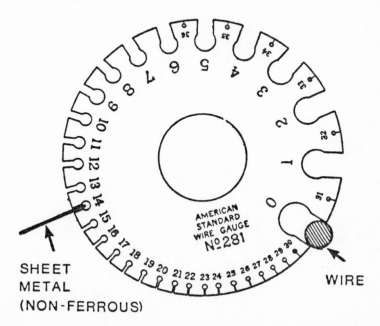

SHEET
METAL
(NON-FERROUS)

WIRE

Figure 3-63.—Using a wire gage to measure wire and sheet metal.

237

Table 3-2.—Wire and Sheet Metal Gages

Gage No.	Birmingham wire gage (B.W.G.) or Stubs iron wire gage, for iron wires, hot and cold rolled sheet steel	American wire gage, or Brown & Sharpe (for non-ferrous sheet and wire)	U.S. Standard gage for sheet and plate iron and steel	Steel wire gage, or the W & M (Washburn & Moen) for steel wire
0	.340	.3249	.3125	.3065
1	.300	.2893	.2812	.2830
2	.284	.2576	.2656	.2625
3	.259	.2294	.2500	.2437
4	.238	.2043	.2343	.2253
5	.220	.1819	.2187	.2070
6	.203	.1620	.2031	.1920
7	.180	.1443	.1876	.1770
8	.165	.1285	.1718	.1620
9	.148	.1144	.1562	.1483
10	.134	.1019	.1406	.1350
11	.120	.0907	.1250	.1205
12	.109	.0808	.1093	.1055
13	.095	.0719	.0937	.0915
14	.083	.0640	.0781	.0800
15	.072	.0570	.0703	.0720
16	.065	.0508	.0625	.0625
17	.058	.0452	.0562	.0540
18	.049	.0403	.0500	.0475
19	.042	.0359	.0437	.0410
20	.035	.0319	.0375	.0348
21	.032	.0284	.0343	.0317
22	.028	.0253	.0312	.0286
23	.025	.0225	.0281	.0258
24	.022	.0201	.0250	.0230
25	.020	.0179	.0218	.0204
26	.018	.0159	.0187	.0181
27	.016	.0142	.0171	.0173
28	.014	.0126	.0156	.0162
29	.013	.0112	.0140	.0150
30	.012	.0100	.0125	.0140
31	.010	.0089	.0109	.0132
32	.009	.0079	.0101	.0128
33	.008	.0071	.0093	.0118
34	.007	.0063	.0085	.0104
35	.005	.0056	.0078	.0095
36	.004	.0050	.0070	.0090

To use table 3-2, you select from the four gages listed in the table the one that applies to the sheet of metal or wire you want to gage. For instance, column 2 of the table tells you that the American Wire Gage shown in figure 3-63 is the one to use for nonferrous sheet or wire. Notice that each of the four gages has its own decimal equivalent for a particular gage number.

To measure wire size, apply the gage to the wire as shown in figure 3-63. Do not force the wire into the slot. Find the slot that refuses to pass the wire without forcing. Then, try the next larger slot until one is found that passes the wire. This is the correct size. Remember, your measurements are taken at the slot portion of the cutout rather than the inner portion of the gage. Now that you have the gage number turn your gage over and read the decimal equivalent for that number.

To measure the gage of a piece of metal, first remove any burr from the place where you

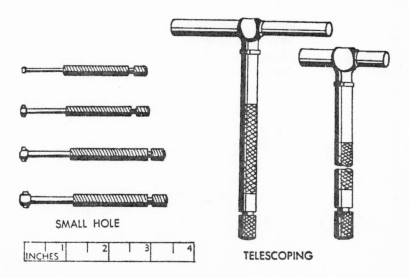

SMALL HOLE

INCHES 1 2 3 4

TELESCOPING

Figure 3-64.—Small hole and telescoping gages.

intend to apply the gage. Then select the appropriate gage for the metal to be measured.

After the right gage has been selected, apply the gage to the wire, or to the edge of the sheet as shown in figure 3-63. The number opposite the slot that fits the wire or sheet is its gage number. The decimal equivalent is stamped on the opposite face of the gage.

TELESCOPING GAGE

Telescoping gages are used for measuring the inside size of slots or holes up to 6 inches in width or diameter. They are T-shaped tools in which the shaft of the T is used as a handle, and the crossarm used for measuring. (See fig. 3-64.) The crossarms telescope into each other and are held out by a light spring. To use the gage the arms are compressed, placed in the hole to be measured, and allowed to expand. A twist of the locknut on top of the handle locks the arms. The tool may then be withdrawn and the distance across the arms measured.

These tools are commonly furnished in sets, the smallest gage for measuring the distances from 5/16 to 1/2 inch, and the largest for distances from 3 1/2 to 6 inches.

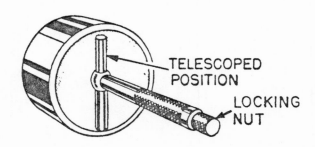

Figure 3-65.—Using a
telescoping gage.

To measure the diameter of a hole from 1/2" to 6" in diameter, select from a set of telescoping gages the one whose range includes the size you need. Loosen the knurled nut at the end of the handle, and telescope the adjustable end of the gage to a size slightly smaller than the hole and retighten the nut. Insert the gage into the hole as shown in figure 3-65, loosen the nut to permit the spring-loaded adjustable end to expand to the hole diameter, and tighten the nut. The spring loaded contact of the adjustable end will assure proper contact. Make sure, however, that the gage is held with the telescoping end at right angles to the axis of the hole to measure the true, maximum diameter. Remove the gage and measure the setting with an outside micrometer caliper.

SMALL HOLE GAGE

For measuring smaller slots or holes than the telescoping gages will measure, small hole gages can be used. These gages come in sets of four or more and will measure distances of approximately 1/8 to 1/2 inch.

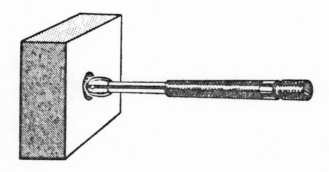

Figure 3-66.—Measuring the diameter of a hole with a small hole gage.

The small hole gage (fig. 3-64) consists of a small, split, ball-shaped member mounted on the end of a handle. The ball is expanded by turning a knurled knob on the handle until the proper feel is obtained (the slight drag of the ball end on the sides of the hole). The gage is then withdrawn (fig. 3-66) and the size of the ball-shaped member on the end of the gage can be measured with an outside micrometer caliper. On some types of small hole gages, the the ball is flattened at the bottom near the centerline to permit use in shallow holes and recesses.

MARKING GAGES

A marking gage is used to mark off guidelines parallel to an edge, end, or surface of a piece of wood or metal. It has a sharp spur or pin that does the marking.

Marking gages (fig. 3-67) are made of wood or steel. They consist of a graduated beam

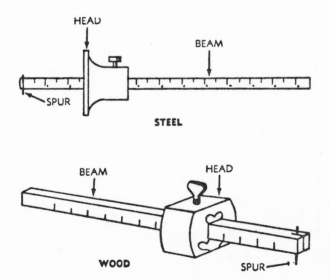

Figure 3-67.—Marking gages.

about 8 inches long on which a head slides. The head can be fastened at any point on the beam by means of a thumbscrew. The thumbscrew presses a brass shoe tightly against the beam and locks it firmly in position. The steel pin or spur that does the marking projects from the beam about 1/16 inch.

To draw a line parallel to an edge with a marking gage, first determine the distance the line must be from the edge of the stock. Adjust the marking gage by setting the head the desired distance from the spur. Although the bar of a marking gage is graduated in inches, the spur may work loose or bend. If this occurs, accurate measurement should be made with a rule between the head and spur. (See fig. 3-68A.) To draw a line after setting the gage, grasp the head of the gage with the palm and fingers as shown in figure 3-68B; extend the

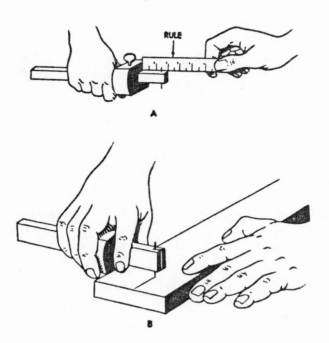

Figure 3-68.—Using the marking gage.

thumb along the beam towards the spur. Press the head firmly against the edge of the work to be marked, and with a wrist motion tip the gage forward until the spur touches the work. Push the gage along the edge to mark the work, keeping the head firmly against the edge of the work.

DIVIDERS

Dividers are useful instruments for transferring measurements and are frequently used in scribing arcs and circles in layout work.

To lay out a circle with a divider, set the divider at the desired radius, using a rule as shown in figure 3-69. Note that the 3-inch radius being set here is being taken at a central portion rather than at the end of the rule. This reduces the chance of error, as each point of the dividers can be set on a graduation.

Figure 3-69.—Setting a divider
to a desired radius.

Place one leg of the divider at the center of the proposed circle, lean the tool in the direction it will be rotated, and rotate it by rolling the knurled handle between your thumb and index finger (fig. 3-70).

Vernier calipers, which have two center points similar to prick punchmarks are particularly useful in setting a divider to exact dimensions. One center point will be found near the zero end of the scale on the rule. The other point is in line with the first and to the left of the zero on the vernier scale. (See fig. 3-71.)

Set and secure the desired setting on the vernier caliper and adjust the divider until both points readily enter the center points on the vernier caliper as shown in figure 3-71.

Figure 3-70.—Scribing a circle
with a divider.

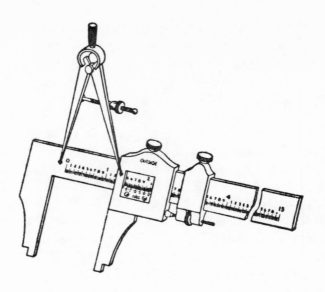

Figure 3-71.—Setting a divider
with a vernier caliper.

PLUMB BOB

A plumb bob (fig. 3-72) is a pointed, tapered brass or bronze weight which is suspended from a cord for determining the vertical or plumb line to or from a point on the ground. Common weights for plumb bobs are 6, 8, 10, 12, 14, 16, 18, and 24 oz.

A plumb bob is a precision instrument and must be cared for as such. If the tip becomes bent, the cord from which the bob is suspended will not occupy the true plumb line over the point indicated by the tip. A plumb bob usually has a detachable tip, as shown in figure 3-72, so that if the tip should become damaged it can be renewed without replacing the entire instrument.

The cord from a plumb bob can be made more conspicuous, for observation purposes, by attachment of a red-and-white target as shown in figure 3-73.

The plumb bob is used in carpentry to determine true verticality when erecting vertical uprights and corner posts of framework. Surveyors use it for transferring and lining up points.

To locate a point which is exactly below a particular point in space, secure the plumb bob string to the upper point, such as A in figure 3-74. When the plumb stops swinging, the point as indicated at B in the illustration, will be exactly below A.

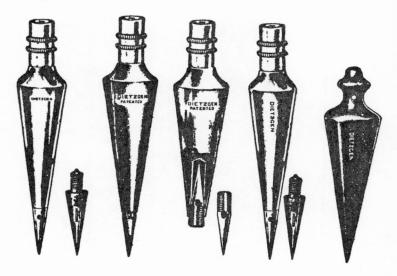

Figure 3-72.—Plumb bobs.

To plumb a structural member, or an electrical conduit, as shown by figure 3-75, secure the plumb line A so that you can look at both the line and piece behind the line. Then, by sighting, line up the member or conduit with the plumb line.

If this cannot be done, it may be necessary to secure the plumb line at some point such as B, and then measure the offset from the line to the piece at two places so that, for example, C and D in figure 3-75 are equal. If the distances between C and D are not equal, adjust the structural member or conduit until they are.

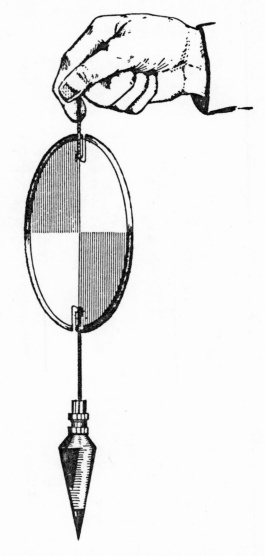

Figure 3-73.—Plumb bob,
cord, and target.

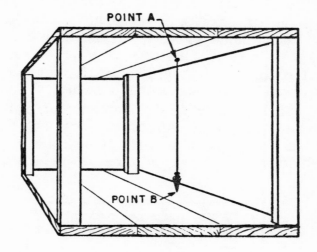

Figure 3-74.—Locating a point
with a plumb bob.

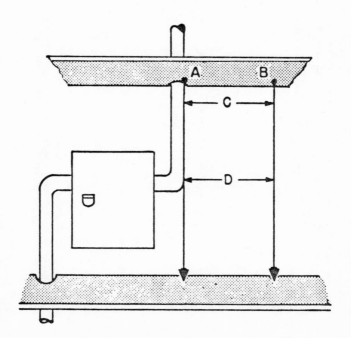

Figure 3-75.—Plumbing a structural
member with a plumb bob.

LEVELS

Levels are tools designed to prove whether a plane or surface is true horizontal or true vertical. Some precision levels are calibrated so that they will indicate in degrees, minutes, and seconds, the angle inclination of a surface in relation to a horizontal or vertical surface.

The level is a simple instrument consisting of a liquid, such as alcohol or chloroform, partially filling a glass vial or tube so that a bubble remains. The tube is mounted in a

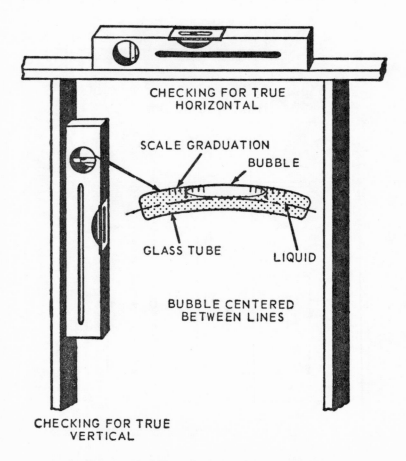

CHECKING FOR TRUE
HORIZONTAL

SCALE GRADUATION

BUBBLE

GLASS TUBE

LIQUID

BUBBLE CENTERED
BETWEEN LINES

CHECKING FOR TRUE
VERTICAL

Figure 3-76.—Horizontal and vertical use of level.

frame which may be aluminum, wood, or iron. Levels are equipped with one, two, or more tubes. One tube is built in the frame at right angles to another (fig. 3-76). The tube indicated in figure 3-76 is slightly curved, causing the bubble to seek always the highest point in the tube. On the outside of the tube are two sets of graduation lines separated by a space. Leveling is accomplished when the air bubble is centered between the graduation lines.

To level a piece of equipment, such as the workbench in figure 3-77, with a carpenter's level, set the level on the bench top parallel to the front edge of the bench. Notice that the level has several pairs of glass vials. Regardless of the position of the level, always watch the bubble in the bottom vial of a horizontal pair. Shim or wedge up the end of the bench that will return that bubble to the center of its

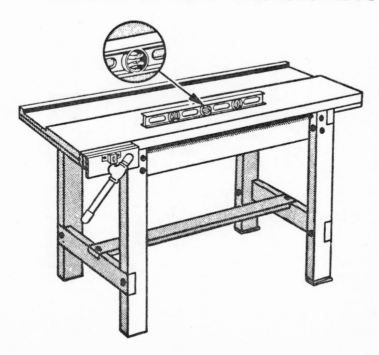

Figure 3-77.—Leveling a bench.

vial. Recheck the first position of the level before securing the shims or wedges.

To plumb a piece of equipment, such as the drill press shown in figure 3-78, place the level on the side and on the front of the main column of the press. Figure 3-78 shows the level on the side. Use shims as necessary to bring the bubble in the lower vial of either pair of the horizontal vials to the center in each case.

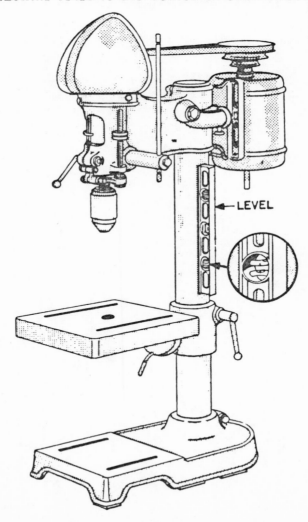

Figure 3-78.—Plumbing a piece of equipment with a level.

Levels must be checked for accuracy. This is readily accomplished by placing the level on a true horizontal surface and noting the vial indication. Reverse the level end for end. If the bubble appears on one side of the graduations with reference to the operator on the first reading and on the other side for the second reading, the level is out of true and must be adjusted.

Do not drop or handle a level roughly. To prevent damage, store it in a rack or other suitable place when not in use.

CHAPTER 4

FASTENING COMPONENTS AND PROCEDURES

This chapter will discuss a variety of fastening devices and procedures so that you will be able to identify, select, and use the proper fasteners on specific jobs. Your knowledge of these fasteners will also enable you to perform assembly and disassembly work accurately, swiftly, and safely with proper tools.

All fasteners are designed for one purpose—to attach components together securely. Some are used advantageously in woodworking. Others have special applications for fastening metal parts. Still others, are used to accelerate fastening and unfastening panels. Let's examine the distinctions between various kinds.

WOODWORKING FASTENERS

Before the development of nail-making, screw-making and bolt-making machinery, wooden members were held together by various types of interlocking joints that were reinforced with glue and wooden dowels. (A dowel is a cylindrical pin which is driven into a hole bored to receive it, and which serves much the same purpose as a nail.) Glued joints and joints fastened with wooden dowels are now confined mainly to furniture.

255

NAILS

Nails achieve their fastening or holding power when they displace wood fibers from their original position. The pressure exerted against the nail by these fibers, as they try to spring back to their original position, provides the holding power.

The usual type of shank is round, but there are various special-purpose nails with other types of shanks. Nails with square, triangular, longitudinally grooved and spirally grooved shanks have a much greater holding power than smooth round wire nails of the same size.

The lengths of the most commonly used nails are designated by the PENNY system. The abbreviation for the word "penny" is the letter "d." Thus the expression "a 2d nail" means a two-penny nail. The penny sizes and corresponding length, and thicknesses (in gage sizes) of the common nails are shown in table 4-1. The thickness of a nail increases and the number of nails per pound decreases with the penny size.

Nails larger than 20d are called spikes and are generally designated by their length in inches (such as 5 inches or 6 1/2 inches); nails smaller than 2d are designated in fractions of an inch instead of in the penny system.

Figure 4-1 shows the more common types of wire nails. The BRAD and the FINISH nail both have a deep countersink head that is designed to be "set" below the surface of the work. These nails are used for interior and exterior trimwork where the nails are "set" and puttied to conceal their location. The CASING nail is used for the same purpose, but because of its flat countersink head, may be driven flush and left that way.

The other nails shown in figure 4-1 are all flat-headed, without countersinks. One of these flat-headed nails (called the COMMON nail) is one of the most widely used in general wood construction. Nails with large flat heads are used for nailing roof paper, plaster board, and similar thin or soft materials. DUPLEX or DOUBLE-HEADED nails are used for nailing temporary structures, such as scaffolds, which are eventually to be dismantled. When using the double-headed nail it is driven to the lower head so that it can be easily drawn at a later time.

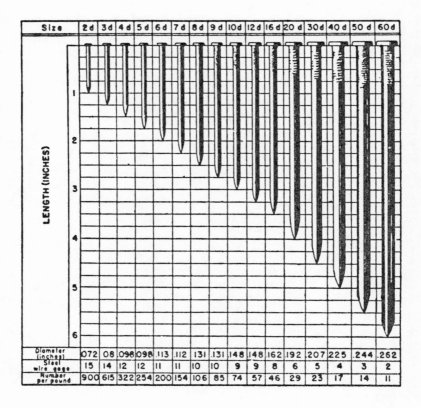

Size	2d	3d	4d	5d	6d	7d	8d	9d	10d	12d	16d	20d	30d	40d	50d	60d
Diameter (inches)	.072	.08	.098	.098	.113	.112	.131	.131	.148	.148	.162	.192	.207	.225	.244	.262
Steel wire gage	15	14	12	12	11	11	10	10	9	9	8	6	5	4	3	2
Number per pound	900	615	322	254	200	154	106	85	74	57	46	29	23	17	14	11

Table 4-1.—Common Nail Sizes

257

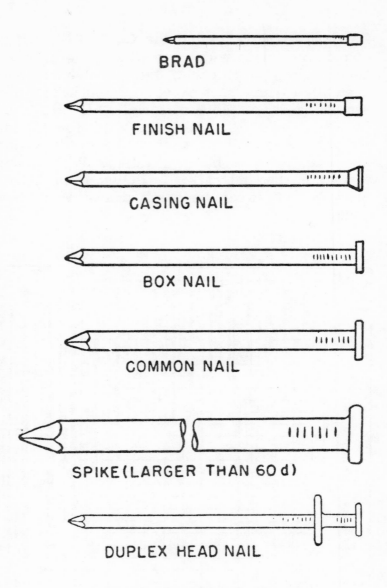

BRAD

FINISH NAIL

CASING NAIL

BOX NAIL

COMMON NAIL

SPIKE(LARGER THAN 60 d)

DUPLEX HEAD NAIL

Figure 4-1.—Nail varieties.

WOOD SCREWS

Screws have several advantages over nails. They may be easily withdrawn at any time without injury to the material. They also hold the wood more securely, can be easily tightened and, generally, are neater in appearance.

Wood screws are designated by material, type of head (fig. 4-2), and size.

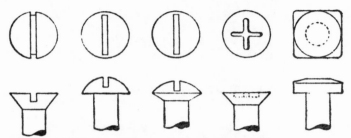

FLAT HEAD   ROUND HEAD   OVAL HEAD   PHILLIPS HEAD   LAG

Figure 4-2.—Woodscrew heads.

Most wood screws are made of steel or brass, but other metals are used as well. Cost or special purpose application will determine the selection of the material to be used.

The size of an ordinary wood screw is indicated by the length and body diameter (unthreaded part) of the screw. Figure 4-3 shows the nomenclature and the three most common types of wood screws. Notice that the length is always measured from the point to the greatest diameter of the head.

Body diameters are designated by gage numbers, running from 0 (for about a 1/16 in. diameter) to 24 (for about a 3/8-in. diameter).

Designation of length and gage number appear as "1 1/4-9". This means a No. 9 screw 1 1/4 inches long.

As a general rule, the length of a screw for holding two pieces of wood together should be such that the body extends through the piece being screwed down so the threaded portion will then enter the other piece. The wood screw simply passes through the hole in the top piece and the threads take hold in the bottom piece. See figure 4-4.

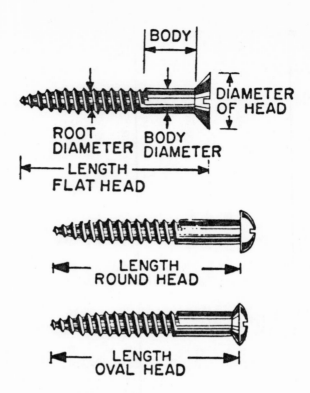

Figure 4-3.—Nomenclature and types of woodscrews.

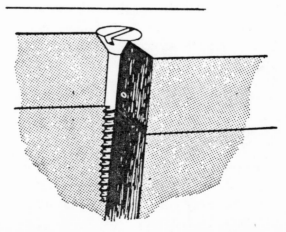

Figure 4-4.—Using a woodscrew to hold two pieces of wood together.

BOLTS

A bolt is distinguished from a wood screw by the fact that it does not thread into the wood, but goes through and is held by a nut threaded onto the end of the bolt. Figure 4-5 shows the four common types of bolts used in woodworking. STOVE bolts are rather small, ranging in length from 3/8 in. to 4 in., and in body diameter from 1/8 in. to 3/8 in. CARRIAGE AND MACHINE bolts run from 3/4 in. to 20 in. long, and from 3/16 in. to 3/4 in. in diameter. (The carriage bolt has a square section below the head, which is imbedded in the wood to prevent the bolt from turning as the nut is drawn up.) The machine bolt has a hexagon or square head which is held with a wrench to prevent it from turning.

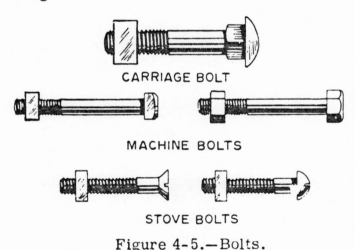

CARRIAGE BOLT

MACHINE BOLTS

STOVE BOLTS

Figure 4-5.—Bolts.

METAL FASTENING DEVICES

Many mechanisms and devices are held together with metal fasteners. Only the more commonly used fasteners will be discussed here so you will know when, where, and how they should be used.

261

Metal parts can be fastened together with various fastening devices, such as rivets, bolts, screws, etc. Rivets provide a more permanent type of fastening whereas bolts and screws are used to fasten together parts that may have to be taken apart later.

BOLTS

Be certain that the grip length of the bolt is correct. The grip length is the length of the un-threaded portion of the bolt shank. Generally speaking, the grip length should equal the thick-ness of the material which is being bolted to-gether. Not more than ONE thread should bear on the material, and the threaded portion of the shank should be showing through the nut. (See fig. 4-6A). In figure 4-6B no threads from the bolt shank show through the nut extremity and too many threads are bearing on the material. In figure 4-6C the nut can't be threaded far enough to apply pressure on the material.

MACHINE SCREWS

The term "machine screw" is the general term used to designate the small screws that are used in tapped holes for the assembly of metal parts. Machine screws may also be used with nuts, but usually, they are screwed into holes that have been tapped with matching threads.

Machine screws are manufactured in a va-riety of lengths, diameters, pitches (threads per inch), materials, head shapes, finishes and thread fits. A complete description of machine screws must include these factors. For exam-ple, "1/2 inch, 8-32, round head, brass, chromium-plated, machine screw." The first number is the length of the screw. Let's ex-amine some of these other factors.

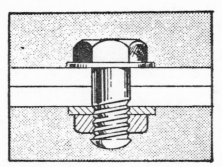

A BOLT GRIP LENGTH CORRECT

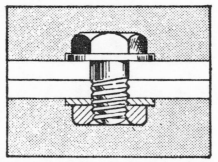

B BOLT GRIP LENGTH TOO SHORT

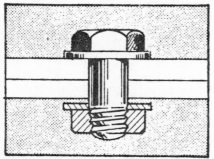

C BOLT GRIP LENGTH TOO LONG

Figure 4-6.—Correct and incorrect grip lengths.

Diameter and Pitch

The diameters of American Standard machine screws are expressed in gage numbers or fractions of an inch as shown in table 4-2. In the preceding paragraph, the "8-32" means that the screw gage is No. 8 and that it has 32 threads per inch. Note, particularly, that the "eight" and "thirty-two" are two separate numbers, indicating two individual measurements; they are never to be pronounced "six-thirty-seconds" or written as a fraction such as 6/32.

Materials and Finishes

Most machine screws are made of steel or brass. They may be plated to help prevent corrosion. Other special machine screws made of aluminum or Monel metal are also obtainable. The latter metal is highly resistant to the corrosive action of salt water.

Head Shapes

A variety of common and special machine screw head shapes are shown in figure 4-7. Some of the heads require special tools for driving and removing. These special tools are usually included in a kit that comes with the machine or installation on which the screws are used.

Fits

At one time each manufacturer made as many threads per inch on bolts, screws, and nuts as suited his own particular needs. For example, one made 12 threads per inch on 1/2" bolts while another might put on 13 or 15 threads per inch. Thus the bolts of one manufacturer would not fit the nuts made by another.

Table 4-2.—Screw Threads per Inch

Diameter		Threads Per Inch			
No.	Inch	Decimal Equivalent	NC	NF	EF
0	----	.0600	---	80	---
1	----	.0730	64	72	---
2	----	.0860	56	64	---
3	----	.0990	48	56	---
4	----	.1120	40	48	---
5	----	.1250	40	44	---
6	----	.1380	32	40	---
8	----	.1640	32	36	---
10	----	.1900	24	32	40
12	----	.2160	24	28	---
---	1/4	.2500	20	28	36
---	5/16	.3125	18	24	32
---	3/8	.3750	16	24	32
---	7/16	.4375	14	20	28
---	1/2	.5000	13	20	28
---	9/16	.5625	12	18	24
---	5/8	.6250	11	18	24
---	3/4	.7500	10	16	20
---	7/8	.8750	9	14	20
---	1	1.0000	8	14	20

The National Screw Thread Commission studied the problem and decided to standardize on a two-thread series, one called the NATIONAL COARSE THREAD SERIES (NC) and the other the NATIONAL FINE THREAD SERIES (NF). The SOCIETY OF AUTOMOTIVE ENGINEERS decided to standardize on some EXTRA FINE (EF) threads to be used in airplanes, automobiles, and other places where extra fine threads are needed. Table 4-2 shows the number of threads per inch for NC, NF, and EF

265

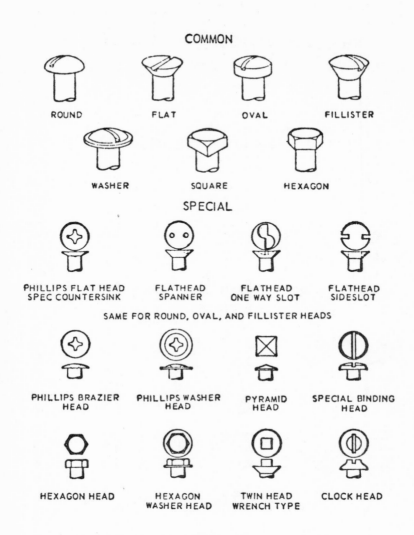

COMMON

ROUND   FLAT   OVAL   FILLISTER

WASHER   SQUARE   HEXAGON

SPECIAL

PHILLIPS FLAT HEAD SPEC COUNTERSINK   FLATHEAD SPANNER   FLATHEAD ONE WAY SLOT   FLATHEAD SIDESLOT

SAME FOR ROUND, OVAL, AND FILLISTER HEADS

PHILLIPS BRAZIER HEAD   PHILLIPS WASHER HEAD   PYRAMID HEAD   SPECIAL BINDING HEAD

HEXAGON HEAD   HEXAGON WASHER HEAD   TWIN HEAD WRENCH TYPE   CLOCK HEAD

Figure 4-7.—Machine screw and capscrew heads.

thread sizes up to 1 inch in diameter. Four classes of fits were also established by the National Screw Thread Commission. They are: Class I, loose fit; Class II, free fit; Class III, medium fit; and Class IV, close fit.

The loose fit is for threaded parts that can be put together quickly and easily even when the threads are slightly bruised or dirty, and when a considerable amount of shake or looseness is not objectionable. The free fit is for threaded parts that are to be put together nearly or entirely with the fingers and a little shake or looseness is not objectionable. This includes most of the screw thread work. The medium fit is for the higher grade of threaded parts where the fit is somewhat closer. The close fit is for the finest threaded work where very little shake or looseness is desirable and where a screwdriver or wrench may be necessary to put the parts together. The manufacture of threaded parts belonging to this class requires the use of fine tools and gages. This fit should, therefore, be used only when requirements are exacting or where special conditions require screws having a fine, snug fit.

CAPSCREWS

Capscrews perform the same functions as machine screws, but come in larger sizes for heavier work. Sizes range up to 1 inch in diameter and 6 inches in length.

Capscrews are usually used without nuts. They are screwed into tapped holes, and are sometimes referred to as tap bolts. Threads may be either NF or NC.

Capscrews may have square, hex, flat, button, or fillister heads (fig. 4-7). Fillister heads are best for use on moving parts when such heads are sunk into counterbored holes. Hex heads are usually used where the metal parts do not move.

The strongest capscrews are made of alloy steel, and can withstand great stresses, strains, and shearing forces. Capscrews made of Monel metal are often specified on machinery that is exposed to salt water.

Some capscrews have small holes through their heads. A wire, called a SAFETY WIRE, is run through the holes of several capscrews to keep them from coming loose.

SETSCREWS

Setscrews are used to secure small pulleys, gears, and cams to shafts, and to provide positive adjustment of machine parts. They are classified by diameter, thread, head shape, and point shape. The point shape is important because it determines the holding qualities of the setscrew.

Setscrews hold best if they have either a CONE POINT or a DOG POINT, shown in figure 4-8. These points fit into matching recesses in the shaft against which they bear.

HEADLESS SETSCREWS—slotted, Allen or Bristol types—are used with moving parts because they do not stick up above the surface. They are threaded all the way from point to head. COMMON SETSCREWS, used on fixed parts, have square heads. They have threads all the way from the point to the shoulder of the head.

THUMB SCREWS are used for setscrews, adjusting screws, and clamping screws. Because of their design they can be loosened or tightened without the use of tools.

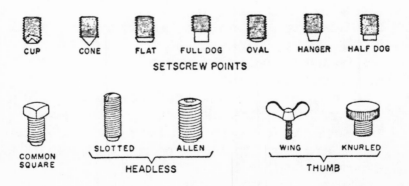

Figure 4-8.—Setscrews and thumb screws.

Figure 4-9.—Common kinds of nuts.

NUTS

SQUARE and HEXAGONAL nuts are standard but they are supplemented by special nuts. (See fig. 4-9.) One of these is the JAM NUT, used above a standard hex nut to lock it in position. It is about half as thick as the standard hex nut, and has a washer face.

CASTELLATED nuts are slotted so that a safety wire or COTTER KEY may be pushed through the slots and into a matching hole in the bolt. This provides a positive method of preventing the nut from working loose. For example, you will see these nuts used with the bolts that hold the two halves of an engine connecting rod together.

WING NUTS are used where the desired degree of tightness can be obtained by the fingers. CAP nuts, are used where appearance is an important consideration. They are usually made of chromium plated brass. THUMB NUTS are knurled, so they can be turned by hand for easy assembly and disassembly.

ELASTIC STOP NUTS are used where it is imperative that the nut does not come loose.

269

These nuts have a fiber or composition washer built into them which is compressed automatically against the screw threads to provide holding tension. They are used extensively on radio, sound equipment, fire control equipment and on aircraft.

WASHERS

Figure 4-10 shows the types of washers used extensively throughout assembly. FLAT WASHERS are used to back up bolt heads and nuts, and to provide larger bearing surfaces. They prevent damage to the surfaces of the metal parts.

SPLIT LOCK WASHERS are used under nuts to prevent loosening by vibration. The ends of these spring-hardened washers dig into both the nut and the work to prevent slippage.

SHAKEPROOF LOCK WASHERS have teeth or lugs that grip both the work and the nut. Several patented designs, shapes, and sizes are obtainable.

FLAT WASHER   SPLIT LOCK WASHER   SHAKE PROOF WASHER

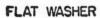

Figure 4-10.—Washers.

KEYS AND PINS

COTTER KEYS (fig. 4-11) are used to secure screws, nuts, bolts, and pins. They are also used as stops and holders on shafts and rods. SQUARE KEYS and WOODRUFF KEYS are used

270

to prevent hand wheels, gears, cams and pulleys from turning on a shaft. These keys are strong enough to carry heavy loads if they are fitted and seated properly.

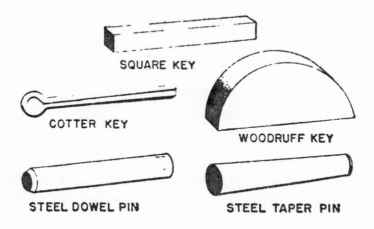

Figure 4-11.—Keys and pins.

TAPER PINS are used to locate and position matching parts. They are also used to secure small pulleys and gears to shafts. They usually have a taper of 1/4-inch per foot. Holes for taper pins must be reamed with tapered reamers. If this is not done the taper pin will not fit properly.

DOWEL PINS are used to position and align the units or parts of an assembly. One end of a dowel pin is chamfered, and it is usually .001 to .002 inch greater in diameter than the size of the hole into which the pin will be driven.

TURNLOCK FASTENERS

Turnlock fasteners are used to secure inspection plates, doors, and other removable panels on items of support equipment and aircraft. These fasteners are also referred to by such terms as quick-opening, quick-acting, and

271

stress panel fasteners. The most desirable feature of these fasteners is that they permit quick and easy removal of access panels and doors for inspection and servicing.

Turnlock fasteners are manufactured and supplied by a number of manufacturers under various trade names. Some of the more common trade names are the Camloc and Dzus (pronounced zoo's) types.

CAMLOC FASTENERS

Camloc fasteners are made in a variety of styles and designs. Regardless of the particular style or shape, the Camloc fastener consists of a stud assembly, receptacle, and a grommet (fig. 4-12).

The stud assembly consists of a stud, a cross pin, spring, and spring cup. The assembly is so designed that it can be quickly inserted into the grommet by compressing the spring. Once installed in the grommet the stud assembly cannot be removed unless the spring is again compressed.

The grommet is a flanged sheet-metal ring made to fit into a hole in the access door or panel. It is ribbed and can be pressed or dimpled into place.

The receptacle consists of a metal forging mounted in a stamped sheet metal. It is riveted to the access opening frame attached to the structure or equipment.

A quarter turn clockwise of the stud screw locks the cross pin into the grooved receptacle. Conversely, a counterclockwise rotation releases the connection between the stud assembly and the receptacle.

DZUS FASTENERS

The Dzus fastener (fig. 4-13) consists of a

272

rotatable stud, which may have a slot for a screwdriver, or a winged fitting on it for hand operation. It also has a permanently mounted spring and a grommet. The stud and grommet are mounted in the door or other removable part, and the spring is riveted to the frame of the access on which the door fits.

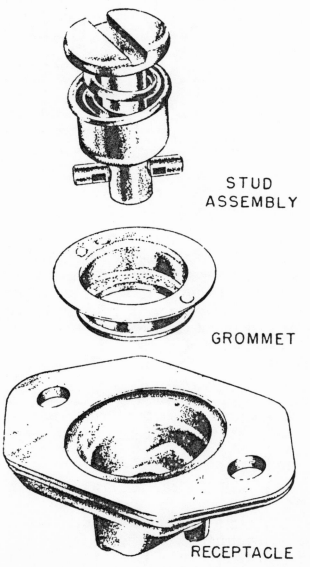

STUD
ASSEMBLY

GROMMET

RECEPTACLE

Figure 4-12.—Camloc fastener.

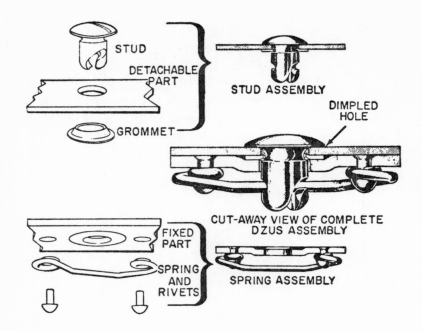

STUD

DETACHABLE PART

GROMMET

STUD ASSEMBLY

DIMPLED HOLE

CUT-AWAY VIEW OF COMPLETE DZUS ASSEMBLY

FIXED PART

SPRING AND RIVETS

SPRING ASSEMBLY

Figure 4-13.—Dzus fastener.

Cams on the stud engage with the spring to lock the fastener in the engaged position. The purpose of the grommet is to retain the stud in the access door. In some installations, the grommet is not used as a retainer; the stud is secured to the access door by a snapring, cup washer, or by dimpling of the metal around the stud.

The quick acting action of the Dzus fastener is achieved when a quarter turn rotation of the stud causes its engagement or disengagement with the spring.

SAFETYING METHODS

Safetying is a process of securing fasteners and other equipment so they do not work loose due to vibration. Loose bolts, screws and nuts or other parts can ruin delicate equipment.

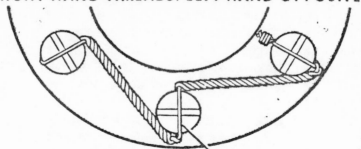

SAFETY METHODS SHOWN ARE FOR
RIGHT HAND THREADS. LEFT HAND OPPOSITE.

SAFETY WIRE OVER HEAD

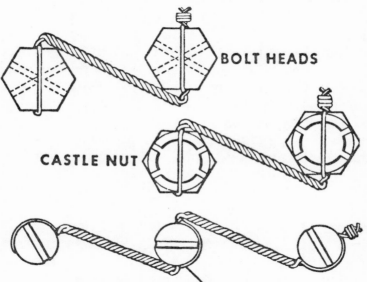

BOLT HEADS

CASTLE NUT

SAFETY WIRE AROUND HEAD
TWIST METHODS

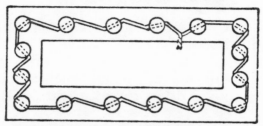

SINGLE WIRE PLAIN

Figure 4-14.—Safety wiring methods.

SAFETY WIRING

Safety wiring is the most positive and satisfactory method of safetying capscrews, studs,
nuts, and bolt heads which cannot be safetied by
any other practical means. It is a method of
wiring together two or more units in such a
manner that any tendency of one to loosen is
countered by the tightening of the wire and the
other unit. Components are safety wired by the
single wire plain method or the twist method
(fig. 4-14).

The single wire plain method may be used
on small components in a closely spaced,
closed geometrical pattern, and in places that
are difficult to reach. When safety wiring
closely spaced components, take advantage of
safety wiring the whole series. The number of
parts in the series safely wired together by this
method depends upon the application; but the
maximum number in the series is limited by a
maximum 24 inch wire length.

The twist method is the most common
method of safety wiring. The technique is
shown in figure 4-15. A group of three should
be the maximum in the series when safety wiring widely spaced components by this method.

The following general rules should be followed
when using the safety wire method to secure
components.

- The safety wire must be new upon each
  application.
- All safety wires must be tight after installation, but not under such tension that
  normal handling or vibration will break
  the wire.
- The wire must be applied so that all pull
  exerted by the wire tends to tighten the
  nut.
- Twists should be tight and even and the

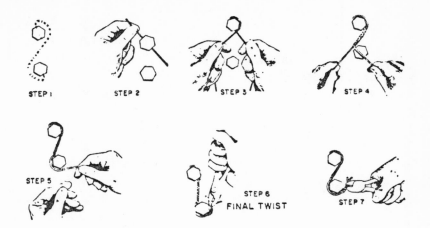

Figure 4-15.—Standard twist safety wire installation procedure.

wire between the nuts as taut as possible without overtwisting. Wire twister pliers should be used if available; otherwise, wire between nuts should be twisted with the hands. The use of regular pliers for twisting will damage the wire. Regular pliers may be used only for the final end twist prior to cutting off the excess wire.

● When castellated nuts are to be secured, tighten the nut to the low side of the selected torque range, unless otherwise specified, and if necessary, continue tightening until a slot aligns with a hole.

COTTER PINS

Some cotter pins are made of low-carbon steel, while others consist of stainless steel and thus are more resistant to corrosion. Regardless of shape or material, all cotter pins are used for the same general purpose—safetying.

Dimension perimeters of a cotter pin are shown in figure 4-16. Whenever uneven prong cotter pins are used, the length measurement is to the end of the shortest prong.

A cotter pin installation is shown in figure 4-17. The cotter pin should fit neatly into the hole with very little sideplay.

In the preferred installation method, the bent prong above the bolt end should not extend beyond the bolt diameter. Additionally, the bent prong should not rest against the surface of the washer. Cut the prongs down to size if necessary.

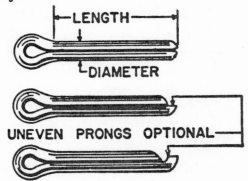

Figure 4-16.—Types of cotter pins.

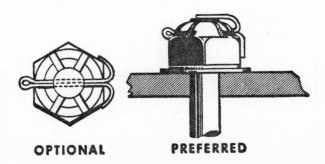

Figure 4-17.—Cotter pin installations.

If the optional wraparound method is used, the prongs should not extend outwards, but should be bent over a reasonable radius to the sides of the nut. Sharpangled bends invite breakage. Usually the initial bending of the prongs of a cotter pin is accomplished with needle nose or diagonal pliers and the best tool for final bending of the prongs is a soft faced mallet.

RIVETS

Rivets are used extensively as a fastening device in aircraft. They are also used to join metal sheet when brazing, welding, or locking techniques will not provide a satisfactory joint.

RIVET TYPES

The major types of rivets used extensively include the standard type and pop rivets. Standard rivets must be driven using a bucking bar whereas the pop rivets have a self heading capability and may be installed where it is impossible to use a bucking bar.

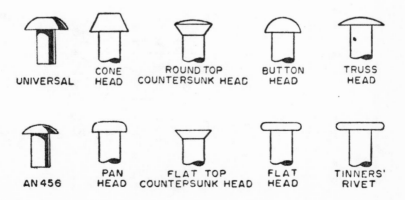

Figure 4-18.—Some common types of rivets.

Standard Rivets

Wherever possible, rivets should be made of the same material as the material they join. They are classified by lengths, diameters, and their head shape and size. Some of the standard head shapes are shown in figure 4-18.

Selection of the proper length of a rivet is important. Should too long a rivet be used, the formed head will be too large, or the rivet may bend or be forced between the sheets being riveted. Should too short a rivet be used, the formed head will be too small or the riveted material will be damaged. The length of the rivet should equal the sum of the thickness of the metal plus 1 1/2 times the diameter of the rivet, as shown in figure 4-19.

When using tinner's rivets, refer to table 4-3 as a guide for selecting rivets of the proper size for the different gages of sheet metal.

The riveting procedure for the standard type of rivet involves three operations: drawing, upsetting, and heading as shown in figure 4-20. The sheets are drawn together by placing the

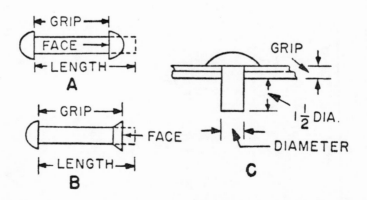

Figure 4-19.—Showing what is meant by "grip" of a rivet.

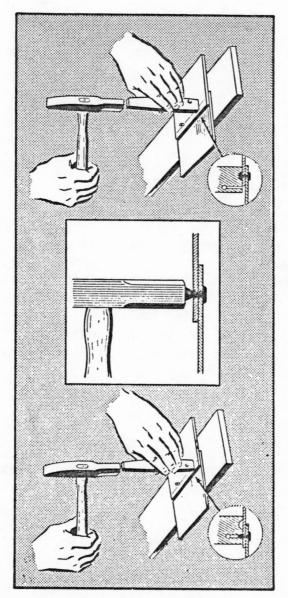

Figure 4-20.—Drawing, upsetting, and heading a rivet.

Table 4-3.—Guide for Selecting Rivet Size for Sheet Metal Work

Gage of sheet metal	Rivet size (weight in pounds per 1000 rivets)
26	1
24	2
22	2 1/2
20	3
18	3 1/2
16	4

deep hole of the rivet set over the rivet and striking the head of the set with a hammer. Upon removal of the set, the end of the rivet is struck lightly to upset the end of the rivet. Finally, the heading die (dished part) of the rivet set forms the head of the rivet when the hammer again strikes the head of the rivet set. The results of correct and incorrect riveting are shown in figure 4-21.

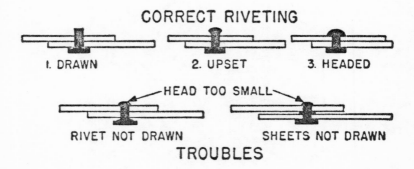

CORRECT RIVETING

1. DRAWN   2. UPSET   3. HEADED

HEAD TOO SMALL

RIVET NOT DRAWN   SHEETS NOT DRAWN

TROUBLES

Figure 4-21.—Correct and incorrect riveting.

CLOSED-END TYPE
HOLLOW-CORE TYPE
DOMED HEAD

SOLID-CORE TYPE
COUNTERSUNK HEAD

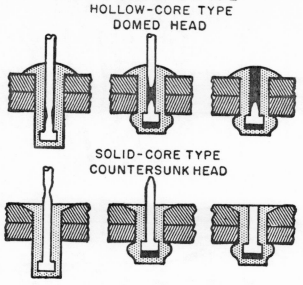

OPEN-END TYPE

DOMED HEAD

COUNTERSUNK HEAD

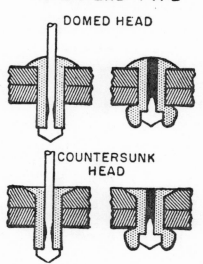

Figure 4-22.—Pop rivets.

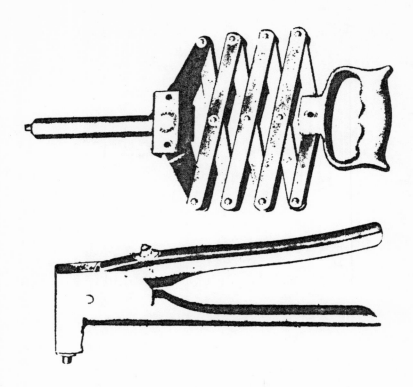

Figure 4-23.—Pop rivet tools.

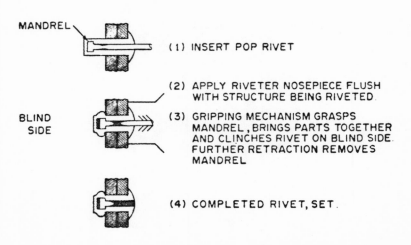

MANDREL

(1) INSERT POP RIVET

(2) APPLY RIVETER NOSEPIECE FLUSH WITH STRUCTURE BEING RIVETED.

BLIND SIDE

(3) GRIPPING MECHANISM GRASPS MANDREL, BRINGS PARTS TOGETHER AND CLINCHES RIVET ON BLIND SIDE. FURTHER RETRACTION REMOVES MANDREL

(4) COMPLETED RIVET, SET.

Figure 4-24.—Setting pop rivets.

Pop Rivets

Pop rivets (fig. 4-22) have two advantages compared to standard rivets in that they can be set by one man and also be used for blind fastening. This means that they can be used where there is limited or no access to the reverse side of the work.

Operation is simple. Drill holes in the parts to be riveted together and align the holes. Insert the pop rivet (a hollow rivet assembled on a solid mandrel) and set it with a pop riveter (fig. 4-23) using the procedure shown in figure 4-24.

There are two basic designs for pop rivets: closed-end and open-end (fig. 4-22). The closed-end type rivet fills the need for blind rivets which seal as they are set. They are gas and liquid tight, when used properly, since a high degree of radial expansion provides excellent hole-filling characteristics and the mandrel head is within the core of the rivet body.

The open-end type is not liquid-tight because the mandrel head which remains in the rivet body is not enclosed within that body as is the closed-end type. This obviously leaves room for possible seepage of liquid or gas.

RIVET SELECTION

The following rules govern the selection and use of rivets in making a repair:

1. Replacements must not be made with rivets of lower strength material unless they are larger than those removed.

2. When rivet holes become enlarged, deformed, or otherwise damaged, use the next larger size as replacement.

285

3. Countersunk head rivets are to be replaced by rivets of the same type and degree of countersink.

4. Rivets selected for specific applications must always be of the type recommended in the repair manual for that particular equipment.

CHAPTER 5
GRINDING OPERATIONS

To keep hand tools in the best usable condition, cutting edges must be sharpened frequently and certain other tools trued or shaped for special purposes. Chisels, punches, drills, tinsnips, screwdrivers, and other hand tools are shaped or sharpened on an abrasive grinding wheel.

Grinding may be defined as the act of shaping or wearing down a surface or sharpening an edge by means of the cutting action of thousands of abrasive grains on the surface of the grinding wheel. Excessive grinding shortens the useful life of a tool.

GRINDING SAFETY

The grinding wheel is a fragile cutting tool which operates at high speeds. Great emphasis must be given, therefore, to the safe operation of bench and pedestal grinders.

What are the most common sources of injury during grinding operation? Hazards leading to eye injury caused by grit generated by the grinding process are the most common and the most serious. Abrasions caused by bodily contact with the wheel are quite painful and can be serious. Cuts and bruises caused by segments of an exploded wheel, or a tool "kicked" away from the wheel are other sources of injury. Cuts and abrasions can become infected if not protected from grit and dust from grinding.

Safety in using bench and pedestal grinders is primarily a matter of using common sense and concentrating on the job at hand. Each time you start to grind a tool, stop briefly to consider how observance of safety precautions and the use of safeguards protect you from injury.

Some guidelines for safe grinding practices are:

1. Secure all loose clothing and remove rings or other jewelry.

2. Inspect the grinding wheel, wheel guards, the toolrest, and other safety devices to ensure they are in good condition and positioned properly. Set the toolrest so that it is within 1/8 inch of the wheel face and level with the center of the wheel.

3. Transparent shields, if installed, should be clean and properly adjusted. Transparent shields do not preclude the use of goggles as the dust and grit may get around a shield. Goggles, however, provide full eye protection.

4. Stand aside when starting the grinder motor until operating speed is reached. This prevents injury if the wheel explodes from a defect that has not been noticed.

5. Use light pressure when starting grinding; too much pressure on a cold wheel may cause failure.

6. Grind only on the face or outer circumference of a grinding wheel unless the wheel is specifically designed for side grinding.

7 Use a coolant to prevent overheating the work.

8. Wear goggles and respiratory filters to protect your eyes and lungs from injury by grit and dust generated by grinding operations.

288

GRINDING WHEELS

A grinding wheel is composed of two basic elements: (1) the abrasive grains, and (2) the bonding agent. The abrasive grains may be compared to many single point tools embedded in a toolholder of bonding agent. Each of these grains extracts a very small chip from the material as it makes contact on each revolution of the grinding wheel.

An ideal cutting tool is one that will sharpen itself when it becomes dull. This, in effect, is what happens to the abrasive grains. As the individual grains become dull, the pressure that is generated on them causes them to fracture and present new sharp cutting edges to the work. When the grains can fracture no more, the pressure becomes too great and they are released from the bond, allowing new sharp grains to be presented to the work.

SIZES AND SHAPES

Grinding wheels come in various sizes and shapes. The size of a grinding wheel is given in terms of its diameter in inches, the diameter of the spindle hole, and the width of the face of the wheel. The shapes of all grinding wheels are too numerous to list in this manual, but figure 5-1 shows most of the more frequently used wheel shapes. The type numbers are standard and are used by all manufacturers. The shapes are shown in cross-sectional views. The specific job will dictate the shape of wheel to be used.

WHEEL MARKINGS AND COMPOSITION

Grinding wheel markings are comprised of six sections. Figure 5-2 illustrates the stand-

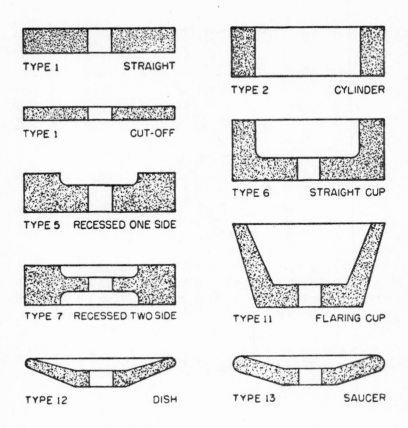

TYPE 1   STRAIGHT

TYPE 2   CYLINDER

TYPE 1   CUT-OFF

TYPE 5   RECESSED ONE SIDE

TYPE 6   STRAIGHT CUP

TYPE 7   RECESSED TWO SIDE

TYPE 11   FLARING CUP

TYPE 12   DISH

TYPE 13   SAUCER

Figure 5-1.—Grinding wheel shapes.

ard marking and possible variations. The following information breaks the marking down and explains each section.

Kind of Abrasive

The first section on the wheel marking (reading from left to right) shows the abrasive type. There are two types of abrasives: natural and manufactured. Natural abrasives, such as emery, corundum, and diamond, are used only in honing stones and in special types of grinding wheels. The common manufactured abrasives are aluminum oxide and silicon carbide. They have superior qualities and are more economical than natural abrasives.

290

Aluminum oxide (designated by the letter A) is used for grinding steel and steel alloys, and for heavy duty work such as cleaning up steel castings. Silicon carbide (designated by the letter C), which is harder but not as tough as aluminum oxide, is used mostly for grinding nonferrous metals and carbide tools. The abrasive in a grinding wheel comprises about 40 percent of the wheel.

Grain Size

The second section on the grinding wheel marking is the grain size. Grain sizes range from 10 to 600. The size is determined by the size of mesh of a sieve through which the grains can pass. Generally speaking, they are rated as follows: Coarse: 10, 12, 14, 16, 20, 24; Medium: 30, 36, 46, 54, 60; Fine: 70, 80, 90, 100, 120, 150, 180; and Very Fine: 220, 240, 280, 320, 400, 500, 600. Grain sizes finer than (240) are generally considered flour. Generally speaking, fine grain wheels are preferred for grinding hard materials, as they have more

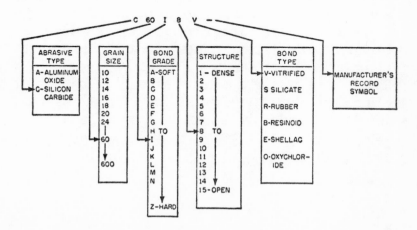

Figure 5-2.—Standard marking system for grinding wheels (except diamond).

291

cutting edges and will cut faster than coarse grain wheels. Coarse grain wheels are generally preferred for rapid metal removal on softer materials.

Grade (Hardness)

Section three of the wheel marking is the grade or hardness of the wheel. As shown in figure 5-2, the grade is designated by a letter of the alphabet; grades run from A to Z or soft to hard.

The grade of a grinding wheel is a measurement of the ability of the bond to retain the abrasive grains in the wheel. Grinding wheels are said to have a soft to hard grade. This does not mean that the bond or the abrasive is soft or hard; it means that the wheel has a large amount of bond (hard grade) or a small amount of bond (soft grade). Figure 5-3 illustrates a magnified portion of a soft grade and a hard grade wheel. You can see by the illustration that a part of the bond surrounds the abrasive grains and the remainder of the bond forms into posts that both hold the grains to the wheel and hold them apart from each other. The wheel having the larger amount of bonding material has thick bond posts and will offer great resistance to pressures generated in grinding. The wheel having the least amount of bond will offer less resistance to the grinding pressures. In other words, the wheel with a large amount of bond is said to be a hard grade and the wheel with a small amount of bond is said to be a soft grade.

Structure

The fourth section of the grinding wheel marking is the structure. The structure is designated by numbers from 1 to 15, as illustrated in figure 5-2. The structure of a grinding wheel refers to the open space between the grains, as shown in figure 5-3. Grains that are very closely spaced are said to be dense; when grains are wider apart, they are said to be open. Generally speaking, the metal removal

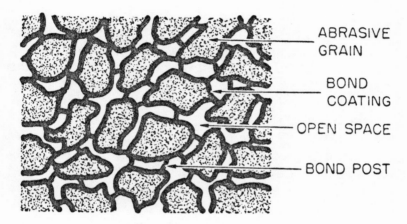

ABRASIVE
GRAIN

BOND
COATING

OPEN SPACE

BOND POST

WHEEL A

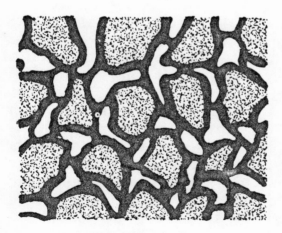

WHEEL B

Figure 5-3.—How bond affects the grade of
the wheel. Wheel A, softer;
Wheel B, harder.

will be greater for open-grain wheels than for close-grain wheels. Also dense or close-grain wheels will normally produce a finer finish. The structure of a grinding wheel comprises about 20 percent of the grinding wheel.

Bond Type

The fifth section on the grinding wheel marking is the bond type. The bond comprises the remaining 40 percent of the grinding wheel and is one of the most important parts of the wheel. The bond determines the strength of the wheel. The 6 basic types of bonds are considered in this chapter.

VITRIFIED bond, designated by the letter V, is not affected by oil, acid, or water. Vitrified-bonded wheels are strong and porous, and rapid temperature changes have little or no effect on them. Vitrified wheels should not be run in excess of 6500 surface feet per minute.

SILICATE bonded wheels are designated by the letter S. Silicate bonded wheels are used mainly for large, slow rpm machines where a cooler cutting action is desired. Silicate bonded wheels are said to be softer than vitrified wheels as they release the grains more readily than the vitrified bonded wheels. This wheel, like the vitrified bonded wheel, is not to be run in excess of 6500 surface feet per minute.

RUBBER bonded wheels, designated by the letter R, are strong and elastic. They are used for the manufacture of thin cutoff wheels and are used extensively for regulating wheels on centerless grinders. Rubber bonded wheels produce a high finish and can be run at speeds up to 16,000 surface feet per minute.

RESINOID bonded wheels are designated by the letter B and are shock resistant and strong. They are used for rough grinding and cutoff wheels. Resinoid wheels also can be run at speeds up to 16,000 surface feet per minute.

SHELLAC bonded wheels, designated by the letter E, give a high finish and have a cool cutting action when used as cutoff wheels. Shellac bonded wheels can be run up to 12,500 surface feet per minute.

OXYCHLORIDE bonded wheels are designated by the letter O. They are not to be run at speeds greater than 6,500 surface feet per minute.

Manufacturer's Record

The sixth section on the grinding wheel marking is the manufacturer's record. This may be a letter or number, or both. It is used by the manufacturer to designate bond modifications or wheel characteristics.

SELECTING AND USING
THE WHEEL

The selection of grinding wheels for precision grinding can be discussed generally in terms of such factors as the physical properties of the material to be ground, the amount of stock to be removed (depth of cut), the wheel speed and work speed, and the finish required. Selection of a grinding wheel having the proper abrasive, grain, grade, and bond is determined by considering one or more of these factors.

An aluminum oxide abrasive is most suitable for grinding carbon and alloy steel, high speed steel, cast alloys and malleable iron. A silicon carbide abrasive is most suitable for grinding nonferrous metals, nonmetallic materials, and cemented carbides.

Generally, the softer and more ductile the material being ground, the coarser the grain selected should be. Also, if a large amount of material is to be removed, a coarse grain wheel is recommended (except on very hard materials). If a good finish is required, a fine grain wheel should be used.

For soft materials, small depth of cut, or high work speed, use a soft grade wheel. If the machine you are using is worn, a harder grade may be necessary to help offset the effects of wear of the machine. Using a coolant also permits the use of a harder grade of wheel.

Table 5-1 lists recommended grinding wheels for various operations.

Before you perform these operations, you should be able, however, to install and dress the wheels properly, whenever required.

INSTALLING THE WHEEL

The wheel of a bench or pedestal grinder must be properly installed; otherwise accidents may occur and the wheel will not operate properly. Before a wheel is installed, it should be inspected for visible defects and "sounded" by tapping lightly with a piece of hard wood

OPERATION	WHEEL DESIGNATION						MATERIAL
	Abrasive	Grain size	Grade	Structure	Bond	Mfg. Symbol	
Cylindrical grinding	A	60	K	8	V	- - - -	High speed steel
	A	60	L	5	V	- - - -	Hardened steel
	A	54	M	5	V	- - - -	Soft steel
	C	36	K	5	V	- - - -	Cast iron, brass, aluminum
	A	54	L	5	V	- - - -	General purpose
Surface grinding	A	46	H	8	V	- - - -	High speed steel
	A	60	F	12	V	- - - -	Hardened steel
	A	46	J	5	V	- - - -	Soft steel
	C	36	J	8	V	- - - -	Cast iron and bronze
	A	24	H	8	V	- - - -	General purpose
Tool and cutter grinding	A	46	K	8	V	- - - -	High speed steel or cast alloy milling cutter
	A	54	L	5	V	- - - -	Reamers
	A	60	K	8	V	- - - -	Taps

Table 5-1.—Recommendations for Selecting Grinding Wheels

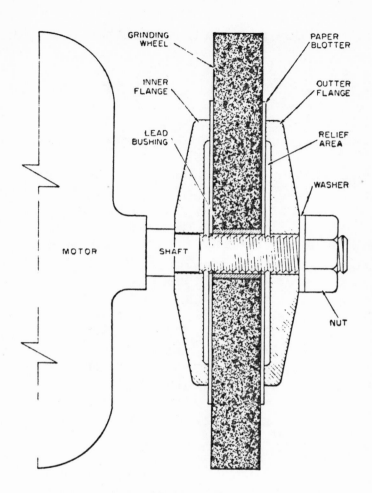

Figure 5-4.—Method of mounting a grinding wheel.

to determine whether it has invisible cracks. A good wheel gives out a clear ringing sound when tapped, but if the wheel is cracked a dull thud is heard. The following information on mounting the wheel should be more readily understood if the reader refers to figure 5-4.

Ensure that the shaft and flanges are clean and free of grit and old blotter material. Place the inner flange in place and follow it with a blotter. NOTE, the blotter thickness for paper must be no thicker than .025 inch and no thicker than .125 inch for leather or rubber. The blotter is used to ensure even pressure on the wheel, and to dampen the vibration between the wheel and shaft when the grinder is in operation. Next mount the wheel, and ensure that it fits on the shaft without play. A .002 to .005 inch clearance should be provided. This may be accomplished by scraping or reaming the lead bushing in the center of the wheel. NEVER FORCE THE WHEEL ON THE SHAFT. Forcing the wheel on the shaft may cause the wheel to crack when placed in operation, or cause the wheel to be slightly out of axial alignment. The next item is another blotter and then the outer flange. NOTE the flanges are recessed so they provide an even pressure on the wheel. The flanges should be at least one-third the diameter of the wheel. Next, install the washer and secure the nut. Tighten the securing nut sufficiently to hold the wheel firmly; tightening too much may damage the wheel.

TRUING AND DRESSING THE WHEEL

Grinding wheels, like other cutting tools, require frequent reconditioning of cutting surfaces to perform efficiently. Dressing is the term used to describe the process of cleaning the periphery of grinding wheels. This cleaning breaks away dull abrasive grains and smooths the surface so that there are no grooves. Truing is the term used to describe the removal of material from the cutting face of the wheel so that the resultant surface runs absolutely true to some other surface such as the grinding wheel shaft.

The wheel dresser shown in figure 5-5 is used for dressing grinding wheels on bench and pedestal grinders. To dress a wheel with this

Figure 5-5.—Using a grinding wheel dresser.

tool, start the grinder and let it come up to speed. Set the wheel dresser on the rest as shown in figure 5-5 and bring it in firm contact with the wheel. Move the wheel dresser back and forth across the face of the wheel until the surface is clean and approximately square with the sides of the wheel.

If grinding wheels get out of balance because of out-of-roundness, dressing the wheel will usually remedy the condition. A grinding wheel can get out of balance by being left sitting with part of the wheel immersed in the coolant; if this happens, the wheel should be removed and dried out by baking. If the wheel gets out of balance axially, it probably will not affect the efficiency of the wheel. This unbalance may be remedied simply by removing the wheel and cleaning the shaft spindle and spindle hole in the wheel and the flanges.

Each time that a wheel is dressed it is necessary that you check the clearance between the tool rest and the wheel. Reestablish the clearance at 1/16-inch as required. Adjustments must be made with the machine secured to preclude possible injury to the operator.

GRINDING METAL STOCK

To grind a straight edge on metal stock (figure 5-6A) adjust the tool rest so that it just clears the wheel and is approximately at the

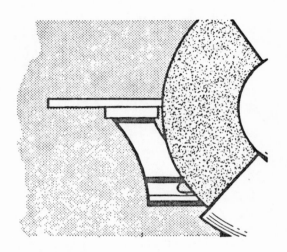

Figure 5-6A.—Grinding a straight edge on metal stock.

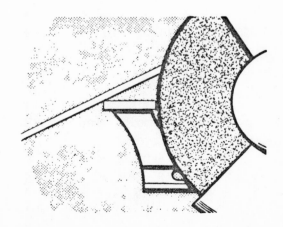

Figure 5-6B.—Grinding a bevel on metal stock.

center line of the wheel. Then, keeping the edge of the stock parallel with the center line of the grinder shaft, pass the stock across the face of the wheel. Grind across the entire width of the piece, using that pressure which will keep the wheel cutting but will not appreciably decrease its speed. Grinding across the entire width of the piece and the wheel wears the wheel evenly and helps prevent overheating.

To grind a bevel on an edge, (figure 5-6B), hold the stock as shown so that it is resting both on the wheel and on the edge of the tool rest. The edge being ground is away from the tool rest and therefore is not liable to get caught between the tool rest and the wheel. Pass the stock across the face of the wheel just as you do when grinding a square edge.

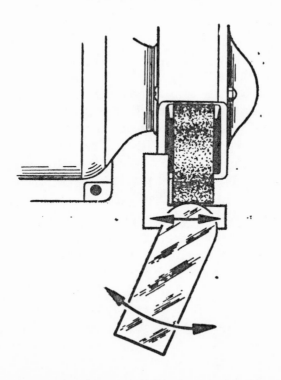

Figure 5-7.—Grinding a rounded
edge on metal stock.

To grind a rounded edge, set the tool rest at the center line of the wheel. With one hand, hold the end of the stock being ground so that you can move it from left to right, across the face of the wheel, as shown by the small double-headed arrow in figure 5-7, and also hold it down firmly on the tool rest. With the other hand swing the arc shown by the longer curved double-headed arrow at the opposite end of the stock. The motion indicated by the curved arrow will produce the rounded edge on the stock. The travel indicated by the short straight double-headed arrow will prevent the wearing of a groove in the wheel which would have to be removed by dressing.

CENTER PUNCH SHARPENING

To sharpen a center punch, cradle the end of the punch between the index finger and thumb of one hand, as shown in figure 5-8, resting that hand on the tool rest of the grinder. Move the punch into light contact with the rotating wheel of the grinder with the center line of the punch forming about a 45° angle with the face of the wheel. This will give the approximate 90° included angle required for a center punch. With the thumb and index finger of the other hand rotate the punch as shown by the directional arrow in figure 5-8. Keep the point cool by using only light pressure on the wheel and by frequently dipping the punch in a can of cooling water. Sharpen a prick-punch in the same way with the exception that, since the included angle should be 30° rather than 90°, the angle between the center line of this punch and the wheel should be about 15°.

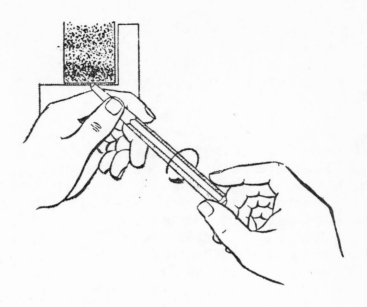

Figure 5-8.—Dressing a center punch
with a bench grinder.

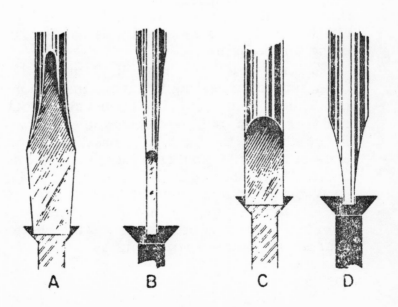

A   B   C   D

Figure 5-9.—Shapes of screwdrivers when
properly dressed.

SCREWDRIVER TIP
DRESSING

Figure 5-9, parts A and C are the front views of a properly dressed screwdriver; 5-9B and 5-9D are the side views.

To dress a common screwdriver, dress the sides so that the blade is symmetrical in shape. Then, square off the end. Check the squareness of the end by resting the tip on the handle of a trysquare and moving the shank of the screwdriver close to the blade of the square. If the blade and the shank appear to be parallel, the tip is square. See figure 5-10.

On the common screwdriver, grind the faces of the blade so that they are parallel or nearly parallel at the tip as shown at B and D in figure 5-9. The thickness of the blade at the tip should be such that the tip will just enter the slot of the screws you intend to turn. With such a tip thickness, and the sides parallel or nearly so, the screwdriver will have the least tendency to climb out of the screw slot when the screw is being turned home.

The screwdriver shown in figure 5-9D has been ground by resting it flat against the grinding wheel. A 6-inch wheel produces about the right grind on a screwdriver used for small screws. Hold the blade high on the circumference of the wheel and rest the shank on the tool rest. See figure 5-11.

When grinding a screwdriver, do not let the tip get too hot or the temper will be drawn. Overheating is discussed later in the section on sharpening metal-cutting chisels.

TIN SNIPS
SHARPENING

To sharpen tin snips on a grinder, open the snips as shown in figure 5-12, resting the

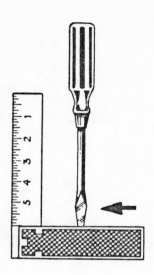

Figure 5-10.—Checking
the squareness of
the end of a
screwdriver.

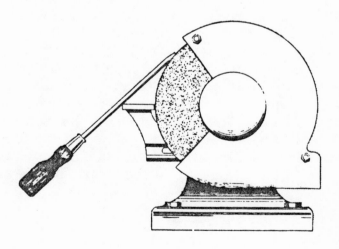

Figure 5-11.—Grinding a screwdriver
tip with a bench grinder.

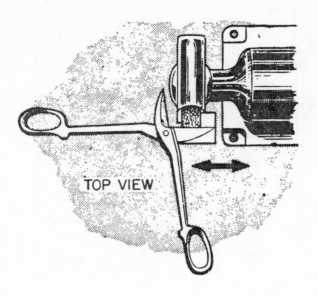

Figure 5-12.—Sharpening snips on
a grinder.

blade on the tool rest. Hold level the handle of
the blade being ground and then rotate the other
blade at whatever angle is necessary to grind
the cutting edge to an included angle of 80° to
85°. Holding the blade lightly against the rotating wheel, move it from left to right across
the face of the wheel. Sharpen first one blade of
the snips and then the other. While sharpening
one blade, be careful to keep the other blade
from coming into contact with the side of the
wheel. Sharpening tin snips requires close and
careful attention; improper techniques may result in wrecking the snips or even in serious
personal injury.

CHISEL HEAD GRINDING

In figure 5-13A you will see a properly
ground chisel head. Keep it that way by frequent
grinding before it begins to mushroom as shown
in figure 5-13B.

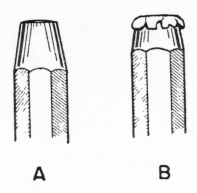

A   B

Figure 5-13.—Good
and bad shaped
chisel heads.

Never use a chisel whose head has been allowed to mushroom. You, or others, can be
injured by chips or metal flying off the head
when it is hammered.

Remove the ragged edges of such a head by
grinding them off. One way to do this is to hold
the head against the wheel as shown in figure
5-14.

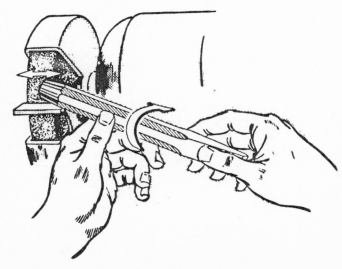

Figure 5-14.—Grinding a chisel head
with a bench grinder.

Turn the chisel with one hand as you apply pressure with the other. Grind across the entire face of the wheel to keep it flat.

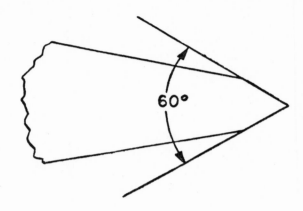

Figure 5-15.—Proper angle for general use cold chisel.

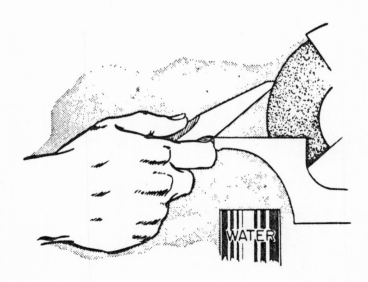

Figure 5-16.—Sharpening a chisel with a grinder.

SHARPENING METAL-CUTTING CHISELS

Metal-cutting chisels are sharpened by grinding. These chisels are designed to cut cold metal, so the general term "cold chisel" is often used. The angle of 60°, shown on the cold chisel in figure 5-15, is for a general-use cold chisel. Increase this angle somewhat for cutting harder metals and decrease it for those that are softer.

To sharpen a metal-cutting chisel, hold the chisel to the wheel, resting it on the tool rest. (See fig. 5-16.) Notice that the index finger, curved beneath the chisel, rides against the front edge of the tool rest. This affords good control of the chisel and will help you to grind a single, equal bevel on each side.

Let the chisel rest only lightly against the wheel when grinding. Less heat will be developed and, because the speed of the wheel is reduced only slightly, the air currents created by the wheel will have the maximum cooling effect. If the temperature of the cutting edge rises to the point where the metal begins to turn blue in color, the temper has been drawn, the cutting edge has been softened, and the edge will not stand up in use. The cutting edge will have to be rehardened, drawn to the proper temper (hardness), and the sharpening continued. As long as you can touch the cutting edge you are grinding with your bare hand and keep it there, you are in no danger of drawing the temper. Notice that it is the temperature of the cutting edge that is important. This means the very tip of the chisel where the bevel is being ground. The chisel at a point an inch or less from the cutting edge may be cool, while the cutting edge itself turns blue from overheating. Check this carefully while grinding.

309

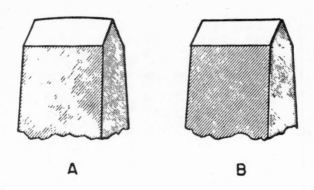

A   B

Figure 5-17.—Two cutting edge
shapes of cold chisels.

Figure 5-18.—Mental alertness is
vital to safety.

Figure 5-17A shows a cold chisel ground with a slight curvature, and figure 5-17B shows a straight cutting edge. Both types of edges are used. The curved cutting edge is ground by swinging either end of the chisel slightly from left to right as the two faces of the cutting edge are being ground.

For shearing metal in a vise the chisel with the straight edge may be better. The chisel with the curvature will probably work better when you are cutting metal on a flat plate.

Be sure you are alert when you work (fig. 5-18). After you have completed your use of the tools, remove any possibility of danger from slipping or tripping (fig. 5-19).

Figure 5-19.—Eliminate potential hazards.

HAND SHARPENING TWIST DRILLS

The following requirements are of greatest importance in twist-drill grinding: (1) equal and correctly sized drill-point angles, (2) equal-length cutting lips, (3) correct clearance behind the cutting lips, and (4) correct chisel-edge angle. All four are equally important when grinding either a regular point (fig. 5-20), which is used for general purposes, or a flat point (fig. 5-21) which is used for drilling hard and tough materials.

Figure 5-22 shows the results of correct lip grinding and how equal drill point angles and two equal length cutting lips help achieve correct drill results.

Figure 5-23 shows a drill being checked during grinding. The drill-point gage is being held against the body of the drill and has been brought down to where the graduated edge of the gage is in contact with one cutting edge. In this way, both the drill-point angle and the length of the cutting edge (or lip) are checked at the same time. The process is repeated for the other side of the drill.

Lip clearance behind the cutting lip at the margin is determined by inspection. This means that you look at the drill point and approximate the lip-clearance angle (see figs. 5-20B and 5-21B), or compare it to the same angle that has been set up on a protractor. The lip-clearance angle is not necessarily a definite angle, but must be within certain limits. Notice that in figure 5-20B this angle ranges from 8° to 12° and that the range given in figure 5-21B is 6° to 9°. Whatever angle in the range is used, however, lip clearance should be the same for both cutting lips of the drill.

There must be lip clearance behind the entire length of the cutting lip which extends from the margin of the drill to the chisel edge. This means that there must be "relief" behind the cutting lip along its entire length.

When lip clearance is being "ground into" a drill, the lip-clearance angle and the chisel edge angle (shown at C in figs. 5-20 and 5-21)

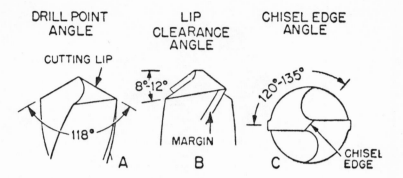

Figure 5-20.—Specifications for
grinding a regular point
twist drill.

will be your guide to the amount of clearance
you have ground into the drill behind the cutting
lip along its entire length. The greater these
angles are, the more clearance there will be
behind their respective ends of the cutting lip.
Too much lip clearance, which occurs when both
the lip-clearance angle and the chisel-edge
angle exceed their top limits, weakens the

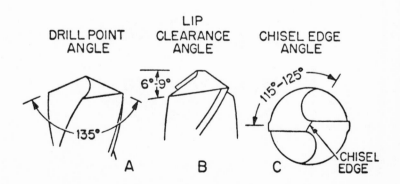

Figure 5-21.—Specifications for grinding
a flat point twist drill.

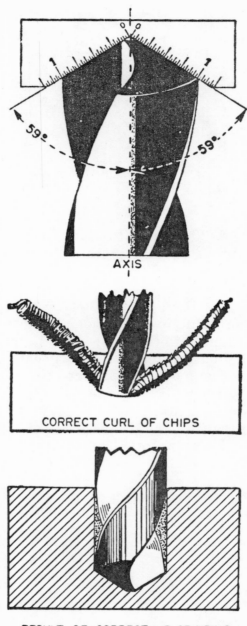

AXIS

CORRECT CURL OF CHIPS

RESULT OF CORRECT LIP GRINDING

Figure 5-22.—Grinding drill lips correctly.

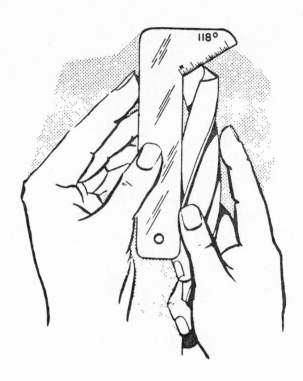

Figure 5-23.—Checking the drill
point angle and cutting edge.

cutting edge or lip by removing too much metal
directly behind it. Too little or no lip clearance prevents the cutting edge from producing
a chip, or cutting, and the drill will not drill a
hole.

To SHARPEN TWIST DRILLS, first get the
grinder ready. If necessary, dress the face of
the wheel so that it is clean, a true circle, and
square with the sides. Before starting the
grinder, readjust the tool rest to 1/16" or less
from the face of the wheel. This is an important safety measure which will help keep
work from wedging between the tool rest and
the face of the wheel.

After starting the grinder and letting it come
up to speed, you can begin grinding the drill

315

point. Hold the twist drill as shown in figure 5-24A, which is a top view of the first step in grinding a drill. The axis of the drill, in the first step, should make an angle of about 59° (half of the drill-point angle) with the face of the wheel as shown in fig. 5-24A. The cutting lip should be horizontal.

The actual grinding of the drill point consists of three definite motions of the shank of the drill while the point is held lightly against the rotating wheel. These three motions are: (1) to the left, (2) clockwise rotation, (3) downward.

Figure 5-24 shows the motion to the left in three views as the angle between the face of the wheel and the drill decreases from about 59° to about 50°.

In figure 5-24 the clockwise rotation is indicated by the advance of the rotation arrows in A, B, and C. Rotation is also pictured by the change in position of the cutting lip as well as that of the tang.

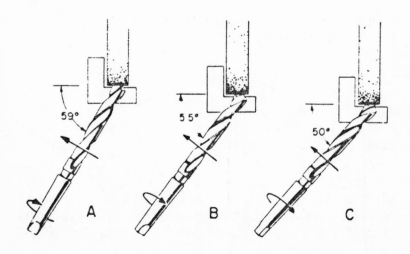

Figure 5-24.—Three steps for grinding
a twist drill with a grinder.

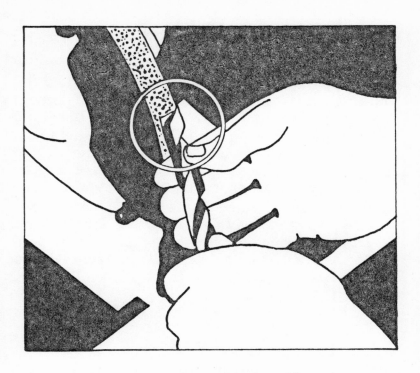

Grinding a twist drill with a grinder
(initial position).

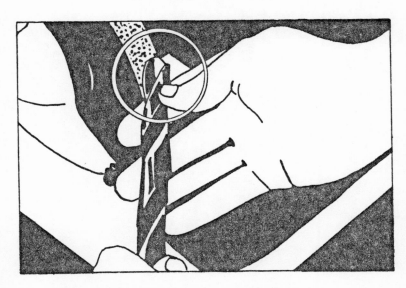

Grinding a twist drill with a grinder
(final position).

SHARPENING A TWIST DRILL
FOR DRILLING BRASS

To grind a drill for drilling brass hold the cutting lip against the right side of the wheel as shown in figure 5-25. Grinding the flute slightly flat, in line with the axis of the drill, greatly reduces the included angle of the cutting lip. This will give the drill a scraping action, necessary for brass, rather than the cutting action used for steel. This scraping action will prevent the tendency, that invariably occurs with drills not ground for brass, to stick in the hole being drilled. This sticking is troublesome especially when drilling through a pilot hole.

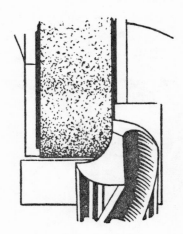

Figure 5-25.—Grinding a twist drill for brass.

THINNING THE WEB OF
A TWIST DRILL

Repeated sharpening, which shortens the drill, or the fact that the remaining length of a broken drill has been resharpened, results in an increase in the web thickness at the point. This may require web thinning. Correct web thinning, when it becomes necessary, is important for satisfactory drilling.

To thin the web of a drill, hold the drill lightly to the face of a round-faced wheel, as shown in figure 5-26A, and thin the web for a short distance behind the cutting lip and into the flutes. This is shown in figure 5-26B. Notice that the cutting lip is actually (but only slightly) ground back, reducing its included angle only a very little and not enough to affect the operation of the drill.

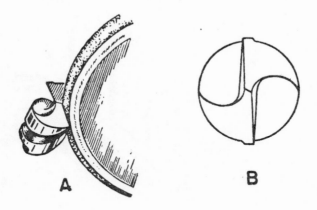

A   B

Figure 5-26.—Thinning the web
of a twist drill.

SHARPENING TWIST DRILL
BY MACHINE

Sharpening a twist drill by hand is a skill that is mastered only after much practice and careful attention to the details. Therefore, whenever possible, use a tool grinder in which the drills can be properly positioned, clamped in place and set with precision for the various angles. This machine grinding (fig. 5-27) will enable you to sharpen the drills accurately. As a result, they will last longer and will produce more accurate holes.

Whether you are sharpening a drill by hand or by machine, it is very necessary that the temperature at the point be kept down. As the point gets hot, it approaches the temperature at which the temper of the steel will be drawn.

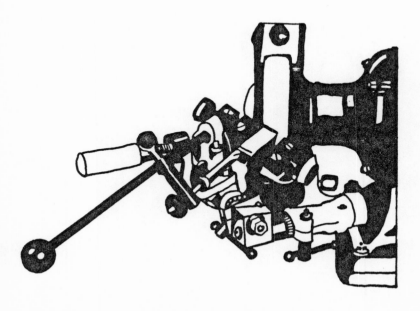

Figure 5-27.—Sharpening a twist drill
with a tool grinder.

Keep the point cool enough to be held in your bare hand. Do this by making a few light passes over the grinding wheel. Take a few seconds to let the point cool and repeat alternate grinding and cooling.

Once you notice the appearance of a blue temper color at the point, it is too late. You have drawn the temper and the steel is now too soft to hold a cutting edge. Then the only thing you can do is to continue the sharpening process, first one lip and then the other, until you have finally ground away the soft tip of the drill. This means that you must grind away all that portion of the tip which is blue. As the blue color indicates softness throughout the entire point of the drill, and not only on the blue surface, resharpening must be continued until all of the blue-colored metal has been ground away. This operation must be done very slowly and carefully, keeping the point cool to prevent continual bluing of the metal.

CHAPTER 6
METAL CUTTING
OPERATIONS

Many handtools and power tools have been designed for the specific purpose of cutting metals quickly and accurately. This chapter will describe some metal cutting operations that can be performed with chisels, drills, taps, dies, reamers, and pipe and tubing cutters.

METAL CUTTING WITH CHISELS

When struck with a heavy hammer, a cold chisel is capable of cutting metal. With chisel and hammer, you can cut wires, bars, rods and other shapes of metal and also cut off the heads of rivets and bolts.

CUTTING WIRE OR ROUND STOCK

Mark off a guideline on the stock and place the work on the top face of an anvil or other suitable working surface. Place the cutting edge of the chisel on the mark in a vertical position and lightly strike the chisel with a hammer. Check the chisel mark for accuracy. Continue to strike the chisel until the cut is made. The last few blows of the hammer should be made lightly to avoid damage to the anvil, supporting surface or to the chisel.

Heavy stock is cut in the same manner except that the cut is made halfway through the stock; the work is then turned over and the cut finished from the opposite side.

CUTTING OFF A RIVET OR BOLT HEAD

Hold the work in a heavy vise or secure it some other way so that the work will not move. (See fig. 6-1A.) Hold the cold chisel with one face of the bevel flat on the surface of the job. Strike the head of the chisel with the hammer as you loosely hold and guide the chisel.

To cut off a rivet head with a cape chisel, select a chisel of about the same size as the diameter of the rivet. Cut through the center of the rivet head, holding one face of the bevel flat on the surface of the job, and then sever the center of the head from the shank or body, as shown in figure 6-1B.

To cut off a rivet head with a side cutting chisel, place the chisel nearly flat on the surface of the work with its single bevel upwards. Drive the cutting edge under the edge of the rivet head just as you would if you were using a cold chisel. (See fig. 6-2A). Notice in figure 6-2B that the cutting edge of the chisel has a slight radius which will tend to prevent the corners from cutting undesirable grooves in the surface of the work.

To remove a rivet head (fig. 6-3) when there is not room enough to swing a hammer with sufficient force to cut the rivet, first drill a hole about the size of the body of the rivet in and almost to the bottom of the rivet head. Then cut off the head with a cold chisel.

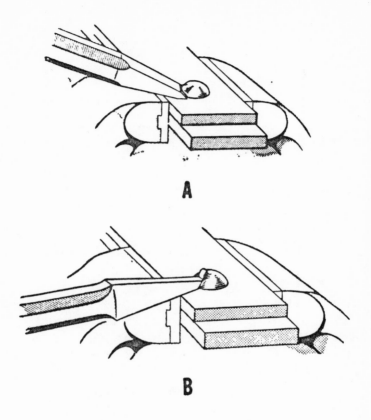

A

B

Figure 6-1.—Cutting off a rivet head
with a chisel

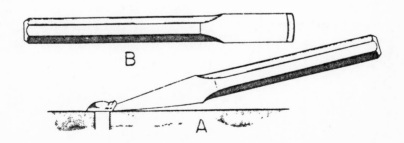

B

A

Figure 6-2.—Cutting off a rivet head
with a side cutting chisel.

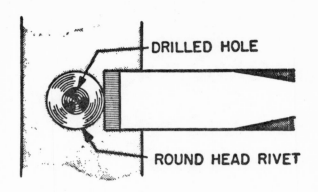

DRILLED HOLE

ROUND HEAD RIVET

Figure 6-3.—Removing a rivet
head in a hard to reach position.

METAL CUTTING WITH DRILLS

In drilling any metal, there are several general steps to be followed. First, mark the exact location of the hole. Second, secure the work properly. Then, use the correct cutting speed and appropriate cutting oil or other coolant, where applicable. Finally, apply pressure on the drill properly. It is assumed that you have selected the correct drill size.

LOCATING THE HOLE

The exact location of the hole must be marked with a center punch. The punch mark forms a seat for the drill point, thus ensuring accuracy. Without the punch mark, the drill may have a tendency to "walk off" before it begins to cut into the metal.

HOLDING THE WORK

Most work is held for drilling by some mechanical means such as a vise or clamps. It is MANDATORY that the work be WELL SECURED.

326

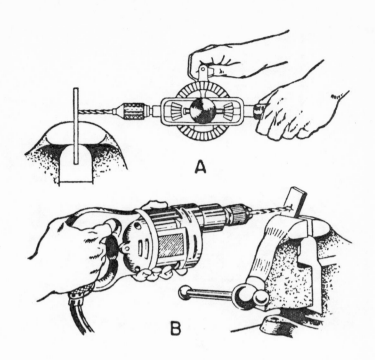

Figure 6-4.—Holding small pieces
in a vise for drilling.

When drilling in small pieces with a hand
held drill, it is best to hold the work in a vise
so that the axis of the drill is horizontal (fig.
6-4). This position provides better control of
the drilling operation and will tend to ensure a
hole which will be square with the surface of the
work.

When drilling in small pieces with a drill
press, hold the work either in a drill press
vise (fig. 6-5), or between V-blocks (fig. 6-6).
CAUTION: BE SURE TO FASTEN THE DRILL
PRESS VISE OR V-BLOCK TO THE DRILL
PRESS TABLE.

When using a drill press to drill holes in the
end of round stock, place the stock in one of the
V-grooves in the stationary jaw of the drill vise
as shown in figure 6-7. These V-grooves will

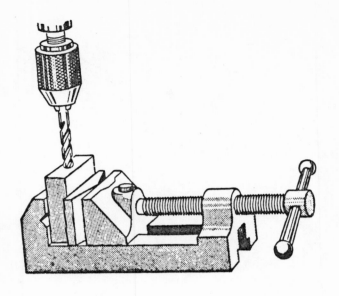

Figure 6-5.—Holding work with
a drill press vise.

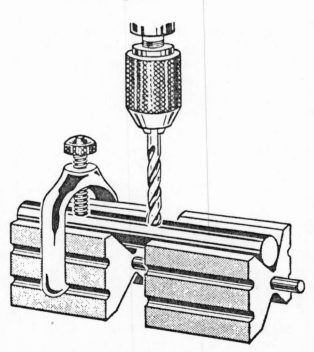

Figure 6-6.—Holding work
in V-blocks.

328

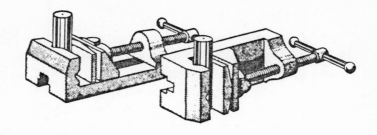

Figure 6-7.—Holding work to drill holes in the end of round stock.

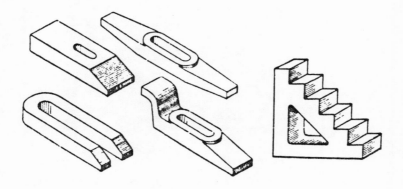

Figure 6-8.—Step block and clamps.

hold the work perpendicular to the table of the drill press. The drilled hole will then be parallel with the axis of the round stock.

Drilling holes in large pieces can be accomplished by holding the work with a step block and clamps (fig. 6-8). A piece of metal of suitable size, with a hole drilled near one end makes a suitable substitute for a clamp.

When holding work with step blocks and clamps, you may use a gooseneck clamp as shown in figure 6-9. Notice that the body of the clamp is approximately parallel with the surface of the drill press table and that the bolt is held close to the work rather than close to the step block. This setup provides the most

329

favorable mechanical advantage. Usually, two or more clamps are used on each setup.

If you are required to hold thin metal, place it on a block of wood to provide support directly beneath the intended hole. This support will also help minimize drill breakage when the feed pressure is applied. Secure the C-clamp as shown in figure 6-10 and drill through the metal and into the wood. Stop drilling when wood chips appear.

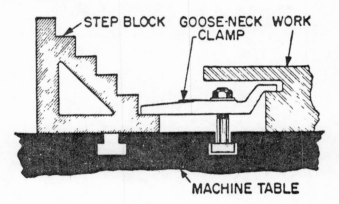

Figure 6-9.—Holding work with step block and clamp for drilling.

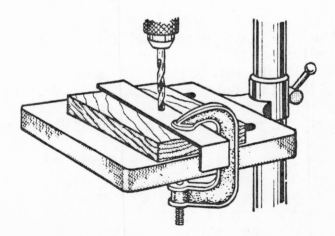

Figure 6-10.—Holding thin gage metal for drilling.

330

Diameter of Drill	Soft Metals 300 F.P.M.	Annealed Cast Iron 140 F.P.M.	Mild Steel 100 F.P.M.	Malleable Iron 90 F.P.M.	Hard Cast Iron 80 F.P.M.	Tool or Hard Steel 60 F.P.M.	Alloy Steel Cast Steel 40 F.P.M.
$\frac{1}{16}$ (No. 53 to 80)	18320	8554	6111	5500	4889	3667	2445
$\frac{3}{32}$ (No. 42 to 52)	12212	5702	4077	3666	3258	2442	1649
$\frac{1}{8}$ (No. 31 to 41)	9160	4278	3056	2750	2445	1833	1222
$\frac{5}{32}$ (No. 23 to 30)	7328	3420	2444	2198	1954	1465	977
$\frac{3}{16}$ (No. 13 to 22)	6106	2852	2037	1833	1630	1222	815
$\frac{7}{32}$ (No. 1 to 12)	5234	2444	1745	1575	1396	1047	698
$\frac{1}{4}$ (A to E)	4575	2139	1527	1375	1222	917	611
$\frac{9}{32}$ (G to K)	4071	1900	1356	1222	1084	814	542
$\frac{5}{16}$ (L, M, N)	3660	1711	1222	1100	978	733	489
$\frac{11}{32}$ (O to R)	3330	1554	1110	1000	888	666	444
$\frac{3}{8}$ (S, T, U)	3050	1426	1018	917	815	611	407
$\frac{13}{32}$ (V to Z)	2818	1316	939	846	752	563	376
$\frac{7}{16}$	2614	1222	873	786	698	524	349
$\frac{15}{32}$	2442	1140	814	732	652	488	326
$\frac{1}{2}$	2287	1070	764	688	611	458	306
$\frac{9}{16}$	2035	950	678	611	543	407	271
$\frac{5}{8}$	1830	856	611	550	489	367	244
$\frac{11}{16}$	1665	777	555	500	444	333	222
$\frac{3}{4}$	1525	713	509	458	407	306	204

Figures are for High-Speed Drills. The speed of Carbon Drills should be reduced one-half. Use drill speed nearest to figure given.

Table 6-1.—Drill Speeds in R.P.M

SPEED INFORMATION

The correct cutting speed for metal drilling depends upon the type of metal and its properties plus the diameter and type of drill (high speed or carbon). See Table 6-1.

DRILLING HINTS

It is necessary to use a cutting oil to lubricate and cool the drill when drilling steel and wrought iron. Cast iron, aluminum, brass and other soft metals may be drilled dry, although at high drilling speeds it is advisable to use some medium to cool these metals. Compressed air, water, and lard oil are examples of such cooling media. Be sure to use goggles whenever you use compressed air.

Always apply pressure on a line which goes straight through the axis of the drill. (Side pressure will enlarge the hole and can break the drill.)

Keep the drill steady and apply enough pressure to keep it cutting. Too much pressure will overload the motor; too little pressure will merely cause the drill to "polish" instead of cut. This will quickly dull the cutting edges of the drill. You will know the pressure is correct when the drill bites continuously without overloading the drill motor.

When drilling large holes, do it in stages. A pilot hole is a good idea, since it serves as a guide for the larger drill and helps to increase accuracy.

THREADS AND THREAD CUTTING

Threads are helical ridges cut into screws, nuts, bolts, or the walls of a hole, so that the action of turning the screw, nut, or bolt gives it endwise as well as rotary motion.

Many thread types exist. These types include bolt threads, machine screw threads and pipe threads. Before we proceed with descriptions of thread cutting procedures, we must become familiar with the terminology to be used.

THREAD TERMINOLOGY

Refer to figure 6-11 and note that the outside diameter of a thread is known as the MAJOR DIAMETER. The diameter across the roots of the thread is called the MINOR DIAMETER. The PITCH is defined as the distance from any point on the thread of a screw to the corresponding point on an adjacent thread. It is usually measured from crest to crest and is expressed by a specific quantity of threads per inch.

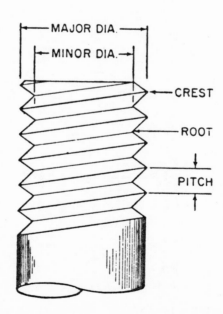

Figure 6-11.—Thread
terminology.

333

TAP DRILL DETERMINATION

If a threaded hole is to be made in a piece of metal, a hole of suitable size must first be drilled. The hole must be somewhat smaller than the size of the bolt to be screwed into it.

How do you determine how much smaller to drill this hole? Figure 6-12 shows the system used for figuring this. The resultant thread is known as a "75% thread" because the diameter of the hole is 75% of the difference between the major and minor diameters, subtracted from the major diameter.

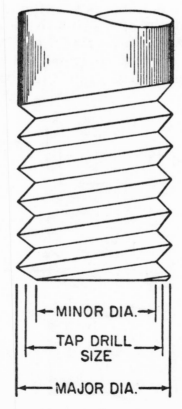

Figure 6-12.—Tap drill size determination.

When the tap hole is the right size, it is a little larger than the root diameter of the tap as shown in figure 6-13. The tap will cut a thread in the work which is only 75 percent as deep as the thread on the tap. The other 25 percent of the depth of thread on the tap provides clearance between the tap hole and the root diameter of the tap. (See fig. 6-14.) This makes tapping easier.

If the tap drill selected is oversize, the tap hole will be oversize, and the tap can cut only shallow threads in the work. (See fig. 6-14.) With less than a full 75 percent depth of thread, stud or capscrew threads usually strip.

If the tap drill selected is undersize, the tap hole will be undersize, being perhaps equal to the root diameter of the tap as shown in figure 6-15. Then there will be no clearance, and the tap will turn hard, tear the threads, and probably break.

The best method to determine the exact size of tap drill to use is to refer to Table 6-2. A chart similar to this generally is included with a set of taps and dies.

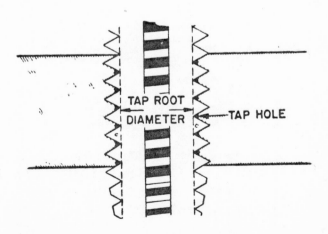

Figure 6-13.—Proper size drilled hole for tapping.

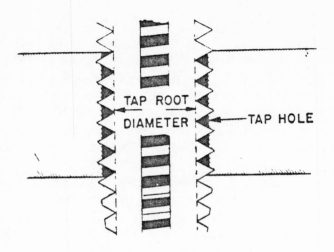

Figure 6-14.—Oversize drilled hole
for tapping.

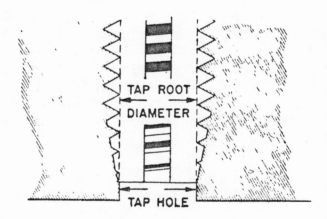

Figure 6-15.—Undersize drilled
hole for tapping.

The working drawing shown in figure 6-16 specifies a 1/2 in. 13 National Coarse (NC) thread to be tapped in a through hole in one part (1/2 in. deep hole in 1/2 in. stock). The same thread is to be tapped in a blind hole in another part (3/4 in. deep hole in 1 in. stock). The 1/2 in. round stock is to be threaded with this same thread to fit the tapped holes.

Refer to Table 6-2 and run down the first two columns until you locate 1/2—13 N.C. Follow this line to the right until you come to the tap drill size, 27/64 in. which will produce approximately a 75 percent full thread. Use the 27/64 in. drill to drill a through hole in the 1/2 in. block and a hole 3/4 in. deep in the 1-in. block as required by the working drawing.

(Thread and Tap Drill Sizes)

Nominal size	Thr'd series	Major diameter inches	Root diameter, inches	Tap drill to produce approx. 75% full thread	Decimal equivalent of tap drill
0-80	N. F.	.0600	.0438	3/64	.0469
1-64	N. C.	.0730	.0527	53	.0595
72	N. F.	.0730	.0550	53	.0595
2-56	N. C.	.0860	.0628	50	.0700
64	N. F.	.0860	.0657	50	.0700
3-48	N. C.	.0990	.0719	47	.0785
56	N. F.	.0990	.0758	45	.0820
4-40	N. C.	.1120	.0795	43	.0890
48	N. F.	.1120	.0849	42	.0935
5-40	N. C.	.1250	.0925	38	.1015
44	N. F.	1250	.0955	37	.1040
6-32	N. C.	.1380	.0974	36	.1065
40	N. F.	.1380	.1055	33	.1130
8-32	N. C.	.1640	.1234	29	.1360
36	N. F.	.1640	.1279	29	.1360
10-24	N. C.	.1900	.1359	25	.1495
32	N. F.	1900	.1494	21	.1590
12-24	N. C.	2160	.1619	16	.1770
28	N. F.	.2160	.1696	14	.1820
1/4-20	N. C.	2500	1850	7	.2010
28	N. F.	.2500	.2036	3	.2130
5/16-18	N. C.	.3125	.2403	F	.2570
24	N. F.	.3125	.2584	I	.2720
3/8-16	N. C.	.3750	.2938	5/16	.3125
24	N. F.	.3750	3209	Q	.3320
7/16-14	N. C.	.4375	.3447	U	.3680
20	N. F.	4375	3726	25/64	.3906
1/2-13	N. C.	.5000	.4001	27/64	.4219
20	N. F.	.5000	4351	29/64	.4531
9/16-12	N. C.	.5625	.4542	31/64	.4844
18	N. F.	5625	.4903	33/64	.5156
5/8-11	N. C.	.6250	.5069	17/32	.5312
18	N. F.	.6250	.5528	37/64	.5781
3/4-10	N. C.	.7500	.6201	21/32	.6562
16	N. F.	.7500	.6688	11/16	.6875
7/8-9	N. C.	.8750	.7307	49/64	.7656
14	N. F.	.8750	.7822	13/16	.8125
1-8	N. C.	1.0000	8376	7/8	.8750
14	N. F.	1.0000	9072	15/16	.9375

Table 6-2.—American National Form Threads

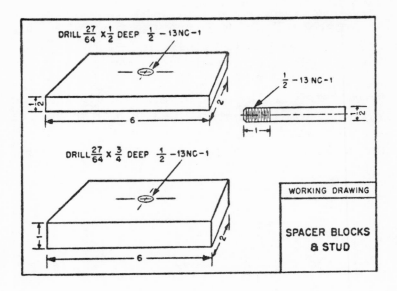

Figure 6-16.—A working drawing for tapping and cutting threads.

CUTTING MACHINE THREADS WITH TAPS

A 50-50 mixture of white lead and lard oil, applied with a small brush, is highly recommended as a lubricant when tapping in steel. When using this lubricant, tighten the tap in the tap wrench and apply the lubricant to the tap. Start the tap carefully with its axis on the center line of the hole. The tap must be square with the surface of the work, as shown in figure 6-17.

To continue tapping, turn the tap forward two quarter turns, back it up a quarter turn to break the chips, and then turn forward again to take up the slack. Continue this sequence until the required threads are cut. After you cut for the first 2 or 3 full turns, you no longer have to exert downward pressure on the wrench. You can tell by the feel that the tap is cutting as you turn it. Don't permit chips to clog the flutes or

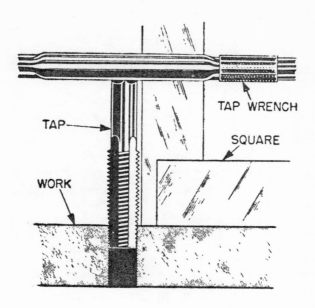

Figure 6-17.—Using a square to ascertain
a tap is square with the work.

they will prevent the tap from turning. When
the tap won't turn and you notice a springy feel-
ing, stop trying immediately. Back the tap up a
quarter turn to break the chips, clean them out
of the flutes with a wire as shown in figure 6-18,
add some more lubricant, and continue tapping.
When the tap has cut threads through the hole,
the tap will turn with no resistance.

To tap a blind hole, start with the taper tap.
For a blind hole you will need all three types—
the taper, plug, and bottoming taps. Be sure
they are the size and thread series you need,
and that the tap hole is the size called for by
the working drawing and Table 6-2.

Begin with the taper tap. Handle it as described and shown before. Figure 6-19A shows
the taper tap just starting to cut. In figure
6-19B it has cut a little farther. In figure 6-19C
it has bottomed in the hole after having cut sev-

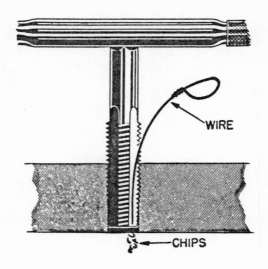

Figure 6-18.—Using a wire to
clear chips from flute
of a tap.

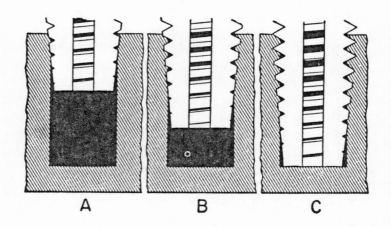

Figure 6-19.—Tapping a blind hole with
a taper tap.

eral full threads near the top of the hole. This completes the work to be done with the taper tap.

In figure 6-20A the plug tap has entered the few full threads cut by the taper tap. At figure 6-20B it has continued these threads a little farther down into the hole. At figure 6-20C it has bottomed in the hole. This is all the work that you can do with the plug tap. It has cut full threads about halfway down the tap hole before bottoming.

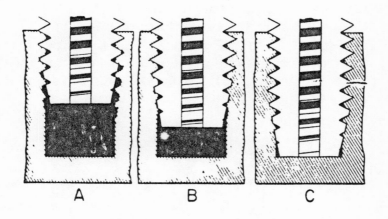

Figure 6-20.—Tapping a blind hole
with a plug tap.

In figure 6-21 the bottoming tap has been substituted for the plug tap. In figure 6-21A it has been run down the full threads cut by the plug tap and is ready to cut more full threads. In figure 6-21B it has cut a few more threads, and in figure 6-21C it has bottomed in the hole. The blind hole has now been completely tapped.

Because these threads are being tapped in a blind hole, chip removal must be done differently. To remove chips, back the tap completely out of the hole very frequently, invert the stock, if possible, and jar out the chips or work them out of the hole with a wire while the stock is in the inverted position. If the work cannot be inverted, blow out the chips with air. Whenever you use air, BE SURE TO USE SAFETY GOGGLES. Chip removal in tapping blind holes is much more difficult to do and is very important because chips will fall ahead of the tap through the flutes and accumulate in the bottom of the blind hole. Until these chips are removed, none of the three taps can complete its work. In tapping blind holes alternate with tapping and chip removal until each of the three taps bottom in the blind hole.

When you have finished using the three taps, brush the chips out of their teeth, oil them well with lubricating oil, wipe off the surplus oil, and replace them in the threading set.

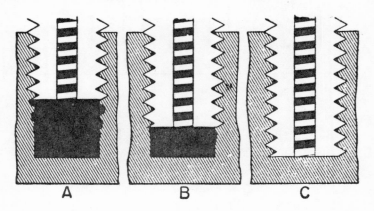

Figure 6-21.—Finish tapping a blind hole with a bottoming tap.

CUTTING MACHINE THREADS WITH DIES

To cut threads on a piece of round stock, first grind a chamfer on the end of the rod as shown in the working drawing in figure 6-16. Then hold the rod vertically in the vise to cut the threads. The working drawing in figure 6-16 calls for a 1/2-13N.C.-1 thread. The 1/2 signifies diameter and the 13 the number of threads per inch. The figure 1 after the N.C. indicates that a class 1 fit is required. A class 1 fit is a loose fit. The fit is controlled while threading the round stock. We tap the threads in the hole first as there is no way to adjust a tap. However, as threading dies are usually adjustable, we can control the fit of the threaded rod in the tapped hole by adjusting the threading die.

The adjustable round split die shown in figure 6-22 has an adjusting screw at A. By tightening this screw and spreading the die slightly, it will cut less deeply into the rod and the fit in the tapped hole will be tighter. The shallow hole at B is placed in the die stock opposite the adjustable handle E and serves as a drive hole. Also, when the adjustable handle is tightened, it holds the split die together and against the adjusting screw to maintain the setting while the die is cutting. The threads or cutting teeth of the die are chamfered or relieved at C to help start the die squarely on the round stock. The die is put into the die stock with the face with the unchamfered teeth against the shoulder, D.

Figure 6-23 is a plain round split die and die stock. At A, where the die is split, there is no adjusting screw. There are shallow holes at B and C, on both sides of the split, opposite which there are setscrews in the die stock at D and E. F is the adjusting screw which is pointed and enters the split A in the die. D and E are the holding setscrews. They have flat points and are tightened after the setting is made with F. D and E hold the adjustment and furnish the drive as they enter the shallow holes B and C shown in figure 6-23.

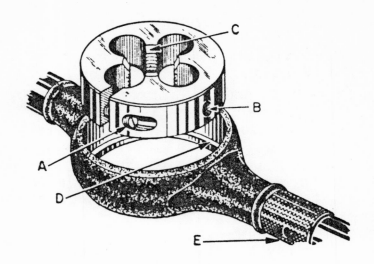

Figure 6-22.—Assembling an
adjustable round split die
to diestock.

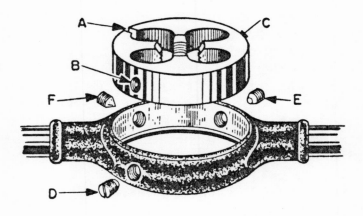

Figure 6-23.—Assembling a plain
round split die to diestock.

Figure 6-24 shows a section of the die in
the die stock and its relation to the chamfer on
the end of the work. The taper on the face of
the die will accept the chamfer on the end of the
work to start the threads square with the common center line.

344

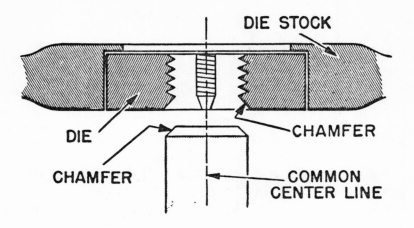

Figure 6-24.—Position of diestock in relation
to chamfer on end of work.

To thread the work, brush some 50-50 white lead and lard oil on the rod. Start the die square with the work. Hold one handle with each hand, apply downward pressure, and turn clockwise until you feel the thread has been started. When the die has started to cut, rotate the die stock two quarter turns, back it off one quarter turn to break the chips, and repeat the cutting (fig. 6-25). When you have cut enough threads so that the rod comes through the back of the die, remove the die and try the rod in the tapped hole.

Adjusting a threading die to produce a thread of the proper fit is a trial-and-error procedure. This was a trial run. If the fit is too loose, cut off and discard the portion of the rod that you threaded. Then expand the die by tightening the pointed setscrews (or the adjusting screw) so that the die will cut shallower threads on the rod and produce a tighter fit.

If the fit is too tight, it will not be necessary to discard the threaded portion of the rod. Contract the die by backing off (loosening) the pointed setscrew (or the adjusting screw) to decrease the size of the split in the die. This will cause the die to remove more metal, when cutting, and produce a looser fit. Then run the die down the cut threads that were too tight. Now test the fit again by turning the threaded end into the tapped hole.

When you have finished the threading job, remove the die from the die stock, carefully clean out all the loose chips, and apply plenty of oil. Wipe off the surplus oil and put the die and die stock away in the threading set where it will be protected and ready for the next job.

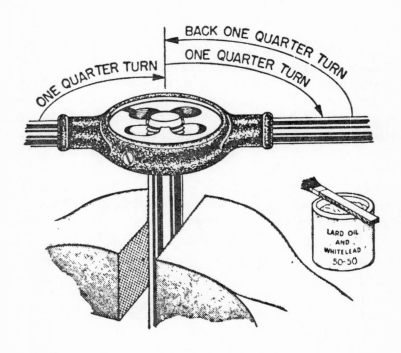

Figure 6-25.—Cutting outside threads on round stock.

RECONDITIONING
MACHINE THREADS

To recondition machine threads, when the damage is not serious, the general practice is to select the proper threading die, one type of which is shown in figure 6-26A. Start the die with the chamfered face of the die which is shown in the figure. Put it in a die stock, and run over the threads that are damaged. For steel, lubricate with a 50-50 mixture of white

A   B

Figure 6-26.—Two thread reconditioning tools.

lead and lard oil, lard oil alone, or lubricating oil if the others are not available. Use no lubricant for brass and copper.

The screw and bolt rethreading die, shown in figure 6-26B, is designed especially for reconditioning threads. The six sets of cutting teeth, in place of the customary four sets on a threading die, provide better alignment while the die is recutting damaged threads. Turn this rethreading die with any type of wrench or hold the die in a vise and turn the threaded piece through it.

When only the first thread or the first 2 or 3 threads are damaged, and a perfect thread is not absolutely necessary, a three-square file can be used to touch up the tops of the damaged threads.

The thread restorer shown in figure 6-27 resembles a square file. Each face is designed to match a certain pitch-screw thread. Two sizes of this tool are available, each one covering eight different machine-thread pitches. Together they cover a range of from 9 threads per inch through 32 threads per inch. Use this thread restorer as you would a file, maintaining the proper angle (that of the threads) as you go over the damaged threads.

Figure 6-27.—Thread restorer.

Tools of this type are available for external pipe threads as well as for machine threads. The thread restorer for internal pipe threads, however, is similar to a tap. This type of thread restorer, whether internal or external, removes metal. Therefore, the thread that remains as a restored thread will not be a perfect or full thread. Where the crest of the original thread was battered over, the crest of the restored thread will be noticeably flat. Threads restored in this manner are, for practical purposes, as strong as new threads and will again enter a nut or tapped hole.

Another type of thread restorer is shown in figure 6-28. This tool is not designed to cut new threads, but only as a maintenance and repair tool. Its action is a reforming action and not a cutting action. Therefore no metal is removed from the thread that is being forced back to its original shape.

Only four sizes of this tool are necessary to cover thread diameters from one-quarter

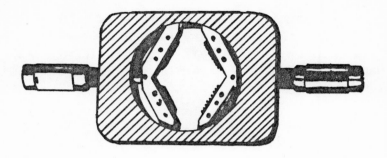

Figure 6-28.—Adjustable thread restorer.

inch to 6 inches. A fifth size takes all diameters from 6 to 12 inches, inclusive. Each size will fit any pitch, left- or right-hand threads, standard pipe or machine thread, within the size limits specified, and no change of blades or dies is necessary. This restorer will not work on Acme threads.

To operate this thread restorer, simply slip it over the threads with the arrow on top, or toward you. Then tighten the jaws or blades to a snug fit into the threads close to the back of the thread where no damage has been done. Then, just as you would remove a nut, turn the tool counterclockwise in the direction of the arrow on right-hand threads. To restore left-hand threads, first flop the tool over so that the face of the tool having the arrow is away from you. Then, after bringing the jaws up snug, run the tool off of the left-hand threads by turning it clockwise so that it will move toward you. Notice that this type of thread restorer normally works from the bottom or back of the thread out toward the end, restoring the threads as it progresses.

In most cases, resotrers slide easily over key ways and milled flats on threaded parts. It may be found that the milled flat is rather wide on large-diameter jobs. In such cases threads can still be restored and the tool will negotiate the flat if you will clamp a half round piece of soft wood on the flat and operate the tool as directed. When this is necessary, it is usually on work of 2-inch diameter or larger. When used on studs or bolts having cotter pin holes, a small wooden plug in the hole will avoid breaking teeth. Keep the restorer clean and well oiled both in use and in storage.

CUTTING INTERNAL PIPE THREADS

Pipe threads are tapered threads to provide an airtight and liquidtight joint. A 3/8" machine thread tap and a 3/8" pipe thread tap are compared in figure 6-29 show their differences. The 3/8" machine thread tap will cut machine threads in a hole so that a 3/8" cap screw, having the same thread can be screwed into the hole. The 3/8" pipe thread tap will cut pipe threads in a hole so that a 3/8" threaded pipe can be screwed into the hole. Because pipe diameters are measured and given as inside diameters, and the wall thickness of the pipe must be taken into consideration, the 3/8" pipe thread tap in figure 6-29 is noticeably larger than the 3/8" machine thread tap. It should also be noted that the pipe thread tap is tapered, but the machine thread tap is not.

The N.P.T., which formerly stood for National Pipe Thread, is still used as a carryover and now refers to the new name for the same thread, American Standard Taper Pipe Thread. This standard taper is 3/4" per foot.

To select the proper tap drill for the pipe tap that you will use to tap a hole to take a

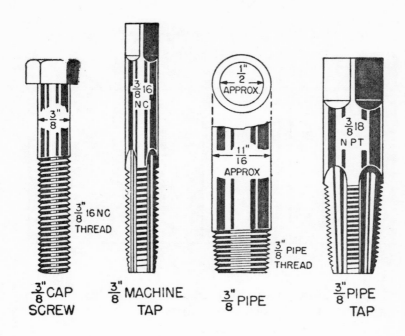

Figure 6-29.—Comparison of machine
thread tap and pipe thread tap.

given size of threaded pipe, refer to table 6-3.
For example, if you want to drill and tap a hole
to take a 3/8" pipe thread, find the 3/8" pipe
tap in the Pipe Tap Size column. Opposite this,
in the Tap Drill Size column, is 19/32", the
proper tap drill to use for a 3/8" pipe tap.

To cut internal pipe threads, drill a tap hole
in the stock to be tapped and, following the sug-
gested procedure for tapping machine threads
described earlier in the chapter under the
heading Cutting Machine Threads With Taps,
run the pipe tap into the tap hole. Notice that
the first few threads on the pipe tap are ground
away. This makes starting easier. Plenty of
lard oil is the standard lubricant for steel. Tap
copper and brass with no lubricant. The depth
to which it is desirable to tap pipe threads is
usually determined by turning the threaded pipe

Table 6-3.—American Standard Pipe Tap Drill Sizes

Pipe Tap Size	Tap Drill Size	Pipe Tap Size	Tap Drill Size
⅛	11⁄32	2	2³⁄₁₆
¼	⁷⁄₁₆	2½	2⅝
⅜	19⁄32	3	3¼
½	23⁄32	3½	3¾
¾	15⁄16	4	4¼
1	1 5⁄32	4½	4¾
1¼	1½	5	5⁵⁄₁₆
1½	1 23⁄32	6	6⅜

into the tapped hole for a trial. As shown in figure 6-30, the last few threads on the pipe should still be visible when the pipe is drawn up tight in the tapped hole. Figure 6-30 shows the values of dimension A (the length of thread on pipe required to make a tight joint) for various sizes of pipe up to 12".

The general practice in tapping holes for pipe threads is to drill the proper size tap hole and then start the pipe tap right into the tap hole. Some men recommend using a pipe reamer, especially when large deep holes are to be tapped. A pipe reamer has the same 3/4" per foot taper as a pipe tap. A reamed pipe tap hole would have the same shape as the pipe tap, and therefore would make tapping easier and reduce wear on the tap.

CUTTING EXTERNAL PIPE THREADS

Usually, both ends of a pipe are threaded with external pipe threads. Notice, in all the figures showing pipe threads, that they are V-shaped. The standard 3/4" taper per foot of pipe threads is equal to 1/16" per inch. Therefore, the taper of the threads on each side of

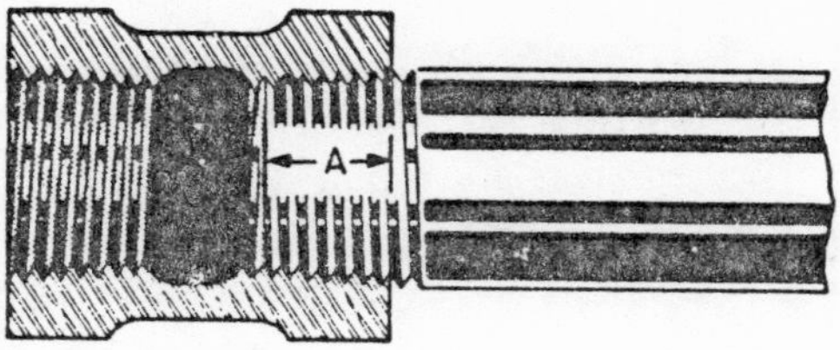

Size of Pipe, Inches	Dimension A, Inches	Size of Pipe, Inches	Dimension A, Inches	Size of Pipe, Inches	Dimension A, Inches
1/8	1/4	1 1/2	11/16	5	1 1/4
1/4	3/8	2	3/4	6	1 5/16
3/8	3/8	2 1/2	15/16	7	1 3/8
1/2	1/2	3	1	8	1 7/16
3/4	9/16	3 1/2	1 1/16	9	1 1/2
1	11/16	4	1 1/8	10	1 5/8
1 1/4	11/16	4 1/2	1 3/16	12	1 3/4

Figure 6-30.—Length of thread on pipe required to make a tight joint.

the pipe is 1/32" taper per inch. This taper cannot be changed. This produces a tight joint. The angle between sides of the threads is 60°, and several threads on the end of the pipe are perfect threads. The next few have V-bottoms but flat tops, and the last few threads have both flat tops and bottoms. Each size of pipe has a certain number of threads per inch, built into the pipe taps and dies.

Adjustable pipe dies have a reference mark on each die which, when lined up with the corresponding reference mark on the die stock, will give a standard-size thread. You adjust the dies one way or the other from the reference mark to cut a thread with the fit you want.

To cut external threads on iron pipe, first determine its nominal size. Nominal size means the "name size" of the pipe such as

1/8", 3/4", and so on. Except in the sizes below 1", nominal sizes correspond closely to inside diameters. For 1" pipe and larger, measure the inside diameter (I.D.) with your rule, to the closest 1/32", and you will have nominal size. For sizes below 1", you can determine nominal size by measuring the outside diameter (O.D.) to the nearest 1/32" and reading the corresponding nominal size in Table 6-4. This method can also be employed for sizes 1" and above in lieu of the I.D. measurement.

To begin cutting, put the die stock on the pipe so that the pipe passes through the guide and enters the tapered face of the pipe die. Turn the die stock clockwise for right-hand

Table 6-4.—Approximate O.D. of Standard Wrought Iron Pipe

Nominal Size	Outside Diameter	Nominal Size	Outside Diameter
1/8	$1\frac{3}{32}$	3½	4
1/4	$1\frac{7}{32}$	4	4½
3/8	$1\frac{1}{16}$	4½	5
1/2	$2\frac{7}{32}$	5	$5\frac{9}{16}$
3/4	$1\frac{1}{16}$	6	$6\frac{5}{8}$
1	$1\frac{5}{16}$	7	$7\frac{5}{8}$
1¼	$1\frac{21}{32}$	8	$8\frac{5}{8}$
1½	$1\frac{29}{32}$	9	$9\frac{5}{8}$
2	$2\frac{3}{8}$	10	$10\frac{3}{4}$
2½	$2\frac{7}{8}$	11	$11\frac{3}{4}$
3	$3\frac{1}{2}$	12	$12\frac{3}{4}$

threads, applying pressure only when starting. It is not necessary to turn the die back and forth as you do when cutting machine threads. Pipe-threading dies can cut continuously because they cut only as many threads on the pipe as there are on the die itself and because there is plenty of room in a pipe die for the chips to escape. After the die has taken hold, it will feed itself. When cutting threads on steel pipe, apply lard oil to the pipe and die where the cutting is actually taking place. Continue turning until the end of the pipe has gone through the die and is flush with the near face. See figure 6-31.

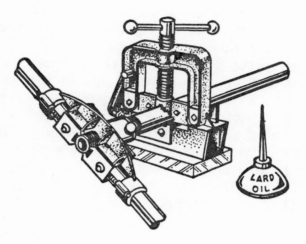

Figure 6-31.—Threading an external pipe thread with a pipe die.

This will give you the length of thread called for in the table in figure 6-30. Notice that, in the assembled pipe joint in figure 6-30 several threads remain on both pipe and fitting to permit further tightening should a leak develop.

REAMING OPERATIONS

Reaming operations are jobs that smoothly enlarge drilled holes to an exact size and finish the hole at the same time. A hole that has been made by drilling is usually slightly oversize. This is quite satisfactory for holes in which bolts or rivets are placed. When greater accuracy and a smooth finish are required, the hole is first drilled undersize and then finished by reaming. Reamers are also used to remove burrs from the insides of pipe.

STRAIGHT HOLES

A solid straight-hole reamer is used for most work, since it is the most accurate and rugged reamer. The straight-hole handreamer is turned by means of a tap wrench that is tightened on the square end of the reamer shank. (See fig. 6-32.) Secure the work in a vise so that the hole to be reamed is perpendicular to the top of the vise jaws. Position the reamer at the top of the hole (fig. 6-33). Straight-hole reamers have a slight taper at the end so that they will fit into the hole easily. Turn the wrench clockwise very slowly until the reamer is centered in the hole.

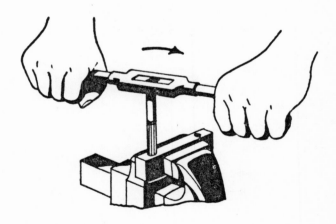

Figure 6-32.—Using a tap wrench
to turn a hand reamer.

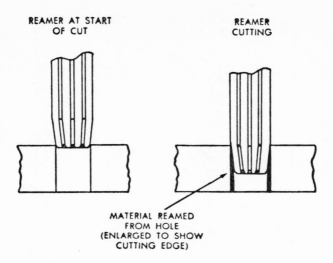

REAMER AT START
OF CUT

REAMER
CUTTING

MATERIAL REAMED
FROM HOLE
(ENLARGED TO SHOW
CUTTING EDGE)

Figure 6-33.—Reaming a hole with
a straight hole reamer.

After the reamer is centered in the hole, turn the wrench clockwise with a steady firm pressure until the reamer has been turned all the way through the hole. When reaming steel, use cutting oil or machine oil to lubricate the tool. When reaming soft iron, do not lubricate the tool. To remove the reamer from the hole turn the wrench clockwise and raise the reamer simultaneously.

NOTE: Turning the wrench too fast or too slowly will cause the reamer to chatter, producing an unevenly reamed hole.

TAPERED HOLES AND PIN INSTALLATION

To install a tapered pin, refer to the blueprint or drawing for the proper size of pin to use. The size will be given as a number and length in inches (table 6-5). For instance, a

Table 6-5.—Standard Taper
Pin Dimensions

NO. OF PIN	DIAMETER AT LARGE END		MAX. LENGTH
	D	D	L
00000	0. 094	³⁄₃₂	¾
0000	. 109	⁷⁄₆₄	⅞
000	. 125	⅛	1
00	. 141	⁹⁄₆₄	1⅛
0	. 156	⁵⁄₃₂	1¼
1	. 172	¹¹⁄₆₄	1¼
2	. 193	³⁄₁₆	1½
3	. 219	⁷⁄₃₂	1¾
4	. 250	¼	2
5	. 289	¹⁹⁄₆₄	2¼
6	. 341	¹¹⁄₃₂	3
7	. 409	¹³⁄₃₂	3¾
8	. 492	½	4½
9	. 591	¹⁹⁄₃₂	5¼
10	. 706	²³⁄₃₂	6
11	. 860	⁵⁵⁄₆₄	7¼
12	1. 032	1¹⁄₃₂	9
13	1. 241	1¹⁵⁄₆₄	11
14	1. 523	1³³⁄₆₄	13

No. 3 pin 1 3/4" long might be specified. Then, when you have the proper pin, measure the diameter of its small end and drill a hole of that size through, for example, the hub of a flange and a shaft while the flange is in place on the shaft. (See fig. 6-34.) Then select the same number of tapered pin reamer, a No. 3 in this case.

Table 6-6 shows specifications of various sizes of reamers. The specifications given opposite the reamer numbers in the left-hand column of table 6-6 are the dimensions of the reamers. The small end of the reamer should just enter the hole you drill and, if the proper size of reamer has been selected, the pin will fit exactly. Turn the tapered pin reamer with a

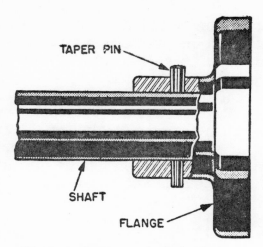

Figure 6-34.—A tapered pin installed in a shaft and flange.

Table 6-6.—Taper Reamer Dimensions

No. of Taper Pin Reamer	Diameter at Large End of Reamer	Diameter at Small End of Reamer	Length of Flute
7/0	0.0666	0.0497	13/16
6/0	0.0806	0.0611	15/16
5/0	0.0966	0.0719	1 3/16
4/0	0.1142	0.0869	1 5/16
3/0	0.1302	0.1029	1 5/16
2/0	0.1462	0.1137	1 9/16
0	0.1638	0.1287	1 11/16
1	0.1798	0.1447	1 11/16
2	0.2008	0.1605	1 15/16
3	0.2294	0.1813	2 5/16
4	0.2604	0.2071	2 9/16
5	0.2994	0.2409	2 13/16
6	0.3540	0.2773	3 11/16
7	0.4220	0.3297	4 7/16
8	0.5050	0.3971	5 3/16
9	0.6066	0.4805	6 1/16
10	0.7216	0.5799	6 13/16

tap wrench slowly and in a clockwise direction only, lifting it out of the hole to clean away the chips while it is still turning. If you reverse the direction of the reamer, chips may be wedged behind its cutting edges, causing them to break. Ream brass dry but apply cutting oil liberally when reaming steel. Try the taper pin in the hole several times as the reaming progresses. Stop reaming when the pin protrudes the same amount on both sides of the hub of the gear.

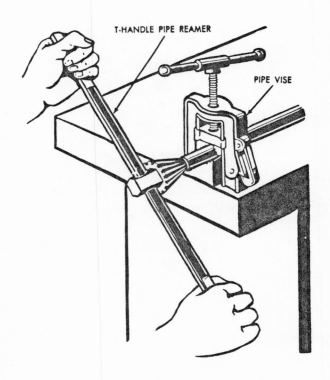

Figure 6-35.—Using a pipe reamer to remove burrs from pipe.

BURR REMOVAL

After a piece of pipe has been cut, the ends should be reamed to remove the burr that is left on the inside of the pipe. This burr, if not removed, will restrict the flow of fluid in the pipe. Besides the pipe reamer you will need a vise to hold the pipe steady. After making sure the pipe is held firmly in the vise, insert the reamer in the end of the pipe and turn the handle. (See fig. 6-35.) Rotate the handle of the reamer clockwise in short even strokes until the burrs inside the cut piece of pipe are completely removed. Remove the reamer from the pipe by rotating it clockwise and reducing applied pressure.

CUTTING PIPING AND TUBING

In performing certain tasks, you may be required to cut pipe or tubing. The main difference between pipe and tubing lies in their wall thicknesses; pipe has thicker walls than tubing. Though pipe cutters are larger than tube cutters, they work on the same principle.

PIPE

You will probably cut more pipes made of iron than any other metal. These pipes must be cut to specific lengths. Before cutting a pipe to length, make sure you have the correct measurement. Figure 6-36 shows three methods of measuring threaded pipe to desired lengths.

The end-to-end method includes measuring the threaded portions of the pipe and measuring the pipe from end to end. The end-to-center method is used on a section of pipe that has a fitting screwed on one end only; measure from the free end of the pipe to the center of the

361

fitting at the other end of the pipe. The center-to-center method is used when both ends of the pipe have fittings; measure from the center of one fitting to the center of the other fitting at the opposite end of the pipe.

The approximate length of thread on 1/2- and 3/4-inch wrought iron or steel pipe is 3/4 inch. On 1-, 1 1/4-, and 1 1/2-inch pipe, it is approximately 1 inch long. On 2- and 2 1/2-inch pipe, the length of thread is 1 1/8 and 1 1/2 inches respectively.

To determine the length of pipe required, take the measurement of installation such as

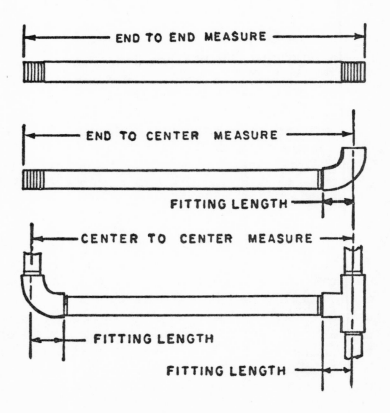

Figure 6-36.—Proper methods for measuring pipe to desired lengths.

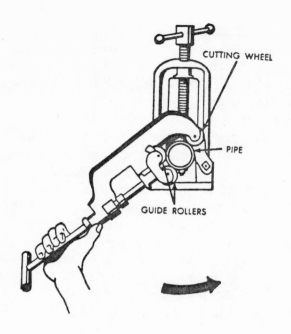

Figure 6-37.—Cutting pipe
with a pipe cutter.

center to center of the pipe requiring two fittings. Measure the size of the fittings as shown in figure 6-36. Subtract the total size of the two fittings from the installation measurement. Multiply the approximate thread length by 2 and add the result to the length obtained. This will give the length of pipe required.

After the length of the pipe has been determined, measure the pipe and mark the spot where the cut is to be made with a scriber or crayon. Lock the pipe securely in a pipe vise.

Inspect the cutter to make sure that there are no nicks or burrs in the cutting wheel. Open the jaws of the cutter by turning the handle counterclockwise. Position the cutter around the pipe at the marked point. Make sure the cutting wheel is exactly on the mark and close

363

the jaws of the cutter lightly against the pipe by turning the cutter handle clockwise. After making contact, turn the cutter handle clockwise one-fourth of a turn more. This will put a bite on the pipe.

Grasp the cutter handle and rotate the cutter as a whole one complete revolution, swinging it around the pipe in the direction indicated in figure 6-37. Turn the cutter handle clockwise one-fourth of a turn more to take another bite on the pipe and rotate the cutter another complete revolution. Keep the cutter perpendicular to the pipe at all times or the wheel will not track properly. Repeat this operation until the pipe is cut. Remove the small shoulder on the outside of the pipe with a file and remove the burr on the inside with a reamer.

STEP ①

SCREW THE CUTTING WHEEL
LIGHTLY AGAINST THE TUBING

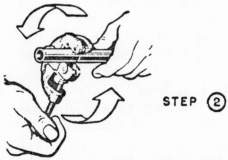

STEP ②

ROTATE THE CUTTER KEEPING A SLIGHT
PRESSURE AGAINST THE CUTTING WHEEL
WITH THE SCREW ADJUSTMENT.

Figure 6-38.—Steps in cutting
tubing with a tube cutter.

TUBING

Copper tubing is one kind of metallic tubing that you can cut readily with a tube cutter. To cut tubing, place the tube cutter with the cutting wheel on the mark where the cut is to be made. Move the cutting wheel into light contact with the tubing. See step 1 in figure 6-38. Then swing the handle around the tubing as you feed the cutting wheel a little for each revolution by turning the screw adjustment. Different wall thicknesses, kinds, and diameters of metallic tubing require different feeds. Step 2, figure 6-38, indicates the direction of rotation. The feed pressure is correct when it keeps the wheel cutting but does not flatten the tubing.

The design of some tubing cutters will permit cutting off a flared end close to the base of the flare. In figure 6-39, notice the groove in the backup roller. Place the flare in this groove so that the cutting wheel rides at the base of the flare. Then cut off the flare as you would cut tubing.

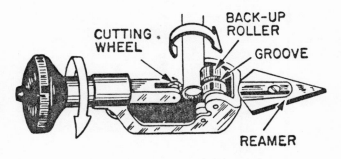

Figure 6-39.—Cutting tubing close to the base of a flare.

Burrs that form may be similar to those formed in pipe cutting. Remove the inside burr with the reamer attached to the tubing cutter opposite the handle (fig. 6-40). In some cases a three-cornered scraper, pocketknife blade, or round file may work better than the reamer. After reaming clean out the chips. Then remove any outside burr with a file.

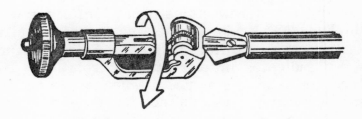

Figure 6-40.—Reaming the burrs from a piece of tubing.

CHAPTER 7

MISCELLANEOUS TASKS

BENDING AND FLARING
METALLIC TUBING

The objective in tube bending is to obtain a smooth bend without flattening the tube. Tube bending is usually accomplished with one of the tube benders discussed in this chapter. In an emergency, however, aluminum tubing under one-fourth of an inch in diameter may be bent by hand.

SPRING BENDERS

External spring-type benders, shown in figure 7-1A, come in sizes to bend 1/4", 5/16", 3/8", 7/16", 1/2", and 5/8" outside-diameter soft copper, aluminum, and other soft metallic tubing. To bend tubing with this type of bender, first select the size that will just slip over the size of tubing you want to bend. Then slip it over the tubing so that it centers at the middle of the proposed bend. Grasp the bender with both hands and make the bend. (See fig. 7-1B.) The restraining action of the bender will prevent the tubing from collapsing at the bend and will produce a smooth curve. To remove the bender, grasp the belled end and pull it off the tubing.

367

Internal spring-type benders, shown in figure 7-1C, come in sizes to bend 3/8", 1/2", and 5/8" outside diameter tubing. This type can be used when both ends of a length of tubing are flared and the external type cannot be applied. To bend tubing with an internal spring-type bender, select the proper size bender and slip it inside of the tubing. Insert it so that the center of its length is at the center of the proposed bend. Grasp the tubing with both hands and make the bend. If the bender sticks out of the end of the tubing, remove it by pulling it out. If not, remove it with a fish wire or other simple means.

HAND TUBE BENDER

The hand tube bender shown in figure 7-2 consists of four parts—handle, radius block

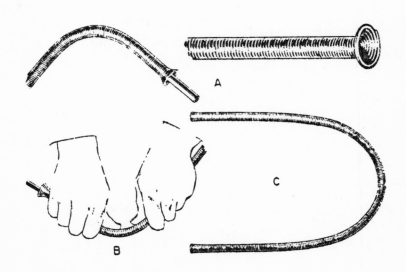

Figure 7-1.—Bending tubing with spring type tube benders.

(mandrel), clip, and slide bar. The radius block is marked in degrees of bend ranging from 0 to 180. The slide bar has a mark which is lined up with the zero mark on the radius block. The tube is inserted in the tool, and after lining up the marks, the slide bar is moved around until the mark on the slide bar reaches the desired degrees of bend on the radius block. Follow the procedure indicated in figure 7-2.

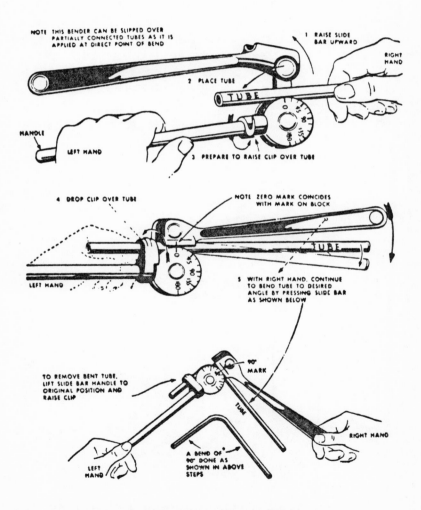

Figure 7-2.—Tube bending.

369

This type of bender is furnished in 3/16", 1/4", 5/16", 3/8", and 1/2" sizes. For larger sizes of tubing similar mandrel-type benders are used. The only difference is that these larger benders are geared for greater mechanical advantage.

FLARING

Tube flaring is a method of forming the end of a tube into a funnel shape so that it can be held by a threaded fitting. A partially threaded flare nut is slipped over the tube, the end of the tube is flared, the flare is seated with the inside of the flare against the end of a fitting which has threads on the outside, and then the flare nut is screwed onto the fitting, pushing the outside of the flare against the seating surface of the fitting.

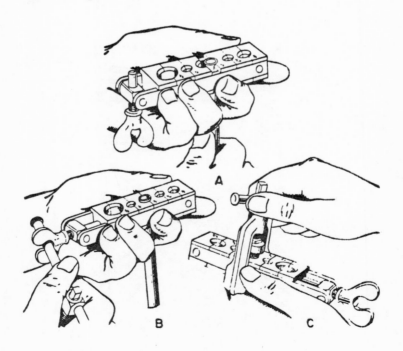

Figure 7-3.—Flaring metallic tubing.

The tube-flaring tool shown in figure 7-3 is one type which is commonly used to flare copper tubing. To flare the end of tubing, first check to see that it has been cut off squarely and has the burrs removed from both inside and outside. Remember to slip the flare nut on the tube before you make the flare. Then, as shown in figure 7-3A, open the flaring tool at the die which corresponds to the size of the tubing being flared. Insert the end of the tubing to protrude slightly above the top face of the die blocks. The amount by which the tubing extends above the blocks determines the finished diameter of the flare. The flare must be large enough so that it will seat properly against the fitting, but small enough so that the threads of the flare nut will slide over it. You determine the correct size by trial-and-error. Then as shown in figure 7-3B, close the die block and secure the tool with the wing nut. Use the handle of the yoke to tighten the wing nut. Then place the yoke over the end of the tubing (fig. 7-3C), and tighten the handle to force the cone into the end of the tubing. The completed flare should be slightly visible above the face of the die blocks.

REMOVING BROKEN BOLTS AND STUDS

When the removal of a broken bolt or stud is required, flood the part being worked on with plenty of penetrating oil or oil of wintergreen. Time permitting, soak the area for several hours or overnight. A week's soaking may loosen a bolt which would otherwise have to be drilled out.

If enough of the broken piece protrudes take hold of it with vise-grip pliers, as shown in figure 7-4, and carefully try to ease it out. If the bolt cannot be turned, further soaking with penetrating oil may help. Or try removing the pliers and jarring the bolt with light hammer blows on the top and around the sides. This may loosen the threads so that the bolt can then be removed with the vise-grip pliers.

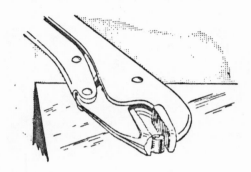

Figure 7-4.—Removing a broken stud with vise-grip pliers.

If a bolt has been broken off flush with the surface as shown in figure 7-5, it is sometimes possible to back it out with light blows of a prick punch or center punch. However, if the bolt was broken due to rusting, this method will not remove it. If it cannot be removed by careful punching first on one side and then the other, a screw and bolt extractor may remove it. (See fig. 7-6B.)

When using this extractor, file the broken portion of the bolt to provide a smooth surface at the center for a punch mark, if possible. Then carefully center punch the exact center of the bolt. (See fig. 7-6A.)

Refer to table 7-1 to select the proper drill size to use according to the size of the broken bolt that you are trying to remove. If possible, drill through the entire length of the broken

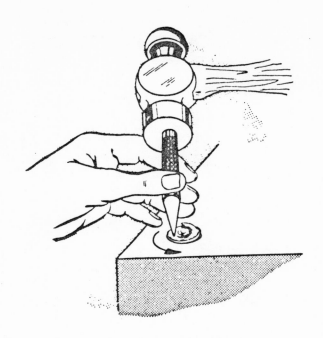

Figure 7-5.—Removing a
broken bolt with a
prick punch.

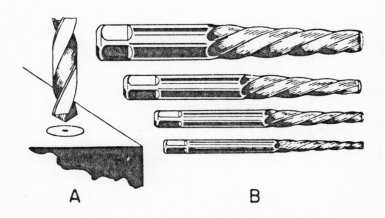

A   B

Figure 7-6.—Screw and bolt extractors
for removing broken studs.

Extractor		Used For—		Use Drill Size Dia., Inches
Size No.	Overall Length, Inches	Nominal Screw And Bolt Size, Inches	Nominal Pipe Size, Inches	
1	2	3/16 - 1/4	--------	5/64
2	2 3/8	1/4 - 5/16	--------	7/64
3	2 11/16	5/16 - 7/16	--------	5/32
4	3	7/16 - 9/16	--------	1/4
5	3 3/8	9/16 - 3/4	1/4	17/64
6	3 3/4	3/4 - 1	3/8	13/32
7	4 1/8	1 - 1 3/8	'1/2	17/32
8	4 3/8	1 3/8 - 1 3/4	3/4	13/16
9	4 5/8	1 3/4 - 2 1/8	1	1 1/16
10	5	2 1/8 - 2 1/2	1 1/4	1 5/16
11	5 5/8	2 1/2 - 3	1 1/2	1 9/16
12	6 1/4	3 - 3 1/2	2	1 15/16

Table 7-1.—Chart for Screw and Bolt Extractors

bolt. Then carefully work some penetrating oil through this hole so that it fills the cavity beneath the bolt and has a chance to work its way upwards from the bottom of the bolt. The more time you let the penetrating oil work from both ends of the broken bolt, the better are your chances of removing it.

When drilling a hole in a stud which has broken off below the surface of the piece which it was holding, as shown in figure 7-7A, a drill guide will center the drill and may be preferred rather than a center punch mark.

When the hole has been drilled, and additional penetrating oil has had time to soak, put the spiral end of the screw and bolt extractor into the hole. Set it firmly with a few light hammer blows and secure the tap wrench as shown in figure 7-7B. Carefully try to back the broken bolt out of the hole. Turn the extractor counterclockwise. (This type of extractor is designed for right hand threads only.)

A screw and bolt extractor can sometimes be used to remove an Allen head capscrew when the socket has been stripped by the Allen wrench. (See fig. 7-8.) When attempting this removal, carefully grind off the end of the extractor so that it will not bottom before the

374

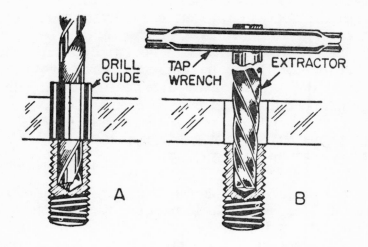

Figure 7-7.—Removing a stud broken
off below the surface.

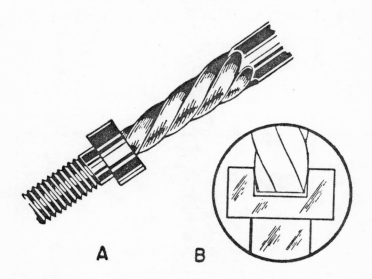

Figure 7-8.—Removing an Allen head
capscrew with a bolt extractor.

spiral has had a chance to take hold. Figure 7-8B shows this end clearance. In doing this grinding operation, great care must be taken to keep the temperature of the extractor low enough so that the tip can be handled with the bare hands. If the hardness is drawn from the tip of the extractor by overheating during the grinding, the extractor will not take hold.

REMOVING A BROKEN BOLT AND RETAPPING HOLE

To remove a broken bolt and retap the hole, file the bolt smooth, if necessary, and center-punch it for drilling.

Then select a twist drill which is a little less than the tap-drill size for the particular bolt that has been broken. As shown in figure 7-9, this drill will just about but not quite touch the crests of the threads in the threaded hole or the

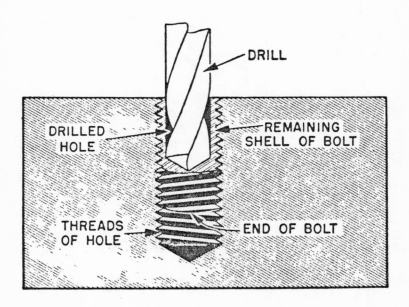

Figure 7-9.—Removing a broken bolt and retapping hole to same size.

376

roots of the threads on the threaded bolt. Carefully start drilling at the center punch mark, crowding the drill one way or the other as necessary so that the hole will be drilled in the exact center of the bolt. The drill in figure 7-9 has almost drilled the remaining part of the bolt away and will eventually break through the bottom of the bolt. When this happens, all that will remain of the bolt will be a threaded shell. With a prick punch or other suitable tool, chip out and remove the first 2 or 3 threads, if possible, at the top of the shell. Then carefully start a tapered tap into these several clean threads and continue tapping until the shell has been cut away and the original threads restored.

In cases where the identical size of capscrew or bolt is not necessary as a replacement, center-punch and drill out the old bolt with a drill larger than the broken bolt, as shown in figure 7-10A. Tap the hole first, and then finish it with a bottoming tap as shown in figure 7-10B. Replace with a larger size capscrew or stud.

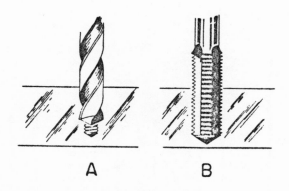

A   B

Figure 7-10.—Removing broken bolt
and retapping hole to larger size.

REMOVING A BROKEN TAP
FROM A HOLE

To remove a broken tap from a hole, generously apply penetrating oil to the tap, working it down through the four flutes into the hole. Then, if possible, grasp the tap across the flats with vise-grip pliers. This operation is shown in figure 7-11. Carefully ease the tap out of the hole, adding penetrating oil as necessary.

If the tap has broken off at the surface of the work, or slightly below the surface of the work, the tap extractor shown in figure 7-12 may remove it. Again, apply a liberal amount of penetrating oil to the broken tap. Place the tap extractor over the broken tap and lower the upper collar to insert the four sliding prongs down into the four flutes of the tap. Then slide the bottom collar down to the surface of the work so that it will hold the prongs tightly against the body of the extractor. Tighten the tap wrench on the square shank of the extractor and carefully work the extractor back and forth to loosen the tap. It may be necessary to remove the extractor and strike a few sharp blows with a small hammer and pin punch to jar the tap

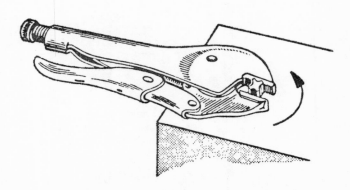

Figure 7-11.—Removing a broken
tap with vise-grip pliers.

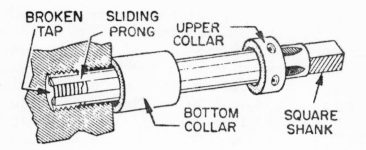

BROKEN TAP SLIDING PRONG UPPER COLLAR BOTTOM COLLAR SQUARE SHANK

Figure 7-12.—Removing a broken
tap with a tap extractor.

loose. Then reinsert the tap remover and carefully try to back the tap out of the hole.

Each size of tap will require its own size of
tap extractor. Tap extractors come in the following sizes: 1/4", 5/16", 3/8", 7/16", 1/2",
9/16", 5/8", 3/4", 7/8", and 1".

When a tap extractor will not remove a
broken tap, it is often possible to do so by the
following method: Place a hex nut over the tap
(fig. 7-13), and weld the nut to the tap. Be sure
to choose a nut with a hole somewhat smaller
than the tap diameter to reduce the possibility

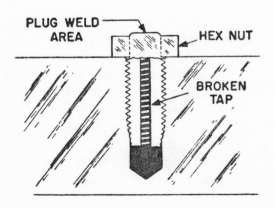

PLUG WELD AREA HEX NUT BROKEN TAP

Figure 7-13.—Using a plug weld
to remove a broken tap.

379

of welding the nut and the tap to the job itself. Allow the weld to cool before trying to remove the tap. When the nut, tap, and job have come to room temperature, it is often helpful to heat quickly the immediate area around the hole with an oxyacetylene torch. This quick heating expands the adjacent metal of the work after which the removal of the tap may be less difficult. If the heating is too slow, the tap will expand with the adjacent metal of the work and there will be no loosening effect.

STRIPPING INSULATED WIRE

Insulation may be stripped from wire by using one of several tools. However, a pocketknife or side cutting pliers are generally used for this work.

When using a pocketknife for stripping insulation, hold the wire in one hand and the knife in the other. Use your thumb to roll the wire over the blade of the knife to cut the insulation almost to the wire itself. (See figure 7-14A.) Then pull off or "strip" the short piece of insulation from the end of the wire. Because any nick in the wire will eventually cause a break, it is important not to cut clear through the insulation. By not cutting completely through the insulation, the blade of the knife never comes into contact with the wire itself, thus preventing any possible injury to the surface of the wire. However, cutting nearly through the insulation weakens it sufficiently so that the insulation can be stripped from the wire.

Another way to perform this operation is, while holding the wire in one hand and the pocketknife in the other, hold the wire against the knife blade and cut the insulation off with several strokes of the blade, working around the wire with each successive stroke. (See fig.

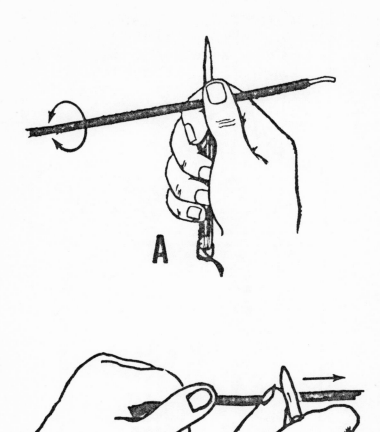

Figure 7-14.—Stripping insulated wire
with a pocket knife.

7-14B.) Notice that the blade is held almost
flat against the insulation. This low angle prevents the blade from cutting into the wire
itself.

Insulated wire can be stripped with the side
cutting pliers, as shown in figure 7-15, by
nicking the insulation all around, being careful
not to break through to the wire itself, and

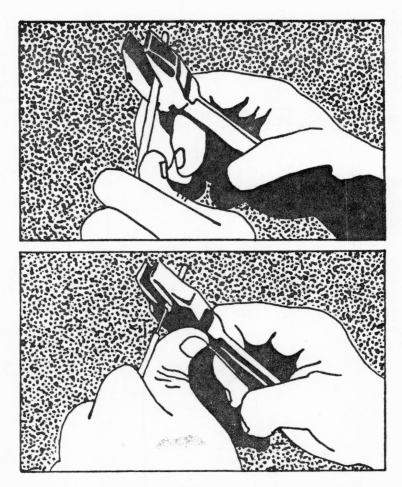

Figure 7-15.—Stripping insulated wire with side cutting pliers.

stripping the short length of insulation off the end of the wire. Notice that, in figure 7-15A, the man's index finger is wedged between the handles of the pliers close to the joint. This affords better control over the cutting edges so that there is less chance that the insulation will be broken completely through. When the nick has been made all around the wire, press your thumb against the side of the pliers to break the insulation at the nick and, without changing the

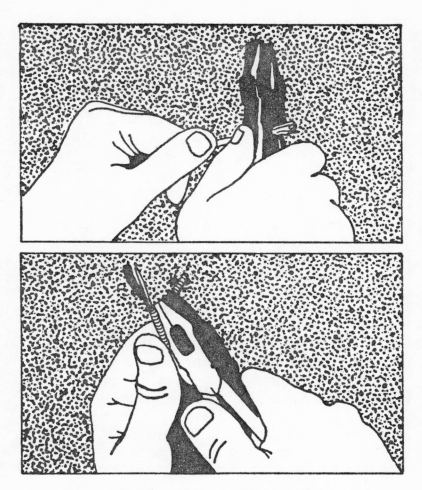

Figure 7-16.—Stripping insulated wire with side cutting pliers (alternate procedure).

grip of the pliers, strip it off the end. (See fig. 7-15B.) Care must be exercised to avoid cutting too far through the insulation and nicking the wire.

Insulated solid wire can also be stripped as shown in figure 7-16. Starting at the end of the wire, grip and crush the insulation between the flat places on the inside of the handles close to the hinged joint. In figure 7-16A, the insulation has been crushed and the wire exposed. Then, as shown in figure 7-16B, grasp the insulation close to the end of the crushed portion and tear it off. Although this method leaves a rather ragged appearing end on the remaining insulation, there is no possibility of damaging the wire.

SOLDERING

Soldering is a metal-joining process in which a lower melting-point metal (called solder) is heated to the point where it melts and wets the joint surface and then is allowed to solidify in place. To enable the solder to wet the surfaces readily and be drawn into fine cracks, the surfaces and the solder must be clean and free of oxide film. When necessary, the cleaning is done with chemicals or abrasives. One cleaning substance frequently used is called flux. Copper, tin, lead, and brass are examples of readily solderable metals. Galvanized iron, stainless steel, and aluminum are difficult to solder and require the use of special techniques which are beyond the scope of this manual.

Soldering is a practical method of forming reliable electrical connections where bare wires are twisted together or are wound on terminals. Soldering is also used to make tight joints, such as lap seams of sheet metal, and to hold parts together physically. Soldered joints, however, do not support loads for long periods of time as well as welded joints do. Where load support is a governing factor, the usual practice calls for riveting, bolting, or using another means of fastening followed by sealing of the joints with solder.

In soldering the readily solderable metals, you only need the solder, a flux, and a heat source. The following paragraphs will be limited to descriptions of the soldering equipment and procedures required for making reliable electrical connections.

SOLDERS

By definition, solders are joining materials or alloys that melt below 800° F. They are available in various forms—wire, bar, ingot, paste and powder. Solders used for electrical connections are alloys of tin and lead whose melting points range between 360° F and 465° F (both endpoints are approximate).

A tin-lead solder alloy is usually identified by two numbers indicating the percentages of tin and lead in the alloy. The first number is the percentage of tin. For example, a 30/70 alloy is made of 30% tin and 70% lead. Likewise, a 15/85 alloy is made of 15% tin and 85% lead. In general, the higher the percentage of tin in a solder alloy, the lower the melting point.

FLUXES

Soldering fluxes are agents which clean solderable metals by removing the oxide film normally present on the metals and also prevent further oxidation. Fluxes are classified as noncorrosive, mildly corrosive, or corrosive, ranging from mild substances such as rosin to chemically active salts such as zinc chloride. Rosin is an effective and nearly harmless flux used for electrical connections that must be reliable, tight, and corrosion free. Rosin flux is available in paste, or powder form for direct application to joints before soldering, or incorporated as the core of wire solders. Unless washed off thoroughly after soldering, salt type fluxes leave residues that tend to corrode metals. Because of their corrosive effects, so-called acid core solders (which incorporate salt-type fluxes) must NOT be used in soldering electrical connections.

SOLDERING TOOLS

The source of heat for melting solder is a soldering gun (electric) or a soldering iron (electric or nonelectric), sometimes called a copper.

SOLDERING GUN

All good quality soldering guns operate in a temperature range of 500° to 600° F. The important difference in gun sizes is not the temperature, but the capacity of the gun to generate and maintain a satisfactory soldering temperature while giving up heat to the joint soldered. The tip heats only when the trigger is depressed, and then very rapidly. These guns afford easy access to cramped quarters, because of their small tip. Most soldering guns have a small light that is focused on the tip working area. (fig. 7-17)

The tip of a soldering gun should be removed occasionally to permit cleaning away the oxide scale which forms between the tip and metal housing. Removal of this oxide increases the heating efficiency of the gun. If for any reason the tip does become damaged, replaceable tips are available.

NEVER USE a soldering gun when working on solid state equipment. Serious damage to diodes, transistors, and other solid state components can result from the strong electromagnetic field surrounding the tip of the soldering gun.

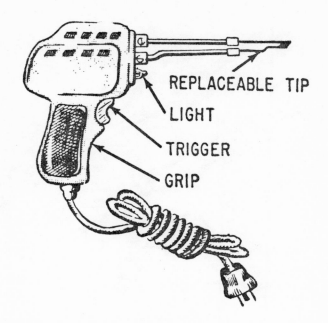

Figure 7-17.—Electric soldering gun.

SOLDERING IRONS

A nonelectric soldering iron (fig. 7-18) is sized according to its weight. The commonly used sizes are the 1/4-, 1/2-, 3/4-, 1-, 1 1/2-, 2-, and 2 1/2-pound irons. The 3-, 4-, and 5-pound sizes are not used in ordinary work. Nonelectric irons have permanent tips and must be heated over an ordinary flame, or with a blowtorch.

The electric soldering iron (fig. 7-18) transmits heat to the copper tip after the heat is produced by electric current which flows through a self-contained coil of resistance wire, called the heating element. Electric soldering irons are rated according to the number of watts they consume when operated at the voltage stamped on the iron. There are two types of tips on electric irons: plug tips which slip into the heater head and, which are held in place by a

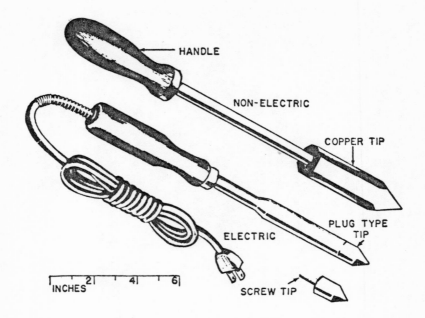

Figure 7-18.—Soldering irons.

setscrew, and screw tips which are threaded, and which screw into or on the heater head. Some tips are offset and have a 90-degree angle for soldering joints that are difficult to reach.

Electric iron tips must be securely fastened in the heater unit. The tips must be clean and free of copper oxide. Sometimes the shaft oxidizes and causes the tip to stick in place. Remove the tip occasionally and scrape off the scale. If the shaft is clean, the tip will not only receive more heat from the heater-element, but it will facilitate removal when the time comes to replace the tip.

TINNING A SOLDERING IRON

If a soldering iron is new or has just been forced, it will need to be tinned (coated with solder). To do so hold it in the vise and "dress" the point with a well-chalked file. By "dressing" is meant filing to remove hammer marks resulting from the forging process and to round off the sharp corners slightly. This is not always required when a tinned iron is to be retinned. Inspection will reveal if it is necessary. Then heat the copper tip hot enough so that it will readily melt solder. Try melting solder with the copper frequently as it is being heated, and as soon as it will melt solder, it is ready for tinning.

To tin the copper, first quickly dip it into rosin or apply rosin core solder to the tip of the iron. The coating of solder is bright and shiny and very thin. It aids in the rapid transfer of heat from the iron to the work.

SOLDERING PROCEDURE

The parts to be soldered must be absolutely clean (free from oxide, corrosion and grease). During the cleaning process, when removing insulation from wire, care must be taken to avoid producing cuts or nicks which greatly reduce the mechanical strength of the wire, especially under conditions of vibration.

The joint should be prepared just prior to soldering since the prepared surfaces will soon corrode or become dirty if it remains exposed to the air.

The parts to be joined must be securely joined mechanically before any soldering is done.

To solder electrical connections (fig. 7-19), hold the soldering iron (copper) beneath the splice being soldered with as much mechanical contact as possible to permit maximum heat transfer. Apply the rosin core solder to the splice. The tinning on the soldering iron aids the transfer of heat to the spliced wire which,

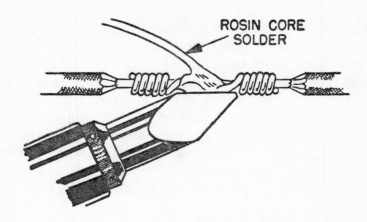

ROSIN CORE
SOLDER

Figure 7-19.—Soldering an electrical
connection.

when hot enough, will melt the solder. Before
this temperature is reached the rosin core will
have melted and run out over the wire to flux
the splice. When the solder has coated the
splice completely, the job is finished. No extra
solder is needed.

A good, well-bonded connection is clean,
shiny, smooth and round. It also approximately
outlines the wire and terminal as shown in figure 7-20.

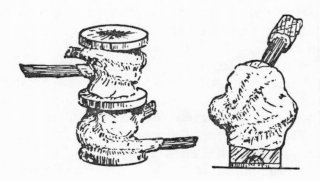

Figure 7-20.—Examples of properly
made soldered joints.

PRECAUTIONS

One sizzling burn experience is usually enough to breed a healthy respect for hot objects. When using a soldering iron or gun always bear in mind the following:

In order to avoid burns, always assume that a soldering iron is hot.

Never rest a heated iron anywhere but on a metal surface or rack provided for this purpose. Faulty action on your part could result in fire, extensive equipment damage, and serious injuries.

Never swing an iron to remove solder because the bits of solder that come off may cause serious skin or eye burns or ignite combustible materials in the work area.

When cleaning an iron, use a cleaning cloth or damp sponge, but DO NOT hold the cleaning cloth or damp sponge in your hand. Always place the cloth or damp sponge on a suitable surface and wipe the iron across it to prevent burning your hand.

Hold small soldering jobs with your pliers or a suitable clamping device. Never hold the work in your hand.

After completing the task requiring the use of a soldering iron, disconnect the power cord from the receptacle and, when the iron has cooled off, stow it in its assigned storage area. Do not throw irons into a toolbox. When storing irons for long periods of time, coat the shaft and all metal parts with rust-preventive compound and store in a dry place.

LUBRICATION

If you grew up in a large city, perhaps the only connection you had with lubrication was taking the family car to the garage or gasoline station for greasing and an oil change. If you grew up on a farm or had a car that you kept in running condition yourself, you are well aware of the need for regular lubrication of all moving parts. If your car ever burned out a bearing, you've had a lesson you are not likely to forget.

FUNCTIONS OF LUBRICANTS

Lubricants are used as coolants, to reduce friction, to prevent wear, and to protect against corrosion.

In mechanical devices, lubrication is necessary to minimize friction between moving parts. Only the presence of a layer or film of lubricant between metal surfaces keeps the metals from touching. Moving parts "ride" on this film. As a result, friction is reduced between the moving parts.

Prolonged operating life is ensured when the thin film of lubricant keeps metal surfaces from direct contact with each other. If the film disappears, you have "hot-boxes," burned out and frozen bearings, scored cylinder walls, leaky packings and a host of other troubles. Appropriate use of proper lubricants minimizes possible damage to equipment.

LUBRICANTS

Lubricants are of two general classes--oils and greases. Oils are fluids; greases are semisolid at ordinary temperatures. For many applications, liquid lubricants are more suitable than greases, particularly if the lubricant can be retained, as in an oil bath, a gear box, or in a forced-feed system. Where conditions are such that oil is not readily retained, or additional protection against corrosion is needed, greases are used.

GREASE GUNS

The types of grease guns shown in figure 7-21 operate on the same principle, but differ in the ways they are loaded. You load one type by removing a cap that comes off with the handle and stem, and filling the body with grease, using a paddle or spatula. As you might expect, this method of loading can be messy, and it also exposes the lubricant to dirt and moisture.

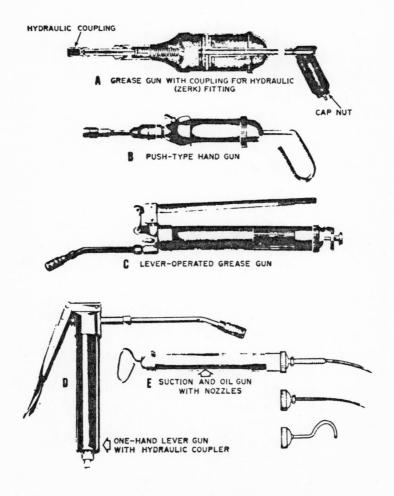

HYDRAULIC COUPLING

A GREASE GUN WITH COUPLING FOR HYDRAULIC (ZERK) FITTING

CAP NUT

B PUSH-TYPE HAND GUN

C LEVER-OPERATED GREASE GUN

D

E SUCTION AND OIL GUN WITH NOZZLES

ONE-HAND LEVER GUN WITH HYDRAULIC COUPLER

Figure 7-21. —Hand-operated grease guns.

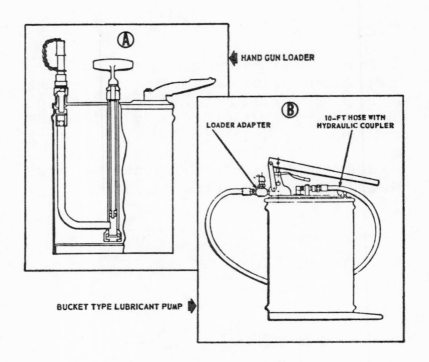

Figure 7-22.—Hand-operated grease pumps.

In a second type, you load by inserting a prepacked cartridge of grease into the body of the gun. This loading method is fast and clean. The gun shown in figure 7-21A also loads fast and clean. You load it by removing the cap nut from the end of the hollow handle and forcing grease in through the handle with a hand gun loader (fig. 7-22A), or a bucket-type lubricant pump (fig. 7-22B).

The hand gun loader is a 25-pound container equipped with a hand-operated pump and a fitting that mates with the opening in the handle of the grease gun. The bucket-type lubricant pump makes use of a loader adapter and loader valve when it is used for loading a grease gun. One pound of lubricant is delivered with every seven full strokes of the pump. The loader will

394

deliver lubricant only when the gun is placed on the loader valve. You can see how much less messy the loader is than the paddle, and how it protects the lubricant against contamination. Besides, you don't have to run back to the storeroom to refill your gun.

Different nozzles can be attached to the grease guns for different types of fittings. The lubricant pump also has various couplers and adapters that attach to the hose, so that the pump can be used on different fittings.

Grease guns can be used for oil if the point to be lubricated has the proper fitting, or an oil gun (fig. 7-21E) may be used.

FITTINGS

Grease fittings are of several types—hydraulic (unofficially called the Zerk fitting), buttonhead, pin-type, and flush (fig. 7-23).

The hydraulic fitting protrudes from the surface into which it is screwed, and has a specially shaped rounded end that the mating nozzles of the grease guns can grip. A spring-loaded ball acts as a check valve. The nozzle will not slip off the fitting during lubrication, but can be easily disengaged by a quick forward-backward movement. Figure 7-23A shows a cross section view of a straight hydraulic fitting and figure 7-23C shows angled hydraulic fittings made tor lubrication points that are hard to reach.

The flush fitting (fig. 7-23B) is flush with (or below) the surface into which it is set, so that it will not interfere with moving parts. It is also used where there is not sufficient clearance to install protruding fittings.

Button-head and pin-type fittings (figs. 7-23D and E) provide a more positive connection with the grease gun. A simple quarter turn of the

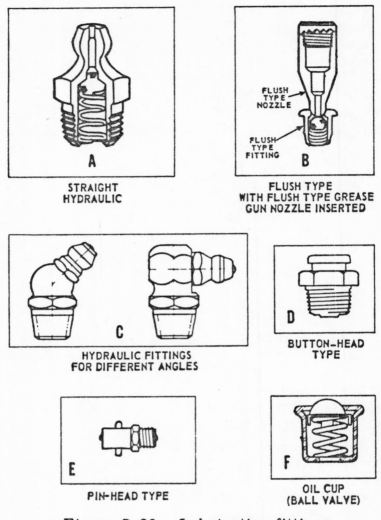

Figure 7-23.—Lubrication fittings.

grease gun on the pin-type fitting locks the connection between the gun and the fitting.

The oil cup with ball valve (fig. 7-23F) is the most popular for oil fittings.

Plastic protective caps often are provided for use on hydraulic fittings to prevent the entrance of dirt and water, and to protect the fittings during ice removal, painting and similar operations. The caps also prevent the greases from hardening in the fitting. If available, use them after you have completed your lubrication task.

USING A HAND-OPERATED GREASE GUN

To use a push-type, hand-operated grease gun, you connect the nozzle of the gun to its corresponding fitting at the lubrication point and work the handle in and out. To connect the gun, align the nozzle and the fitting end-to-end and push on the gun handle so the nozzle slips over the hydraulic fitting or into the flush fitting. At the same time that the nozzle mates with the fitting, the handle moves inward to build pressure inside the gun to force grease out of the nozzle and into the fitting. Then, let up on the handle a moment. A spring in the gun will then force the handle out a little way and prepare the gun for another inward stroke of the handle.

When you connect the push-type gun to a hydraulic fitting, the nozzle grips the fitting and is held firmly only as long as the nozzle and fitting are aligned or until pulled free. In connecting the gun to a flush type fitting, however, you must keep a steady pressure on the fitting because the nozzle doesn't grip the fitting (fig 7-23B).

LUBRICATING PROCEDURE

As with other routine jobs, it helps to have a standard operating procedure that you can habitually follow. Here's one that will be helpful when lubricating.

1. First, consult the lubrication chart to

397

learn the location of each fitting.

2. After locating a fitting, clean it with a lintless cloth.

3. Apply the correct amount of the specified lubricant. (Be careful of the amount you apply—too much will cause excessive heat in the bearing and strain the grease retainers, while too little is on a par with too late.)

4. Wipe all excess grease from around the fitting.

Appendix

Wood Properties for Selected Construction Projects

PROJECT	DECAY RESISTANT	FREE FROM WARP	STIFFNESS	STRENGTH	HARDNESS	MISCELLANEOUS QUALITIES	WOODS POSSESSING EXCELLENT QUALITIES FOR SPECIFIED PROJECT	WOODS POSSESSING GOOD QUALITIES FOR SPECIFIED PROJECT
DOORS	●		●			Resistant to fire and sound transmission; Ability to hold special hardware	Oak, Birch	Ponderosa Pine, Southern Yellow Pine, Spruce, Gum, Douglas-fir
CABINET DOORS	●					Pleasing Grain	Maple, Oak, Birch, Cherry	Douglas-fir, Southern Yellow Pine, Gum, Ponderosa, Pine, Magnolia, Poplar
SHELVING	●	●	●				Ash, Birch, Maple, Oak, Walnut, Poplar, Douglas-fir, Redwood, Ponderosa Pine, Sugar Pine, Idaho White Pine	Hemlock, Spruce, Western Larch, Particle Board
PANELING	●				●	Pleasing Grain	Oak, Redwood, Cypress, Walnut, Cedar, Ash, Birch, Pine	

Use				Characteristics	Recommended Woods	Alternative / Other Woods
STAIRWAYS	●	●	●	Pleasing Grain; wear-resistant	Oak, Birch, Maple, Walnut, Beech, Ash, Cherry	Douglas-fir, Southern Yellow Pine, Gum, Sycamore (these are to be used only for basement stairways or for stairways which will be covered)
INTERIOR TRIM (NATURAL FINISH)	●			Pleasing texture and grain	Oak, Birch, Maple, Cypress, Cherry, Sycamore, Beech, Walnut. Knotty Surface: Cedar, Ponderosa Pine, Spruce, Sugar Pine, Gum, Lodgepole Pine	Douglas-fir, West Coast Hemlock, Western Larch, Southern Yellow Pine, Redwood, Aspen Magnolia
INTERIOR TRIM (PAINTED FINISH)	●			Fine, uniform texture; Absence of knots and pitch; Freedom from shrinkage	Northern and Idaho White Pine, Ponderosa Pine, Sugar Pine, Poplar	Hemlock, Redwood, Spruce, White Fir, Magnolia, Gum, Basswood, Beech, Maple, Tupelo, Douglas-fir, Western Larch, Southern Yellow Pine
EXTERIOR TRIM	●	●		Good Weathering Characteristics and painting qualities; Easy working characteristics	Cedar, Cypress, Redwood, Northern and Idaho White Pine, Ponderosa Pine, Sugar Pine	West Coast Hemlock, Poplar, Spruce, Douglas-fir, Western Larch, Southern Yellow Pine
FRAMES & SASH	●	●		Moderately free from shrinkage; Good painting qualities; Easy working characteristics	Cypress, Cedar, Redwood, Northern and Idaho White Pine, Ponderosa Pine, Sugar Pine	Douglas-fir, Western Larch, Southern Yellow Pine, White Oak

PROJECT	DECAY RESISTANT	FREE FROM WARP	STIFFNESS	STRENGTH	HARDNESS	MISCELLANEOUS QUALITIES	WOODS POSSESSING EXCELLENT QUALITIES FOR SPECIFIED PROJECT	WOODS POSSESSING GOOD QUALITIES FOR SPECIFIED PROJECT
SIDING	●	●				Good painting and easy working characteristics	Western Red Cedar, Cypress, Redwood	Northern and Idaho White Pine, Sugar Pine, White Cedar, West Coast Hemlock, Spruce, Poplar
DECKING & OUTDOOR STEPPING	●	●	●			Non-splintering; Excellent painting characteristics, Wear-resistant	White Oak, Locust, Walnut	Douglas-fir, Western Larch, Southern Yellow Pine, Redwood, Cedar
EXPOSED PLATFORMS & PORCHES	●	●	●	●		Wear-resistant; Splinter-resistant	Redwood, Locust, White Oak	Cedar, Douglas-fir, Western Larch, Southern Yellow Pine, Rock Elm
SHINGLES	●					Splinter-resistant	Cedar, Cypress, Redwood	Northern and Idaho White Pine, Ponderosa Pine, Sugar Pine, White Oak
PLANK ROOF DECKING	●	●	●				Solid or laminated wood decking of Southern Yellow Pine, Douglas-fir, or other softwood (1⅝" to 3⅝" thick)	Structural Insulating Roof Deck

Use	Property	Preferred species	Other species
FENCE POSTS		Black Locust, Osage Orange, White Oak, Cedar, Cypress, Redwood	Douglas-fir, Western Larch, Southern Yellow Pine, Beech, Birch, Elm, Hemlock, Spruce, White Fir, Basswood, Cottonwood, Gum, Tupelo, Poplar, Lodgepole Pine
GATES; FENCES	Good Bending Strength; High weathering characteristics	Douglas-fir, Western Larch, Southern Yellow Pine, Redwood, White Oak	
ROOF SHEATHING	Easy working qualities	Douglas-fir, Western Larch, Southern Yellow Pine	Hemlock, Ponderosa Pine, Spruce, Lodgepole Pine, Aspen, Balsam Fir, White Fir, Northern and Idaho White Pine, Sugar Pine, Redwood, Poplar
WALL SHEATHING	Easy working qualities	Cedar, Hemlock, Northern and Idaho White Pine, Redwood, Aspen, Spruce, Balsam, White Fir, Basswood, Lodgepole Pine, Poplar, Sugar Pine, Ponderosa Pine	Douglas-fir, Southern Yellow Pine, Western Larch, Cedar, Redwood, Sitka Spruce, West Coast Hemlock, White Fir
SUBFLOORS		Douglas-fir, Western Larch, Southern Yellow Pine, Ash, Oak	Hemlock, Ponderosa Pine, Spruce, Lodgepole Pine, Aspen, Balsam Fir, White Fir, Northern and Idaho White Pine, Sugar Pine, Poplar

Good bending strength

INDEX

S